I Am Not A Man, I Am Dynamite!

Friedrich Nietzsche and the Anarchist Tradition

John Moore, editor

with Spencer Sunshine

AUTONOMEDIA

Book design: Ben Meyers
Nietzsche stencil: Kevin Pyle

Thanks to Erika Biddle

ISBN 1-57027-121-6

Autonomedia
PO Box 568
Williamsburgh Station
Brooklyn, NY 11211-0568
email: info@autonomedia.org
www.autonomedia.org

Printed in Canada

Anarchy Unbound

A Tribute to John Moore

Jonathan Purkis

The essays in this collection each offer a unique contribution to an emerging area of political philosophy and in a sense serve as their own introduction to it. Why they were assembled and how one situates them within contemporary libertarian thought is another matter altogether, and one which requires a tribute to its contributing editor John Moore, who died suddenly in October 2002, aged 45.

John's writings occupy a special place within anarchism. He once described his work as 'anarchist speculations' about power, epistemology and ontology, for people to consider, refine, revise and act upon, rather than as absolute truths that should be adhered to.[1] His speculations not only resist easy intellectual classification within libertarian thought itself, but they have frequently challenged existing modes of political expression. On the one hand this has resulted in a series of innovative publications that seek to re-examine the intellectual assumptions of Enlightenment philosophy, of Modernism, of anti-authoritarian thought in general, and of anarchism in particular. On the other, John's work poses questions about the possibilities of libertarian aesthetics and the need for consistency between revolutionary form and content. A re-evaluation of the relationship between Nietzsche and anarchism can be seen to be something of a logical extrapolation of a commitment to these questions, which he raised in earlier pieces on Fredy Perlman and Max Stirner.[2]

The work of Nietzsche is complicated and contradictory and has enjoyed a somewhat similar relationship with anarchists and anarchist theory over the last hundred years. It is in the context of post-structuralism and the various attempts to link it with anarchist thought in the arts and social sciences that John's interest in Nietzsche in recent years should be seen. In a review article "All Nietzscheans Now?" for *Anarchist Studies* in 2001, he notes the tendency for contemporary theorists (including some anarchists) to retreat from the potentialities offered by Nietzsche's deconstruction of morality, truth and justice, and fall back on Enlightenment rationality. The strands of Nietzsche's work lead in all directions, but many can be appropriated to better understand the manifestations of power and the extent of the transformations that are necessary for the liberatory project to be realised. Here we find a clue to the kind of thinker that John was—one increasingly unconcerned with pre-existing categories and coherent ideological positions. It is noticeable that in much of his later work, the term 'anarchy' is preferred to that of 'anarchism,' and 'insurrection' to that of 'revolution,' to signal a break from some of the more deterministic and dated analyses left over from the 'classical' era of libertarian politics. This is especially true of his reclamation—along with several contemporaries—of the word 'chaos.'

Looking back, John's work has always been in this vein. When I first met John at the (London-based) Anarchist Research Group in the late 1980s, his first collection of writings—*Anarchy and Ecstasy* (1989)—was causing a few ripples. Brought up on the standard canon of anarchism, I remember being fascinated, intrigued and perhaps a little alarmed as to what it all meant. Tom Cahill's review of these essays in the *Bulletin of Anarchist Research* affectionately described it as the work of a "dedicated oddball; a serious weirdo" and wondered what 'they' might think. 'They,' I think, being some hypothetical 'rump' of British anarchism, likely to find evocations of primal mythology, medieval millenarians, or the imaginative possibilities of dance, song and laughter a little bit incompatible with the collective political struggles around class and state political power. Unsurprisingly, much of British anarchism seemed moribund to John and it was only the emerging radical ecological politics of the early 1990s which seemed remotely connected with the kind of issues that he wanted to explore.

At this time, the work of Fredy Perlman, especially *Against His-story, Against Leviathan!* (1983) began to play a part in shaping John's analyses of civilisation and the deeply entrenched ways in which power is perpetuated in everyday life. His utilisation of Perlman's work has helped introduce his writing to a new generation of activists, and as readers of the editorial introduction to the 1992 (Aporia Press) version of *The Machine Against the Garden* will testify to, in a lot more of a critical fashion than some have suggested. John co-founded the Primitivist Network in Britain in 1994 and wrote accessible and well-distributed articles such as "A Primitivist Primer," yet he refused to eulogise the pre-Neolithic era. The primitive should be a source of inspiration, not of answers, and should be a part of the process of cultural remembering that informs all struggle. In this respect, there are moments of insurrection against Leviathan which are worthy of recall, as are the intense moments of *being* in the world—memories of childhood pleasure, recapturing the first feelings of love: all of these can assist in the process of *becoming* and reinvigorate sterile political discourse.

The focus on language forms a central part of John's later work on aesthetics and subjectivity, that draws upon theorists such as Hakim Bey, John Zerzan and in particular the Situationists. For John, it is these writers whose work constitutes a second 'wave' of anarchist thought (based on a different epistemology from that of the classical era), not the post-structuralist 'anarchism' of Foucault, Deleuze or Lyotard whose commitment to the abolition of power is indifferent or of secondary consideration. Similarly, Kristeva's post-structural work on the possibilities of revolutionary poetic language and form are actually anticipated in the work of Max Stirner. In Stirner's *The Ego and its Own* we have an example of a truly radical text in both form and content. Debates about revolutionary texts and their integration into everyday life reoccur in John's work, particularly an engagement with what the Situationists called 'lived poetry' and the formation of subjectivity under the 'totality.'

This collection of essays is evidence that not only was John engaged in a serious epistemological project but a methodological one as well: a commitment to reinstating forgotten, obscure or problematic figures in the history of anti-authoritarian thought, whose ideas offer new directions and alternative visions today. Whilst the focus here is Nietzsche and I have mentioned Stirner and Perlman already, John also included Henry Bailey Stevens and John Carroll as figures worthy of significant reconsideration. Such people might be seen as reference points in a beautiful and bizarre intellectual counter-history of modernity, which details all of the iconoclastic, eccentric, irrational figures who do not appear to 'fit in.' More often than not, these 'theoretical oddballs' have been castigated or ignored, particularly because of their departure from the rationalist hegemony of Enlightenment thought. Yet to really comprehend the nature of power—which can both motivate potential libertarians as well as seduce millions into obedience—an engagement with 'irrationality' becomes mandatory for anarchist theorists. John's utilisation of Carroll's non-materialist 'anarcho-psychological' critique might therefore be seen to form part of an as-yet-to-be-fully-realised anarchist historical methodology. It is within this context that John regarded Nietzsche as a pivotal part of an alternative 'episteme' of modernity to those of capitalist liberal-rationalism and Marxist socialism, one that embraces the irrational, the psychological and the anti-ideological. This was what he termed 'maximalist anarchism' where nothing is "off limits for investigation and revision."[3]

John's own contribution to this collection is a logical continuation of earlier work on anarchist aesthetics, texts and their potential to prefigure an anarchist future. Again he is working with the notion of 'lived poetry'; that people can transform their lives aesthetically as part of the liberatory project. He notes how gradually Nietzsche moved towards a position of accepting the connections between art and activism, rejecting along the way 'narcotic art' (which anaesthetises its audiences) and even 'ludic art' (that helps heal one from the excesses of the controlling structures of society). What Nietzsche calls 'Dionysian art' involves turning one's life into a work of art, not just for its own sake but to engage with the very oppressive forces that prevent the emergence of such a possibility in the first place.

At the end of his essay John argues that Nietzsche had himself embraced Dionysian art, even though he struggled with the idea. It is suggested that Nietzsche employed anarchistic textual strategies in creating the anti-authoritarian Zarathustra. Given that much of John's writing was committed to exploring the relationship between form and content, it is fitting that this his last work should be devoted to developing these ideas further.

I Am Not A Man, I Am Dynamite! is an inspiring and challenging collection. It is also a testimony to the enthusiasm, popularity and vision of an editor devoted to opening up exciting new discursive spaces, of which some of the most important have been his own work.

Notes

1 John Filiss, interview with John Moore (2001).
   Online at www.insurgentdesire.org.uk/jminterview.htm (accessed October 2004).
2 "Public Secret: Fredy Perlman and the Literature of subversion" appeared in Jonathan Purkis & J. Bowen, eds., *Twenty-first Century Anarchism* (London: Cassell, 1997). "Lived Poetry: Stirner, Anarchy, Subjectivity and the Art of Living" was first drafted in 2000 but reworked for Jonathan Purkis & J. Bowen, eds., *Changing Anarchism: Anarchist Theory and Practice in a Global Age* (Manchester: Manchester University Press, 2004).
3 John Moore, "Maximalist Anarchism/Anarchist Maximalism" (2001).
   Online at www.insurgentdesire.org.uk/moore.htm (accessed October 2004).

Friedrich Nietzsche

Guy A. Aldred

The fascination exerted upon an ever-growing number of followers by that brilliant, if somewhat erratic genius, Friedrich Nietzsche, serves to bring out not only the several points of attraction and repulsion characterising his philosophy of revolt, but also the extent to which he has been misunderstood. In the Emersonian sense, this last-mentioned fact alone would serve to establish Nietzsche's greatness. And yet, even where one feels the greatest uncertainty as to Nietzsche's teaching, the pregnancy of his style and the intellectual force accompanying the directness of his appeal to sentiment intoxicates the reader for months by virtue of his egoism.

The self-preservation instinct which all recognise as being the first law of Nature is shown by Nietzsche to be the last law of ethics. Between the right of self-assertion, intellectually expressed, and social self-realisation in the service of all, he draws no line of demarcation. To him they are one and the same. Absolute independence of external authority, the being without God or master, the sovereignty of 'being' over 'doing,' are the challenges he throws out to the mediocre who suffer themselves to be the victims of legalised disorder. Nor does he hesitate to attack the various phases of expertism. With him, rights take the place of duties, since to the superman the performance of duties will be the highest right.

It being given to the many not to understand the essence of this philosophy of Communistic individualism, Nietzsche's 'egoism' has been confounded with a decadent Spencerian individualism. In turn a follower of Schopenhauer, Wagner, and August Comte, Nietzsche founded a system that was not so much a reaction against the ideals of his former masters as a further development and unification of their respective theses, and only apparently opposed to their primary teachings of philosophic, nirvanic egoism. Where there is a difference, the difference is more of a temperamental character than anything else. The ultimate purposelessness of being was as much emphasised by Nietzsche as by Schopenhauer; the elevation of humanity was as essential a part of his system as it was of Comte's; but Nietzsche brought temperamental characteristics to

This piece originally appeared as an article, "The Message of Nietzsche," in *Freedom*, June 1907, and as the pamphlet *Nietzsche—Apostle of Individualism* (London: Bakunin Press, nd).

bear upon the unity of the two systems. In other words, essentially a religious teacher and apostle of iconoclasm, opposed to the metaphysical world erected by theologians as also by many a scientist and philosopher, Nietzsche's philosophical system was nonetheless based upon an unconscious conservation of the teachings of the very philosophers to whose systems his was supposed to have been opposed.

Man as we know him, with his respect for conventional morality and controlled by external rules of conduct, was something to be surmounted. The super-earthly hopes, whether of scientist or philosopher or theologian, that animate man in the transition stage were to be consigned to the vortex of oblivion. The philosophers' and scientists' advice to man to take refuge from the miseries of those around him by regarding the world of science and art and lofty aspirations—the ideal subjective world—as atonement for the evils of the objective world, was thought by Nietzsche but little improvement on the objective paradise of the theologian. It was not that Nietzsche deprecated this ideal subjective world, but only that he wanted all men to rise to this level, coupled with an assertion of their individuality. His was a system based on an extension and conservation of the ideals that found their expression in this subjective world. But his egoism was directly opposed to the egotism of such philosophers. They would ask men to put up with their sordid conditions, to continue to be the slaves of others, so long as they could experience the "realities" of this subjective world of idealism. But Nietzsche could see no reality in this subjective idealism if it was divorced from the self-assertion of the individual or opposed to his physical well-being. The scientist who was of this school of philosophy divorced knowledge and truth from the happiness of the individual, and would have you disbelieve in his being self-contained. Nietzsche, even if he embraced the ultimate pessimism of Schopenhauer, also emphasised the *reality* of man's being *to man*. Truth and knowledge, therefore, were only valuable as they became subservient to the reality of self-contained being, only useful in so far as they administered to the individual's freedom from oppression of and by others.

All roads lead to Rome, and all Nietzsche's aphorisms lead to one end—the superiority of the superman. But the superiority spelt a new social system, and was as much a social regeneration as an individual advance. For whilst domination of man over man continued, the superman could not be. The superman was superior to man because he would be so placed as to be neither man-slave nor man-master. Freed from the desire and the economic power to dominate, he would be neither dominator nor dominated. But in so far as differing hereditaries would produce different traits, the idiosyncrasies of each individual would vary, and hence this lack of officialdom would spell freedom, variety, and consequent genius. For where freedom and variety are, there is genius also. Hence man would be happy without regard to external canons of morality, serving his fellows in so healthy a manner as not to regard it as "service," benefitting the rest of his fellows by daring to be himself. Such is the greatness and grandeur of the philosophy propagated by Nietzsche, a philosophy bidding man be true to himself, and to cease to be either the exploiter or the exploited of science, of misdirected industry, and bestial luxury.

By those who have not mastered him, Nietzsche is looked upon as the decadent individualist; but to the student he is the herald of the highest Socialist principles, the herald of revolt and freedom, the deep thinker who realised that Socialism must inevitably be identical with absolute individual freedom. As such, his memory will ever be dear to those who, coupling Freethought ethics with Socialist economics, spell the combination, "Anarchist Communism"—the brotherhood and sisterhood of humanity that depends for its happiness on the authoritarianism of none. And what higher Socialism could men have than that which bids them at all times be themselves, and to serve men, not because of the pressure of circumstances, but because such acts as would benefit the community spring from the higher inner principle of true being?

Nietzsche and the Libertarian Workers' Movement

Daniel Colson

The history of a given thing is, in general, a succession of the forces that take hold of it, and the coexistence of the forces that strive to take hold of it. A single object, a single phenomenon changes meaning according to the force that is appropriating it.[1]

This introductory remark of Deleuze to the work of Nietzsche should suffice to underline the importance of this philosopher to all those who have sought to one day transform the world in which we live. History provides a wealth of examples of struggles and of notions of struggle having entirely changed meaning and value: "national" struggles, for example, taken up in turn by movements of the ultra-left and extreme-right; "pacifism," revolutionary in 1916, collaborationist in 1942; ecology and the backing this movement has today as to the issues it unifies, the currents that it attracts or which it opposes; the takeover bid the extreme-right is making of a certain number of the ultra-left ideas of the last thirty years: the rallying of leftist and ultra-leftist militants to the extreme-right, and vice versa (although more rarely); etc.

Each event, each and every aspect of life and of reality is always capable of changing meaning and, says Nietzsche, requires much foresight and vigilance, plus an aptitude for interpretation and evaluation. No phenomenon draws its value and meaning from itself alone. There is no meaning and value in itself. No external authority, no supreme court can assess, guarantee and define these once and for all. No providence or historical reason can assure them of meaning. The Russian Revolution can be transformed into a bloody tyranny. Militant French anarchists before 1914 into fervent patriots after it. Pacifists and non-violent types into collaborators of a machine of war and oppression hitherto unknown. Ultra-leftists without a fatherland into defenders of the countryside, the Basque béret, the accordion and local cheeses. Nothing is ever fixed once and for all. Everything must be repeatedly addressed, reinterpreted and remade.

This piece originally appeared in a different form in *EchoGryffe* 2-3, 1993. Translated from the French by Paul Hammond.

One or many Nietzsches?

This conflict around the meaning and value of things is also to be found in connection with the work of Nietzsche. It can be the object of a variety of interpretations.

The extreme-right interpretation, for instance. This is generally characterised by the literal reading of a certain number of images or metaphors: the "blonde-haired brute" celebrated at the beginning of *On the Genealogy of Morals*; or then a literal reading of Nietzsche's vocabulary: "masters," "slaves," "aristocrats," "will to power" (as a desire for power and domination),[2] "overman" (which would suppose, therefore, the existence of "undermen"); etc. The appearance of a more intelligent extreme-right thinking cannot be excluded. And neither is it excluded that the polyvocality of the Nietzsche text may authorise this. Yet, historically, the feebleness of this reading is perceptible in the fact that it has required the falsification and censoring of his manuscripts: the assembling and invention of a book he never wrote (*The Will to Power*); the censorship and destruction of a great many texts against anti-Semitism, the German Reich and Pan-Germanism; or, then again, the aphorism in *Ecce Homo* where Nietzsche, after having spoken so often of the "instincts," "race" and the nobility of the blood, invents a Polish origin for himself and repudiates any link with his mother and his sister, in his eyes the very image of the "German" type he denounces elsewhere.[3] This literal and unintelligent, extreme-right interpretation of Nietzsche's thought is also found, paradoxically, among a certain number of philosophers who could be described as "left-liberals"—if the word "left" still had any meaning today—anxious to combat the contestatory thought of the sixties and seventies.[4]

Another possible interpretation: the Christian reading of Nietzsche. More cognisant of the texts themselves, and favourable to Nietzsche, it salutes the importance of his thought and, in a willfully recuperative gesture which is nothing if not forthright, strives to link this to a particular Christian mysticism (the "yes to life" of Nietzsche as an echo of the Virgin Mary's "fiat," etc).[5]

And there's yet another interpretation, one which interests us more particularly here: a somewhat remote, individualist, explicitly anarchist reading and, later on, a reading we might qualify as "libertarian" and linked to the renewal of libertarian ideas during the last thirty years, though external to the anarchist movement per se. Foucault and Deleuze are its best-known French representatives.

The Nietzsche the libertarians discovered from the first is an individualist Nietzsche; and it is essentially the more individualist anarchist circles who referred to him very early on. Pelloutier, one of the founders of the *Bourses du travail* movement,[6] certainly read him during his more individualist phase.[7] Libertad, and the "Libertarian Discussion Groups" he founded in 1902, referred to Stirner as well as to Nietzsche.[8] This individualist and anarchist reading of Nietzsche, as amiable as it is misguided, is found in Georges Palante, the *Cripure* of Louis Guilloux.[9] Nietzsche lends himself to such a reading. There is a whole psychological typology in Nietzsche, a thinking through of the body, of the individual-society opposition. Yet the inconvenient thing about this interpretation is that it cannot avoid what any superficial reading can lead to in terms of posturing and unbearable affectation, ultimately comparable (although clearly less antipathetic) to that of the extreme right. This all-too-simplistic, individualist Nietzscheanism endlessly runs the risk of being confined to a form of dandyism and elitism in which each person strives to construct an image of himself as an aristocrat of thought, nourished by a scorn for others, and reduced to a simple, willfully aesthetic representation.

The reading of Nietzsche by authors like Deleuze and Foucault or, less well-known, Sarah Kofman or Michel Haar, offers a far more interesting interpretation of the individualist dimension of Nietzsche's writings, but also of their collective dimension.[10] In effect, as M. Haar reminds us, the will to power, the plurality of forces, instincts and drives, is not particular to the individual, whether this be in relation to his body or his unconscious. It applies to everything. "All force, all energy, whatever it may be, is will to power, in the organic world (drives, instincts, needs), in the psychic and moral world (desires, motivations, ideals) and in the inorganic world itself, to the extent that life is only a particular instance of the will to power."[11] Whilst individual, the will to power is also collective, in direct relation to a world in which individualism is only a particular point of view and may take many forms.

As an historical and practical movement, the libertarian movement had every reason to recognise the collective and social dimension of Nietzsche's thought, and not to restrict itself to the strictly individualist aspect of this. Yet this was not the case, for two main sets of reasons.

To begin with, for reasons internal to anarchism, and which belong to its own history. The main theorists, precursors or founders of anarchism as an explicit current—Stirner, Proudhon and Bakunin—obviously knew nothing of Nietzsche. It would have been necessary for them to disentangle themselves (as all did, each in his own way) from Hegelianism, the dominant current of thought at that time. As Claude Harmel points out, Stirner and Bakunin's thinking has certainly more in common with Nietzsche's than with Hegel's.[12] But the anarchist "intellectuals" who came after—Kropotkin, Reclus, Guillaume—and who, chronologically, could have known Nietzsche's writings, were not philosophers. Geographers, the first two; educationalist, the third, they were only remotely interested in philosophy per se. As to turn-of-the-century militant anarchist thinking: being highly autodidactic (in France at least) it rarely extended, some individualists apart, beyond the tiny militant circle of the reviews and newspapers of the period. Generally scientist and encyclopaedic, it stuck to an idealist, rationalist vision far removed from a philosophy like Nietzsche's—or Stirner's, Bakunin's and Proudhon's for that matter. For these narrow circles anarchism was, first of all, an "ideal" project without direct relation (as a theoretical expression) to the movements which were then rendering it possible; an "ideal" that it was necessary to "apply" by privileging explanation, education, adhesion and, for some, organisation.

To these important reasons, specific to the libertarian movement, we must add others which this time have to do with the writings of Nietzsche and the history of their reception. The texts of Nietzsche were known very early on in France and quickly became the object of numerous commentaries, often related to the rediscovery of Stirner.[13] Yet this welcome was essentially literally, aesthetic and moral. The provocative, poetic and fragmentary form of Nietzsche's writings did not lend itself well, in the beginning, to a theoretical reading. And it was somewhat tardily, commencing in the 1930s with the works of Jaspers, Löwith and Heidegger in Germany, or Bataille and Klossowski in France, that a philosophical reading was undertaken, a reading capable of producing a wider interpretation which goes beyond a strictly and immediately individualist approach.[14] Another obstacle to the social and revolutionary revival of Nietzsche lay in the vocabulary and metaphors he uses and, more generally, in the political, historical and scientific references which serve him for elaborating his thought. How could the anarchists, syndicalists and revolutionaries in general recognise themselves in formulations where, in opposition to dominant moral and populist interpretations, Nietzsche sides with the "strong" and the "masters" against the "weak" and the "slaves" who, according to him and against all appearances, have triumphed over the "masters"?[15]

"It is necessary to protect the strong against the weak," says Nietzsche: a paradoxical and provocative formula which only a philosophical interpretation can render intelligible. We now know how, for Nietzsche, "masters" and "slaves" go to make up "types," applicable to a large number of situations and calling, each time, for great subtlety of evaluation and interpretation. Masters and slaves are rarely where we take them to be; and these qualities owe nothing to the signs and representations which claim to fix and express them. A "master" for Nietzsche is an affirmative and active force who creates his own values, who does not define himself in relation to other forces, who is autonomous. The "slave" is a negative and reactive force. He submits to others out of envy and hatred, and it is in relation to them that he defines himself. Filled with resentment and guilt, he only exists through the attention and judgement of others. The utilisation of these types is extremely varied in Nietzsche. For him, a savant, however great he may be, is, with his objectivity and his tutelage to "facts," a slave. An anti-Semite filled with envy and resentment (insofar as he is actually anti-something) is also a slave. It is true that the historical figure Nietzsche frequently employs when speaking of the "master" is the Greek warrior-type celebrated by Homer in *The Iliad*, or the Aryan "barbarian," Vandal or Goth of 19th century historiography. But, as he tells it, this figure is the philosopher and the creative artist, too. For Nietzsche, philosophers like Spinoza, Schopenhauer or Heraclitus are "masters." It is likewise true that for him the people, democracy, the egalitarianism of the voter, the crowd and the masses, always ready to give in to the first tub-thumping charlatan who promises them the moon, are also slaves. But as even the most superficial knowledge of the libertarian movement encourages us to believe, this judgement contains nothing that might shock the anarchists. And it is precisely here that Nietzsche's analysis is interesting; in particular when we confront it with what we may know, historically, of the different forms of the libertarian workers' movement and, behind that (or after it), of what any libertarian movement can hope to be.

Nietzsche's thought and the libertarian workers' movement

Anarcho-syndicalism and revolutionary syndicalism only theorised their practices to a minor degree and, *a fortiori*, rarely made appeal to any philosophical reference with which their militants felt uncomfortable. The intellectuals Sorel, Berth, etc., who claimed to speak for the latter, might well refer to Bergson, though more rarely to Nietzsche. This surely calls for retrospective interpretation here. We may formulate it thus.

Contrary to appearances, if the masses in thrall to politicians or fascinated by charismatic leaders (from Mussolini to Mao Zedong) indisputably belong to what Nietzsche calls the "slaves," then the workers' movement known as anarcho-syndicalism, revolutionary syndicalism or direct action, along with what sociology demonstrates of the values and lifestyle of the classes which gave them birth, undoubtedly belong to the kind of "masters" and "aristocrats" such as Nietzsche conceives them. To support this thesis we could easily multiply the points of convergence: apropos of the working classes of the 19th and 20th centuries, the value systems they develop, their relation to the world and to other people; apropos of the so-called anarcho-syndicalist workers' movements above all, from the frequently-vilified "active minorities" to the mixture of individualism and collective action which characterises them, taking in its also improperly-understood conception of the "strike" as "revolutionary gymnastics." We will restrict ourselves here to considering three aspects: separatism, federalism and direct action.

1) Separatism

When Nietzsche distinguishes between the "masters" and the "slaves" it is to explicitly oppose himself to Hegel, to his way of dialectically uniting the two terms. For Nietzsche the antagonism between masters and slaves is only a secondary effect, or (if not) merely a slavish point of view. There is nothing dialectical in their relationship, in a rapport where, worse still, the active principle would be on the side of negation, of the one who denies himself in order to affirm himself. How could an affirmation be born of a negation, of nothingness? For Nietzsche this is truly slave thinking. For him it is, on the contrary, advisable to adopt the point of view of the "masters" (in the meaning he attributes to this word), to grasp how that which distinguishes them from the slaves is precisely a separation, a differentiation. The antagonism between the masters and the slaves presupposes a relation of differentiation on the part of the masters, not as a struggle which links and binds them, but as a separation which detaches and sets them apart. It is here, and from this point of view, that we can understand why the libertarian workers' movement has always been so radically different from Marxism (a variant of Hegelianism) and its conception of class struggle, insofar as it yields precisely to the differentiating movement of the strong and the masters of which Nietzsche speaks.

In the anarcho-syndicalist or revolutionary syndicalist conception the working class must, in effect (and in a preemptive and fundamental manner) constitute itself as an autonomous, independent force, endowed with all the services and institutions necessary to it, which depend only on it and on what it becomes. It must secede, and radically so, and thereby have nothing more to do with the rest of society. In the historiography of this libertarian tradition within the history of the working class, this movement of differentiation has the transparently clear name, from the Nietzschean point of view, of "worker separatism." The workers' movement must "separate" itself from the rest of society.

To begin with, it is not a question of a conception or of an intellectual project, but of an effective practice, as the study of any remotely important Bourse du travail shows in the case of France.[16] Within this conception the workers' organisations can make non-binding agreements, affirm and develop their strength ("revolutionary gymnastics"); they do not aim at any reasonable compromise because such things are defined by a framework which has already been "transcended," or at any "satisfaction" which would come defined by the economic and social order from which they obtained it, and which would depend on what the latter can contrive. Even when they sign agreements, the workers are not in the role of plaintiff. They content themselves with provisionally obtaining a part of their "rights," while waiting to obtain them all, then to producing these rights themselves, freely, in their totality, with no other guarantors than themselves.[17] If they ask nothing it is because the workers feel no need for the old world they seek to destroy, which they scorn and ignore. Their revolt is a pure affirmation of forces and of the movement which constitutes these. And it is only in a derived manner that they combat the reactive and reactionary forces which oppose themselves to this affirmation. They ask nothing from anybody, but everything from themselves, from their capacity to express and to develop the power of which they are the bearers. Their relationship to the outside world is one of "pretension" (in the original sense of the world), the pretension of one day occupying the whole social space, through a radical transformation of the bourgeois order as regards its values, morals, economic and political system.

And so we reencounter, in another form, the trajectory of Nietzsche, perceptible after *Zarathustra* and later in his will to overturn all values (not in the sense of turning them into their opposites, but in the sense of destroying the tablets of the law), to cut history in two and to institute an entirely new world. As with Nietzsche, the libertarian workers' project, being affirmative and differential, is inscribed within the messianic trajectory we find almost everywhere in societies on the way towards industrialisation, from Spanish anarchism to the Jewish messianism of Central Europe which M. Löwy describes.[18]

The theme of the general strike, and its popular expression as the "big uprising," the "settling of scores," well illustrates this radical conception of revolutionary struggle, as conceived by the libertarian workers' movement. With the general strike the working class brings everything to a standstill simply by folding its arms. Like the trumpets of Jericho, this is its way of causing the walls of the existing order to come tumbling down, by demonstrating the immense force of the workers. Within this conception of the "revolution" the working class in effect has nothing to demand, nothing to say to whoever the other side may be, since it claims to be everything and, above all, something so entirely new that nobody can give it anything since it is the working class who is in full posses- sion. As all the observers of the time clearly perceived, this way of seeing things has nothing autistic or pacifist about it. The revolutionary militant workers are not blind to the fact that, once shaken, the old social and economic order will not miss the opportunity, being a negative and reactive (reactionary) force, to try and suppress at any price a force as foreign as the one it makes up. As formi- dably certain as they might be of the power they possess, they know that they will have to pitilessly destroy such enfeebled forces which, while on the defen- sive, are all the more dangerous because they emanate from a "dying society."[19]

It is not a question, here, of knowing if such a project (effectively tried out in Spain) was realisable or not. It is enough (whether, deep down, such a proj- ect touches us or not) to observe how libertarian working-class forces were able to ascribe to a movement which has echoes of Nietzschean thinking about it, to partake of a will which according to Nietzsche characterises the "masters," the "aristrocrats" and the "strong" who triumph over the mediocrity, cowardice and gregariousness of minor leaders and passive crowds.

2) Federalism

Another point of contact between Nietzsche and the libertarian workers' movement is federalism. Being affirmative, Nietzsche's trajectory is perforce "multiple" because "it belongs, essentially, to the affirmation of being multiple and pluralist itself, and as the negation of being one, or clumsily monist."[20] The will to power does not designate a unified force, a central principle from which everything would emanate. As Haar shows, it refers "to a latent plurality of drives, or to complexes of forces about to unite with or repel each other, to asso- ciate with or dissociate themselves from each other."[21] In defining itself, the will to power harmonises and hierarchises the multiple forms of chaos; it does not destroy or reduce these, does not resolve their difference or their antagonism in the manner of Hegelian dialectic. "Affirmative and forceful, the will to power will make appeal to variety, difference and plurality."[22] This conception of the will to power is particularly useful for understanding the forms the workers' movements of the anarcho-syndicalist or revolutionary syndicalist type have assumed.

For a start, it would be necessary to confront this conception with a certain aspect of Proudhon's thought, an aspect the libertarian workers' movement immediately understood because it bore directly on its own practice and expe- rience: namely, the idea of autonomy. Proudhon is not only the socialist theo- retician who insists the most on the necessity for different components of the working class to become radically autonomous from the rest of society. He is, without doubt, the only one to think about the plurality of forces which make up the working class, to conceive of the latter as a multiple reality. Contrary to Marx, Proudhon always speaks of the working "classes" and not "the" working class or "the" proletariat. While for Marx the "working class" is merely the abstract—because instrumentalised—moment of a reason at work in history, for Proudhon working-class forces are always concrete and living forces in a state of flux, which may disappear and spring up again in other forms, change nature, be absorbed, dominate other forces or be dominated by them, in an incessant movement of transformation in which nothing is ever established and definitive. Marx is right to say that Proudhon never understood Hegel. "Serial dialectic" has in effect very little in common with Hegelian dialectic. For Proudhon, the differences and oppositions between the multiple forces which make up any society, along with everything else, do not have to be resolved, neither dialectically nor in any other way, since in their incessant transformation they are all necessary to life.

Extremely diverse, according to region and country, the development and functioning of the so-called direct action workers' movement completely vindicates Proudhon's and Nietzsche's analyses of the modalities of the affirmation of "power" (Proudhon) or the "will to power" (Nietzsche). In effect, and limiting ourselves to the specific experiences of the French workers' movement, working-class federalism is always characterised by the conflictual union of extremely diverse forces. Associations of miners, musicians, cabinetmakers, typographers, carpenters, "odd-job men," plumbers and roofers, etc.: all of them types of workers' groupings, the embodiment of a particular way of being; all of them specific forces, struggling to unite and affirm themselves in a much larger force which itself draws all its strength from what constitutes it by way of a combination of distinct forces. This multiplicity of forms and syndical forces united within the framework of the labour exchanges is not just linked to the different industrial branches or activities (mines, metallurgy, music, postal services, etc.). With greater or lesser intensity, it is equally at work within each professional sector. Thus, in an average-size industrial area like Saint-Etienne we can, from 1880 to 1914 and for metallurgy alone, count more than forty specific syndicalist forms, be they ephemeral or long-lasting, distinct or implicated with each other, adherent or not (according to the moment) to the town's Bourse du travail, and each one the embodiment of a way of being and a re-vindicative logic and an inherent mode of functioning.

These syndical forms are not just different in relation to each other. Each force constituting itself as a power within the workers' movement is itself a composition of forces that are just as multiple and singular: the geography of the locality over which it is deployed, modalities of organisation, the kinds of militant, number of adherents, the rhythms and modalities of how it functions, its links with the rest of the profession, the relative proportion of trade-union members, the nature of professional expertise, sorts of tools, types of enterprise, organisation of the work, origins of the labour force, etc. The basic structure of any Bourse du travail (which only admits one of each type) is not a specific force alone, different to all the others. It is itself the ever-imbalanced "resultant"[23] of an extremely complex composition of equally-autonomous forces which may, to varying degrees within the interplay of relations at the core of the Bourse du travail, directly shape itself (or oppose itself) in relation to other components or compounds of components of this Bourse; this composition of forces is at once social and human, but also technical and material. In effect, and along with B. Latour,[24] we could, in order to define the multiple constitutive identities of the forms of worker groupings, speak of "hybrid" identities and collectives which pay no respect at all to the false opposition between nature and culture, world and society, in a relationship to the world in which the least regrouping, since it consistently makes appeal to the totality of the real in order to exist, is constitutive, as Proudhon says, of a "particular society."

In echo of Nietzsche, one of the essential characteristics of libertarian movements resides in their capacity to permit all the forces which constitute them to express themselves, to affirm and endlessly seek to evaluate the meaning of their composition, to experiment and struggle among themselves to determine the hierarchy of values of which their composition is the embodiment. From this space—negatively, that is, from the outside—comes a sense of disorder, of unceasing conflict which is seen, for example, in the day-to-day life of the Bourses du travail and, more generally, the workers' organisations of a libertarian kind induce. In a Bourse like Saint-Etienne's, everything is the object of discussion, conflict, scission and reconciliation, of differential affirmation. This includes serious problems, such as the question of the war and the Sacred Union in 1915, for instance; but also of apparently more futile problems, as in 1902, when the administration council endlessly and heatedly discussed if one of the labour exchange secretaries, caught kissing the concierge, had the right to give in this way to his amorous penchants or not.[25] Another, even more significant, sign of this originality in the forms of worker associations of the libertarian kind is the enormous difficulty in codifying the multiplicity and incessant change of relationships in the legal statutes, within a formal logic which functions abstractly and externally. From 1919 to 1921 the Saint-Etienne Bourse du travail vainly tried to reformulate an internal ruling that was no longer complied with. Over those two years, six successive versions, each time on the point of being "printed," were hotly debated; but no consensus or stabilisation of the internal and external situation emerged for long enough for a sufficiently-final version to reach the printer's, where it could rejoin the vast cemetery of dead letters.

3) Direct action

This discrepancy between abstract and external forms of law, and what goes to make up the life of workers' movements of a libertarian persuasion, enables us to draw attention to one last point of comparison between Nietzsche and the reality of such movements: direct action. It is well known that for anarcho-syndicalism and revolutionary syndicalism the workers' forces must always act directly, without intermediaries, without "representatives" and without "representation." The term "representation" must be understood here in its widest sense. From the libertarian point of view this means not only refusing political representation, but any form of representation at all, which is perceived as inevitably abstract and manipulative, detached from the real forces of which it claims to give an account, which it claims to "represent" and finally replace. This is how we may understand another dimension of the libertarian workers' movements, a dimension which is often confusing, because seemingly contradictory: their anti-intellectualism. Enamoured of culture, science and of knowledge in general, yet believing along with Proudhon that "the idea is born of action, and not action of reflection,"[26] anarcho-syndicalist and revolutionary syndicalist militants tend to constantly reject any theoretical formulation or science which, coming from outside and proceeding from its own *raison d'être*, would seek to define what they are and what it is they seek.[27]

Once again we encounter, in almost identical terms, an attitude and certain practices which directly echo the thought of Nietzsche, and his ferocious critique of representation, whether it be "political" or "scientific," whether it challenges State, Church or Knowledge. We know that for Nietzsche, science and politics are reactive forces which aim to "separate the active forces from what they are capable of," to render them powerless, to deny them as such by annexing them to other ends.[28]

This is true of a science and knowledge which, "starting as a simple means subordinated to life... becomes systematised as an end in itself, a higher power, a final arbiter."[29] And it is even more true of the human sciences, of their "disavowal of action, of anything active."[30] Like the State, the Churches—but also the races, people and classes which it tends to anchor and substantiate—science displays a particular "taste" for "substituting the real relations of forces by an abstract relation which is thought to express them all, like a kind of 'measure.'"[31] Because it is opposed to life, because it is reactive, the science of the savants and philosophers, those "seekers after thought," "highly-strung and cadaverous," "consumed with ambition" of whom E. Coeurderoy spoke,[32] can only kill what it speaks of, what it takes hold of:

> All that philosophers have handled for thousands of years have been concept-mummies; nothing real escaped their grasp alive. When these honourable idolators of concepts worship something, they kill it and stuff it; they threaten the life of everything they worship.[33]

The same is true of politics and of religion, those other ways of fixing and representing an active force in order to annex it to a mendacious reactive order. "State is the name of the coldest of all cold monsters. Coldly it tells lies too; and this lie crawls out of its mouth: 'I, the State, am the people.'"[34] "The State is a hypocritical hound... it likes to talk... to have us believe that its voice comes from the belly of things." As for the Church, "that is a kind of State, the most mendacious kind."[35] Science, Church, State—it is always a question of annexing the real to the lie of signs and of representation, "movement" to "substance," active to reactive forces.[36] As Deleuze says of the Hegelian or utilitarian nature of the human sciences:

> In this abstract relation, whatever it is, one is always led to replace

real activities (creating, talking, loving, etc.) by a third party's viewpoint on these activities: one confuses the essence of the activity
with the prerogative of a third party, and it is assumed that the latter must profit from this or have the right to reap the benefits of it
(God, objective spirit, humanity, culture, or even the proletariat...).[37]

Allusive in Deleuze's case, yet virulent in Nietzsche's—in his critique of
"socialism" and "anarchism"—this reference to the mystificatory nature of the
"proletariat" or of the "working class" contains nothing (at least from this point
of view) that would surprise a reader of Proudhon and, along with him, the
numerous militants who, in the thick of the fray, have tried to think in anarcho-
syndicalist or revolutionary syndicalist terms. On the contrary, one could say,
since in a certain way, and however little or much attention we pay to what the
one or the other is saying, it precisely furnishes, against all the evidence, a final
indication of what could have brought them together.

We know how, for the Nietzsche of Deleuze, "culture" is a "generic activity,"
a "prehistory" of man which enables him to "speak" rather than to "reply," to be
his own "master," a "law" unto himself, but which, historically, has been "taken
over by alien forces of a completely different kind."[38]

Instead of generic activity, history presents us with races, peoples,
classes, Churches and States. Grafted onto generic activity are social
organisations, associations, communities of a reactive kind, para-
sites which contrive to colonise and consume it.[39]

This "generic activity," this "activity of man as a generic being,"[40] which
races, peoples, classes, Churches, States and other individuating forms manage
to colonise and consume so easily, is elsewhere related by Deleuze, in an ampler
and altogether more offensive way, to what he calls "univocal being." A "power"
irreducible to the social forms and the individuals it helps to produce, "univocal
being":

functions in them as a transcendental principle, a plastic, anarchic
and nomadic principle which is contemporaneous with the process
of individuation and which is just as capable of dissolving and
destroying individuals as it is of temporarily constituting them.[41]

Deleuze is correct to underline the "anarchic" dimension of this conception
of "being" as "power," to consider "univocal being" under the "plastic" sign of an
"anarchy of beings," of a "sovereign anarchy" in which each unique being is, in
the affirmation of its existence, the "equal" of all the others because it is "immediately present in all things, without intermediary or mediation."[42]

In effect, we rediscover this distinction in Proudhon, and in almost the same
terms. On the one hand, we encounter "action," the origin of any "idea" and all
"thought," in its doubly warlike and productive form: the "war" without which

man "would have lost... his revolutionary faculty" and reduced his life to a "pure community," a "sheep-like civilisation";[43] "work," the "plastic force of society," "always identical in plan" and "infinite in its workings, like creation itself."[44] On the other hand, we encounter the appropriation of collective force and of man's power of action by a variety of forms of social individuation which claim to be "absolute":

> Embodied in the individual person, the absolute gradually evolves with increasing autocracy in the race, in the city, the corporation, the State, the Church; it appoints itself king of the humanitarian collectivity and of the aggregate of creatures. Having arrived at such heights, the absolute becomes God.[45]

Yet this opposition between "action," a "plastic force infinite in its applications," and the multifarious forms of the absolute which seek to fix and annex it, is not unique to either Nietzsche or Proudhon. We encounter it in just as categorical a way in the writings of the leaders of revolutionary syndicalism, in texts, furthermore, written hurriedly for a mass audience, and within a context in which all the reasons were seemingly present to aggrandise and absolutise the "working class," the "proletariat" and "syndicalism" itself.

Let us lend an ear to V. Griffuelhes, secretary of the French CGT from 1901 to 1910, as he sets about the dangerous exercise (from the point of view of Nietzsche and Proudhon) of defining "syndicalism." What does Griffuelhes say?

> Syndicalism is the working-class movement which seeks to gain full possession of its rights to the factory and the workshop; aimed at producing the emancipation of labour, it affirms that such a conquest will be the result of the personal and direct effort exercised by the worker.[46]

An astonishing phrase, given the usual banalisation of words and ways of looking, which manages in two propositions to condense a significant number of the characteristics of revolutionary syndicalism and anarcho-syndicalism without ever annexing them to an identity, a form of representation or an organisation. "Personal and direct effort," "conquest," "emancipation," "affirmation," a tension aiming at the "full possession of its rights": the "generic activity" Deleuze speaks of in relation to Nietzsche finds a content and a formulation here which immediately fixes the definition of "syndicalism." For Griffuelhes syndicalism is neither a thing nor, *a fortiori*, a representative or organisation (of the working class, in this instance). Syndicalism is a "movement," the "movement" of the working class.

This formulation doubtless profits from a contemporary infatuation with notions of action and movement.[47] Yet under Griffuelhes' pen there is nothing conventional or mechanical about it, as the next part of the text shows. In an extremely Proudhonian, and just as astonishing, way, Griffuelhes immediately goes on to discuss, not capitalism, the bosses or the bourgeoisie, but the question of "God" and "Power":

> For the priests' confidence in God, for the politicians' confidence in a Power inculcated in the modern proletariat, syndicalism substitutes confidence per se; for that action labeled as tutelary of God and of Power, it substitutes direct action.[48]

Previous to and in echo of what we have already said about worker separatism, the movement of the working class is the force which immediately enables it to launch into movement, its "confidence per se" opposed to confidence in some other force, that of the priests' God or the politicians' Power. But the movement of the working class is, above all, that "direct action" which Griffuelhes, in a slightly obscure manner, opposes to another kind of "action," a "labeled" action, "labeled as tutelary of God and of Power," because it is submitted to their shadow and their domination.

The next part is even more interesting. For four paragraphs, Griffuelhes continues denouncing God and the Church, Power and the State. And then, confronted by an apparently minor—yet concrete and practical—difficulty, he suddenly breaks off. What must syndicalism's attitude be when faced with "workers imbued with religious ideas or confident in the reforming potential of the rulers?"[49] In other words, what's to be done with those workers labeled as Christians or reformists? Here again an obvious answer seems to impose itself, one the Comintern hymn will popularise ("You're a worker, no? Join us, be not afraid"). Another label has to be opposed to the Christian one, the worker label, in order to valorise the anteriority and superiority (from the viewpoint of history and determinations of the real) of the condition of "worker." Griffuelhes, though, does not choose this obvious and reassuring answer, but rather the passive order of things, identities and representations. For better or worse, he resolutely rejects it as contrary to the goal being sought and, above all, to what revolutionary syndicalism can do.

If syndicalism has no need to spurn Christian workers it is not because they are "workers," but on the contrary or in a different way, because it is advisable to carefully distinguish between "movement, action on the one hand, the working class on the other."[50] The fact of belonging to the working class guarantees nothing since, as it happens, workers can be "Christians" or "socialists."[51] The difference lies in "action" and "movement," both capable of acting on things and labels, of blurring their frames of reference and their limits, of sweeping "workers," "Christians," "socialists," "anarchists," but also "masons," "foundry workers" and "pastry cooks," or even "Greeks," "Germans" and "Spaniards," along in a process which has more difficult objectives since it seeks to transform the workshop, the factory and the society as a whole. And as it was necessary to drive this essential idea home—not only the superiority of the movement and action specific to syndicalism in respect of worker identity and its representations, but their difference in kind—Griffuelhes immediately returns to the subject:

Syndicalism, let us repeat, is the movement, the action of the working class; it is not the working class itself.[52]

Griffuelhes does not define what he understands by "direct action," this "movement" and this "action" which differs so clearly from all identities, be they of class, métier, nationality or religious conviction. But another CGT leader, E. Pouget, gives a definition which wholly confirms the affinity, linking it to Proudhon's "plastic force," to the "generic activity" and "univocal being" of Nietzsche and Deleuze. What is direct action for Pouget?

Direct Action, a manifestation of working-class force and will, is materialised, according to the circumstances and the context, by acts which may be extremely anodyne, just as they may be exceedingly violent... There is... no specific form to Direct Action.[53]

"A manifestation of working-class force and will," direct action has no "specific form." Its only "materiality" is in "acts" as changing as "the circumstances and the context." Strictly speaking, and like Deleuze's "univocal being" or Nietzsche's "generic activity," it is "unassignable," doubly unassignable:

—spatially, in such and such a practice, such and such an organisational form, such and such a group employing it;

—but also temporally, in breaking free from order and from the agency of clocks and calendars, planned strategies and actions, distinctions between present and future, between what is possible and what is not. As Pouget writes:

The tactical superiority of Direct Action lies precisely in its *incomparable plasticity* [our emphasis]; the organisations which promote its practice do not confine themselves to waiting, in hieratic pose, for social change. They endow passing time with all possible combativity, sacrificing neither the present to the future, nor the future to the present.[54]

• • •

As the characteristics of direct action indicate, the affinity between Nietzsche's thought and libertarian movements is certainly not peculiar to the workerist and syndicalist forms of the latter. This, at least, is what remains to be shown, and I will content myself, in conclusion, with illustrating it by a personal example; a limited example, but one in which the interest Nietzsche represents for thought and for the libertarian workers' movement may (perhaps) be seen.

In 1992, the action and agitation of a few dozen squatters in an area of Lyons (La Croix-Rousse) seemed, over a period of weeks, capable of extending its forms of action and its demands not only right across the city but, at times, to the whole social question, to the question of the world we live in or the worlds we could live in. The failure of this movement, its vanishing as suddenly as it had appeared, and the feeling of having missed a ("political"?) opportunity, provoked, after the event, and hence in a truly "reactive" manner, various bitter and despondent discussions, often couched in terms of error and responsibility (or irresponsibility).

Once again Nietzsche's analyses offer the possibility of accounting in libertarian terms for what happened and what was at stake. At a given moment the Croix-Rousse squatters' movement constituted a particular and unique force, irreducible to any other comparable or completely different movement. This force, or rather this composition of forces, went as far as it could. It certainly opened up other possibilities, at the city scale, to do with the issue of housing, the kind of society in which we live. Yet these possibilities went beyond the specificity of the squatters' movement. Other forces would have had to exist or to be created and link up with the squatters; not in a strategic way, but as forces capable of combining with the first and of forming a much larger force with it. That was not the case, and this is nobody's fault. To reproach the squatters with not having done what they were incapable of doing, given who they were, was, after the event, a negative and reactive absurdity, something one loses sleep over as one is waiting for the dawn to be able to act anew.

From the libertarian viewpoint Nietzsche proposes, it was just as absurd to reproach the squatters' movement for having spent so much time, just as in the Bourses de travail of an earlier age, in discussing everything—the power relations within their movement, emotional and amorous relations, people's personal behaviour. These internal discussions, this will to allow all the forces and compositions of forces of the squatters' movement to express themselves, was constitutive of that movement. They contributed in an essential way to assuring the very existence and effectiveness of the movement, as, in the last analysis, they did the limits of this effectiveness. A force must not be separated from what it can do, to the profit of other, inevitably reactive forces, but neither must it be asked to do more than it can.

Notes

1 Gilles Deleuze, *Nietzsche et la philosophie* (Paris: Presses Universitaires de France, 1962), p. 4. English trans. *Nietzsche and Philosophy* (New York: Columbia University Press, 1983).
2 Let's remember that for Nietzsche "power" is clearly not the goal of "will," precisely to the extent in which the latter seeks nothing that is exterior to itself, and that any exteriority could only belong to the domain of "representation" and appearance. "Power" is not the objective or the "object" of will, but its "subject." As Deleuze says, "Power is that which is sought in will." The will to power is not "appropriative" but "creative." (Ibid., p. 97.)
3 Nietzsche explains that "it is with one's kin that one has the least kinship; it would be the worst sign of baseness to want to feel oneself 'akin' to one's kin." Friedrich Nietzsche, *Ecce Homo*, "Why I Am So Wise," in *Oeuvres complètes* (Paris: Gallimard), vol. 3, p. 249. English trans. *On the Genealogy of Morals and Ecce Homo* (New York: Vintage, 1967).
4 *Cf.*, de Ferry, Renaut, Comte-Sponville, Taguieff, etc., *Pourquoi nous ne sommes pas Nietzschéens* [*Why We Aren't Nietzscheans*] (Paris: Grasset, 1991).
5 *Cf.*, for example, P. Valadier, *Nietzsche l'athée de rigueur* [*Nietzsche, the Strict Atheist*] (Paris: Desclée de Brouwer, 1975).
6 The *Bourses du travail* (literally, "labor exchanges") were a complex phenomenon. They acted as a combination hiring hall, worker education center and meeting place, in addition

to providing social benefits for members. The Bourses tried to organize all workers in their geographical region, regardless of specific trade or profession. Each one was autonomous and had its own internal structure, although in 1893 they linked together as the Federation des Bourses du Travail. In 1902 the federation became part of the Confédération Général du Travail (CGT), the French syndicalist union. [—*S.S.*]

7   Particularly during his collaboration with the international review *La Société Nouvelle* [*The New Society*], published in Brussels. On this point, *cf.*, J. Julliard, *Fernand Pelloutier et les origines du syndicalisme d'action directe* [*Fernand Pelloutier and the Origins of Direct-Action Syndicalism*] (Paris: Seuil, 1971), p. 98.

8   J. Maitron, *Le mouvement anarchiste en France* [*The Anarchist Movement in France*] (Paris: F. Maspero, 1975), vol. I, p. 421.

9   Louis Gilloux, *Cripure* (Paris: Gallimard, 1962); on Palante and Nietzsche, *cf.*, M. Onfray, *Georges Palante, essai sur un Nietzschéen de gauche* [*Georges Palante: Essay on a Left-Nietzschean*] (Bédée: Éditions Folle Avoine, 1989).

10 S. Kofman, *Explosion I De l'"Ecce Homo" de Nietzsche* (Paris: Editions Galilée, 1992), English trans. *Explosion* (London: Continuum/Athlone, 1999); M. Haar, *Nietzsche et la métaphysique* (Paris: Gallimard, 1993), English trans. *Nietzsche and Metaphysics* (Albany: SUNY Press, 1996).

11 Ibid., p. 27.

12 C. Harmel (a pacifist who rallied to Pétain and collaboration with Germany during the war), *Histoire de l'anarchie, des origines à 1880* [*A History of Anarchy From Its Origins to 1880*] (Paris: Éditions Champ Libre, 1984), pp. 159, 435.

13 R. Catini, "Marx, Stirner et son temps," in *Max Stirner* (Paris: L'Age d'Homme, 1979), pp. 73ff.

14 K. Jaspers, *Nietzsche: An Introduction to the Understanding of His Philosophical Activity* (Paris: Gallimard, 1950). English trans. (Tucson: University of Arizona Press, 1965); originally *Nietzsche; Einführung in das Verständnis seines Philosophierens* (Berlin: W. de Gruyter, 1936); K. Löwith, *Nietzsche: The Philosophy of the Eternal Return* (Paris: Calmann-Lévy, 1991). English trans. (Berkeley: University of California Press, 1997); originally *Nietzsches Philosophie der ewigen Wiederkehr des Gleichen* (Stuttgart: W. Kohlhammer Verlag, 1935/1956). For Bataille and Klossowski, *cf.*, the review *Acéphale*, January 1937.

15 Without speaking of Nietzsche's violent attacks on "anarchism," as this was represented in the writings of Dühring, in particular.

16 *Cf.*, Daniel Colson, *Anarcho-syndicalisme et communisme, Saint-Etienne 1920-1925* [*Anarcho-syndicalism and Communism in Saint-Etienne, 1920-25*], CEF-ACL (Saint-Étienne: Publications de l'Université de Saint-Etienne, 1986).

17 On the opposition between workers' "law," internal to worker action, a conscious expression of the "forces" which constitute it, and the "law" of the State and of bourgeois society, external to working-class life, *cf.*, in what concerns the thought of Proudhon, P. Ansart, *Naissance de l'anarchisme* [*The Birth of Anarchism*] (Paris: Presses Universitaires de France, 1970), pp. 128ff., and the same author's *Marx et l'anarchisme* [*Marx and Anarchism*] (Paris: Presses Universitaires de France, 1969), pp. 314ff.

18 M. Löwy, *Rédemption et utopie, le judaïsme libertaire en Europe centrale* (Paris: Presses Universitaries de France, 1988), English trans. *Redemption and Utopia: Libertarian Judaism in Central Europe* (London: Athlone, 1992).

19 *Cf.*, J. Grave, *La société mourante et l'anarchie* [*The Dying Society and Anarchy*] (Paris: Stock, 1893).

20 Gilles Deleuze, *Nietzsche* (Paris: Presses Universitaires de France, 1965), p. 25. English trans. in *Pure Immanence: Essays on a Life* (New York: Zone Books, 2001).

21 Ibid., p. 12.

22 Ibid., p. 29.

23 On the Proudhonian notion of "resultant," *cf.*, P. J. Proudhon, *De la Justice dans la Révolution et dans l'Église* [*On Justice in the Revolution and the Church*] (Paris: Rivière, 1932), vol. III, pp. 409ff.

24 Bruno Latour, *Nous n'avons jamais été modernes, essai d'anthropologie symétrique* (Paris: Éditions La Découverte, 1991), English trans. *We've Never Been Modern* (Cambridge: Harvard University Press, 1993).

25 A narrow majority voted that the secretary be deprived of his office.

26 Proudhon, *De la Justice*, vol. III, p. 71.

27 *Cf.*, Daniel Colson, "Anarcho-syndicalisme et pouvoir," in *Un anarchisme contemporain Venise 1984* [*An Anarchism for Today: Venice 1984*], vol. I, 1985; and "La Science anarchiste" in *Réfractions*, no. 1, December 1997.

28 Deleuze, *Nietzsche*, p. 98.

29 Ibid., p. 114.

30 Ibid., p. 83.

31 Ibid., p. 84.

32 E. Coeurderoy, *Oeuvres* [*Works*] (Paris: Stock, 1910), vol. I, p. 11.

33 Friedrich Nietzsche, *Twilight of the Idols*, in *Oeuvres philosophiques complètes* (Paris: Gallimard), vol. VIII, p. 75. English trans. (New York: Penguin, 1968).

34 Nietzsche, *Thus Spoke Zarathustra*, in *Oeuvres philosophiques complètes*, vol. VI, "On the New Idol," p. 61. English trans. (New York: Penguin, 1954).

35 Ibid., "De grands évènements" ["On Great Events"], p. 152.

36 "Thought fraudulently introduces Being as a cause and it does this everywhere. It sees only actions and active beings everywhere, it believes in the will as cause; it believes in 'ego,' in 'ego' as Being, in 'ego' as substance." Nietzsche, *Twilight of the Idols*, p. 78.

37 Deleuze, *Nietzsche*, p. 84.

38 On this subject, ibid., pp. 157-58.

39 Ibid.

40 Ibid., p. 153.

41 Gilles Deleuze, *Différence et répétition* (Paris: Presses Universitaires de France, 1968), p. 56. English trans. *Difference and Repetition* (New York: Columbia University Press, 1995).

42 Ibid., p. 55. Whatever their tactical motives and legal status, this is how we may think, theoretically or concretely, of both Proudhonian "federalism" and the revolutionary syndicalist obligation to give, in their congresses, an equal voice to all trade unions, however large or small.

43 P. J. Proudhon, *La Guerre et la Paix* [*The War and the Peace*], *Oeuvres complètes*, p. 32.

44 P. J. Proudhon, *De la Création de l'Ordre* [*On the Creation of Order*], p. 241 and *De la Justice* [*On Justice*], vol. III, p. 89.

45 Ibid., p. 175.

46 Victor Griffuelhes, *Le syndicalisme révolutionnaire* [*Revolutionary Syndicalism*] (Paris: CNT-AIT, nd [1910]), p. 2.

47 From Bergson to Sorel, taking in M. Blondel.

48 Griffuelhes, ibid., p. 2.

49 Ibid., p. 3.

50 "To spurn them would be to confuse different factors: movement, action (etc)." Ibid.

51 Ibid., p. 4.

52 Ibid., p. 3.

53 Emile Pouget, *L'Action Directe* (Paris: Éditions CNT-AIT, nd), p. 23.

54 Ibid., p. 11.

"Nietzsche was an anarchist"

Reconstructing Emma Goldman's Nietzsche Lectures

Leigh Starcross

Between 1913 and 1917, Emma Goldman gave a series of public lectures throughout the United States on the subject of Nietzsche, and the importance of his theories in terms of contemporaneous anarchist issues. In all, she appeared during this period on at least twenty-three occasions, from Los Angeles to New York, speaking on the relation of Nietzsche's thought to the themes of atheism, anti-statism and (given the context of the First World War) anti-nationalism/militarism.

It would seem, then, that Goldman's evaluation of Nietzsche is merely a matter of public record, and that one need only consult the texts of these lectures in order to ascertain the exact nature of her claims as to Nietzsche's relevance to anarchism; unfortunately, this is not the case. Due to police raids on the offices of *Mother Earth*,[1] the anarchist newspaper which Goldman co-edited, any materials deemed to be seditious or to undermine the American war effort were confiscated. Apparently, Goldman herself searched, but with no success, for copies of her lectures.[2] Thus, the actual texts of her Nietzsche talks were lost to posterity.

Despite this, other existing references make it possible to gather a sense of the fundamentality of Nietzsche for Goldman in terms of constituting a modern anarchist praxis, as well as the debt she acknowledged to him whilst forming her own brand. Brief references to him are dispersed throughout Goldman's essays. But it is her autobiography, *Living My Life* (published in 1930, many years after the lectures), which makes clear Nietzsche's formative influence upon her, one that evidently provided an impetus not only intellectually, but in her personal life as well. Also surviving are contemporaneous accounts, supplied in the newspapers *Free Society* and *Mother Earth* itself, concerning several of her Nietzsche lectures. Although frustratingly cursory, these reports do give some indication of the general content and tenor of her lectures on this subject.

When combined with her comments pertaining to Nietzsche in both her autobiography and essays, these reviews help to provide the only remaining clues as to what Goldman might have had to say about this philosopher in her lectures. In doing so, one gains an understanding of the important role Nietzsche's thought can play in informing anarchist theory and practice, which, after all, was the message that Goldman was so anxious to convey.

Goldman dates her first encounter with Nietzsche's work to the period of her brief sojourn in Vienna, during the years 1895 and 1899 whilst studying nursing and midwifery there.[3] Apart from her studies, she also visited London and Paris where she lectured and attended clandestine anarchist meetings, thereby beginning to attain an international reputation amongst the revolutionary milieu. In this way she came to meet already celebrated anarchists such as Kropotkin, Michel and Malatesta; but her autobiography makes it evident that the authors to whom she was introduced through her reading during that time, Nietzsche among them, were just as important to her in terms of being an anarchist.

This was allied to her insistence that things of a cultural nature—music, drama, literature—had equal possibilities in terms of the revolutionary as things of a more directly political nature. While in Europe, for example, apart from anarchist gatherings, she attended Wagnerian opera, saw Eleonora Duse perform, and heard Levy Bruhl and Sigmund Freud lecture. Here also, she discovered the works of Henrik Ibsen, Gerhart Hauptmann, and von Hofmannsthal, as well as Nietzsche. These writers Goldman praises particularly for "hurling their anathemas against old values,"[4] an act she found compatible with the anarchist spirit.

Indeed, such names as those listed above were at that time amongst those most touted by the European avant-garde. An intellectual, writer or artist, in order to consider him/herself a 'modern' and in tune with the *zeitgeist*, had to be *au fait* with their works. Nietzsche was taken up by *fin-de-siècle* bohemians, particularly in the German-speaking world, as an exemplar of iconoclasm. He seemed to be a prophet calling for the clearance of the debris and weight of the oppressive past, its morality, religion, conventions and institutions. At the end of the 19th century this was associated with the rejection of one's heritage and traditions, of the old world order of 'the father'; but the phenomenon lasted until the First World War, amongst, most notably, the German Expressionists.[5]

As an anarchist, however, Goldman was unusual in her enthusiasms; and given the added factors of being a woman and a Jew, her interest in Nietzsche is perhaps all the more remarkable. Nevertheless, being timely culturally made her rather untimely politically, as she was to find when she tried to share her excitement about Nietzsche ("the most daring" of the "young iconoclasts"[6]), with the anarchist most close to her at the time, Ed Brady. She wrote to him in raptures over Nietzsche as representative of "the new literary spirit in Europe," and "the magic of his language, the beauty of his vision."[7] However: "Ed evidently did not share my fervour for the new art... he urged me not to tax my energies with idle reading. I was disappointed, but I consoled myself that he would appreciate the revolutionary spirit of the new literature when he had a chance to read it for himself."[8]

In America, years later, this would be Goldman's same hope for the audiences of her Nietzsche lectures; and for other anarchists, who, like Brady, could not understand how revolutions must be cultural as well as political. For Brady and their relationship, however, as she soon discovered, there was no hope. His ideas about politics as well as literature were mired in the 'classical,' and like other anarchists at that time, he couldn't see how the one had anything to do with the other. The passage in *Living My Life* which describes how and why Goldman ended her relationship with Brady is worth quoting at length because it illustrates the strength of her convictions concerning her stance as both anarchist and 'modern':

> It was caused by Nietzsche... One evening... James Huneker was present and a young friend of ours, P. Yelineck, a talented painter. They began discussing Nietzsche. I took part, expressing my enthusiasm over the great poet-philosopher and dwelling on the impression of his works on me. Huneker was surprised. "I did not know you were interested in anything outside of propaganda," he remarked. "That is because you don't know anything about anarchism," I replied, "else you would understand that it embraces every phase of life and effort and that it undermines the old, outlived values." Yelineck asserted that he was an anarchist because he was an artist; all creative people must be anarchists, he held, because they need scope and freedom for their expression. Huneker insisted that art has nothing to do with any ism. "Nietzsche himself is proof of it," he argued; "he is an aristocrat, his ideal is that of the superman because he has no sympathy with or faith in the common herd." I pointed out that Nietzsche was not a social theorist but a poet, a rebel and innovator. His aristocracy was neither of birth nor of purse; it was of the spirit. In that respect Nietzsche was an anarchist, and all true anarchists were aristocrats, I said.[9]

Here Goldman defends Nietzsche's concepts and their importance in the face of misunderstanding, as she would do later in her essays and lectures. Brady's response typifies the resistance with which she became familiar:

> "Nietzsche is a fool," he said, "a man with a diseased mind. He was doomed from birth to the idiocy which finally overtook him. He will be forgotten in less than a decade, and so will all those pseudo-moderns. They are contortions compared with the truly great of the past."[10]

In her fury over the incident, Goldman decided to leave Brady: "You're rooted in the old. Very well, remain there! But don't imagine that you will hold me to it... I'll free myself even if it means tearing you out of my heart."[11] Obviously, for Goldman, the Nietzschean task of the transvaluation of all values was one that she passionately took to heart. In order to realise a project both 'modern' and anarchist she was evidently willing to question and/or reject anything no matter how difficult for her personally.

Immediately following this episode, Goldman embarked on a lecture tour arranged by the anarchist circle based around the journal *Free Society*. As part of this, she presented a talk in Philadelphia in February, 1898, entitled "The

Basis of Morality,"[12] in which she cited Nietzsche in arguing against the oppression of totalising moral and legal systems. *Free Society* carried a report of her comments:

> Comrade Goldman maintained that all morality is dependent upon what is known to moralists as the "materialistic conception," that is to say, the ego. She said she was thoroughly in accord with Nietzsche in his *Twilight of the Idols* when he wrote that "our present morality is a degenerate idiosyncrasy which has caused an unutterable amount of harm."[13]

Also citing Kropotkin and Lacassagne, Goldman "denied the right of Church or State to frame a code of ethics to be used as the basis of all moral action."[14] This ploy of placing political references side by side with literary ones typifies Goldman's discursive practice, and is evidence of her belief that artistic expression could provide insights and revolutionary inspiration equal to or even greater than overtly political tracts.

In her later essays, Goldman attributed a more profound influence in this respect to art and literature rather than propaganda, i.e., purely political discourse. In publishing the anarchist monthly, *Mother Earth*, from 1906 onward, she hoped to provide in part a forum for the discussion of theory as well as presenting "socially significant" art.[15] This attitude finds its clearest expression in her 1911 preface to *Anarchism and Other Essays*:

> My great faith in the wonder worker, the spoken word, is no more. I have realized its inadequacy to awaken thought, or even emotion. Gradually... I came to see that oral propaganda is at best but a means of shaking people from their lethargy: it leaves no lasting impression... It is altogether different with the written mode of human expression... The relation between the writer and the reader is more intimate. True, books are only what we want them to be; rather, what we read into them. That we can do so demonstrates the importance of written as against oral expression.[16]

For these reasons, Goldman continually reiterates that Nietzsche's chosen modes of expression—poetic, literary, even visionary—are as fundamentally important as the actual content which they convey. Hers represents an important insight concerning the limits of political discourse, and one which is still relevant today.

Time and time again, in both her essays and lectures, Goldman can be found defending Nietzschean concepts in much the same way as she did when faced with Brady's resistant prejudices. She was keen to clear up certain unfortunate misconceptions about Nietzsche's ideas that were circulating just before America's entry into the First World War—misconceptions compounded later by the Nazis long after the philosopher had ceased to be a guiding force amongst intellectuals and artists. These misunderstandings mainly concern Nietzsche's most well-known and controversial concept, that of the *Übermensch*, as well as his ideas concerning an 'aristocratic' type of individualism, which Goldman saw as being close to Stirner's. Thus, she explains her frustration when confronted with ignorant misreadings of Nietzsche:

> The most disheartening tendency common among readers is to tear out one sentence from a work, as a criterion of the writer's ideas or personality. Friedrich Nietzsche, for instance, is decried as a hater of the weak because he believed in the *Übermensch*. It does not occur to the shallow interpreters of that giant mind that this vision of the *Übermensch* also called for a state of society which will not give birth to a race of weaklings or slaves.[17]

She goes on to disparage "the same narrow attitude" which reduces Stirner's brand of individualism to the debased formula "each for himself, the devil take the hind one."[18]

Likewise, in promulgating atheism in the stead of Christianity (or the Judaism she had rejected early on), Goldman bases her oppositional stance on the individualism of Nietzsche and Stirner, whom she asserts "have undertaken to transvalue the dead social and moral values of the past."[19] Both philosophers, she claims, opposed Christianity because:

> They saw in it a pernicious slave morality, the denial of life, the destroyer of all the elements that make for strength and character. True, Nietzsche has opposed the slave-morality idea inherent in Christianity on behalf of a master morality for the privileged few. But I venture to suggest that his master idea had nothing to do with the vulgarity of station, caste or wealth. Rather did it mean the masterful in human possibilities, the masterful in man that would help him to overcome old traditions and worn-out values, so that he may learn to become the creator of new and beautiful things.[20]

These concerns are reiterated in Goldman's next major lecture series which occurred during the period 1913-1917. Many of her talks from these years are specifically on Nietzsche or directly related topics.[21] Although the texts of these lectures are no longer extant, it appears from scanty records that at times the content of the talks may have been virtually identical, although the titles were sometimes changed to suit a particular audience or to make them more current. For instance, at various times she addressed an audience on the subject "Nietzsche, the Intellectual Storm Center of Europe," "Nietzsche, the Intellectual Storm Center of the European War," "Friedrich Nietzsche, the Intellectual Storm Center of the Great War" or "Nietzsche and the German Kaiser."[22]

These lectures, combined with her other anti-conscription and antiwar activity, were to eventually result, in 1917 (the year of America's entry into the

Great War), with her and Alexander Berkman's arrests on the charge of 'conspiracy' to obstruct the draft, and their subsequent unfortunate deportation to a newly communist Russia.

Other of her talks in this series concern the relevance of Nietzsche's thought to a variety of contemporaneous anarchist concerns: individualism, atheism, anti-statism, and anti-moralism. The rest, although not directly related to Nietzsche, witness Goldman's desire to inform discussion of social issues—e.g., women's suffrage, birth control, free love—with the Nietzschean/Stirnerian concepts of individualism. As she put it, "My lack of faith in the majority is dictated by my faith in the potentialities of the individual. Only when the latter becomes free to choose his associates for a common purpose, can we hope for order and harmony out of this world of chaos and inequality."[23]

On July 25, 1915 in San Francisco, Goldman delivered "Nietzsche, the Intellectual Storm Center of the War,"[24] the gist of which was described in *Mother Earth*. From this account it is clear that Goldman found herself yet again faced with the task of countering ill-informed accusations concerning the philosopher's thought, including the charge that "the man who had advocated 'the Will to Power' should... be held responsible for the present carnage in Europe."[25] The *Mother Earth* report relates the way in which Goldman summarily dealt with such false assertions:

> Miss Goldman pointed out that Friedrich Nietzsche's 'superman'— if he emerged at all—must emerge from a revised conception of present standards; that Nietzsche's vision was above and beyond the concepts of today... She quoted Nietzsche's *Thus Spake Zarathustra* to show... his attitude toward the uniformed brand of debility we term 'aristocracy'... No one having heard Miss Goldman's interpretation could longer list Nietzsche on the side of short-sighted aspiration. She made plain that he stood for the fathoming of depths which at present are hardly conceivable; and that those who dispute this fact prove merely that they do not understand Friedrich Nietzsche.[26]

Goldman makes a similar point in an undated essay, "Jealousy: Causes and a Possible Cure":[27]

> The 'beyond good and evil' philosopher, Nietzsche, is at present denounced as the perpetrator of national hatred and machine gun destruction; but only bad readers and bad pupils interpret him so. 'Beyond good and evil' means beyond prosecution, beyond judging, beyond killing, etc. *Beyond Good and Evil* opens before our eyes a vista the background of which is individual assertion combined with the understanding of all others who are unlike ourselves, who are different.[28]

Mother Earth also reported on a lecture, given in Philadelphia in 1915, entitled "Friedrich Nietzsche, the Intellectual Storm Center of Europe,"[29] in which Goldman again tackles this subject. The newspaper comments:

> At present Nietzsche serves nations and individuals (who do not read him and would not understand him if they did) with an excuse for every form of self-centered pitiless brutality and greed. "I am a Nietzschean," is said in extenuation of a great many selfish acts. But for a synthetic interpretation of the real Nietzsche and for an exposition of his philosophy one listens to Emma Goldman in silence.[30]

That this topic was seen as something of a speciality of Goldman's is also apparent from this journalist's commentary: "It is in this lecture more than in the others that Miss Goldman gives us of herself. Rarely, if ever, does one find a speaker more in harmony with the subject."[31]

And Goldman was more than able to make her favourite subject harmonise with whatever current events made relevant, whatever the issues or debates of the time made most pressing. Yet, it was certainly never the case that she was merely jumping on bandwagons. Always there is a definite sense that Goldman was setting her own agendas and determining her own priorities in terms of an anarchist praxis.

In her lectures and essays one witnesses a blending of Nietzschean individualism with Kropotkinian collectivism which makes her thought distinctive. It is this which allows her to advocate the primacy of the self and its autonomy, while simultaneously interesting herself in the social, e.g., women's issues, childhood, education, relationships between the sexes.[32]

But it is her insistence that the autonomous self must never be sacrificed in terms of the collective that sets her stance apart from that of communism or socialism, or even from certain types of anarchism, such as syndicalism, which view the masses or the workers in a revolutionary light. In this, as ever, Nietzsche was her example:

> Friedrich Nietzsche called the state a cold monster. What would he have called the hideous beast in the garb of modern dictatorship? Not that government had ever allowed much scope to the individual; but the champions of the new State ideology do not grant even that much. "The individual is nothing," they declare, "it is the collectivity which counts." Nothing less than complete surrender of the individual will satisfy the insatiable appetite of the new deity.[33]

But Goldman was also at pains to distinguish what she termed "individuality" from the dominant American ideology's beloved concept of "rugged individualism."[34] The latter she rejects as "only a masked attempt to repress and defeat the individual and his individuality," a doctrine which represents "all the 'individualism' for the masters, while the people are regimented into a slave

caste to serve a handful of self-seeking supermen."[35] A similar theme may well
have been the subject of her lecture given in May of 1917 in New York entitled
"The State and its Powerful Opponents: Friedrich Nietzsche, Max Stirner, Ralph
Waldo Emerson, David [sic] Thoreau and Others."[36]

As an anarchist who was simultaneously Russian (Lithuanian), German, and
a Yiddish-speaking Jewish female *émigré*, Goldman's thought was clearly intellectually, culturally and linguistically distinct from that of American radicalism,
as practised by, for example, Benjamin Tucker. The American heritage of dissent
derived its character from a combination of Protestantism, Emersonian/Thore-
auian individualism and Jeffersonian democracy; philosophies to which Goldman's anarchism owed little. Like other European *émigrés* in the anarchist
milieu she inhabited, she had left the past of the Old World behind, only to find
herself rootless in the New World. Accordingly, her political philosophy had origins other than those of the native-born American radical tradition. Goldman
reformulated Stirner's concept of the self and Kropotkin's collectivism and combined them with the Nietzschean project of the transvaluation of all values,
applying the resulting melange to an American socio-cultural context.[37]

If Goldman's combined attention to individualism and the social is unusual,
so is her interest in the timely whilst yet valuing the untimely. Although she
shared an interest in Nietzsche with many of her contemporaries, she did so in
a rather different sense. For *fin-de-siècle* intellectuals or early 20th century
Expressionists, for example, Nietzsche's *Übermensch* represented the superiority
of the creative genius over the conventions of the common herd, or bourgeois
ideology. Some German artists and writers, although opposing the old world
order of the state and its decrepit institutions, even went so far as to hail the
First World War, initially at least, as an instance of supposedly Nietzschean
destruction out of which would be born a new world free from the constraints
of tradition and history.[38]

This represents, of course, just the sort of wrong-headed approach to
Nietzsche that Goldman was ever at pains to point out is not compatible with
the overall spirit of the philosopher's thought, nor with that of anarchism. This
is because Goldman read Nietzsche, not so much as one primarily concerned
with being in tune with the *zeitgeist*, or merely with being a 'modern'; but
rather, first and foremost, as an anarchist. It is this that separates her readings
of Nietzsche from the majority of her contemporaries. She remarks:

> The "arrived" artists are dead souls upon the intellectual horizon.
> The uncompromising and daring spirits never "arrive." Their life
> represents an endless battle with the stupidity and the dullness of
> their time. They must remain what Nietzsche calls "untimely,"
> because everything that strives for a new form, new expression or
> new values is always doomed to be untimely.[39]

Likewise, whilst engaging with contemporaneous countercultural trends
and addressing social and political issues which were then very much of the

moment, Goldman's Nietzsche lectures, in the spirit of the philosopher himself, quite apparently aim to deliver untimely messages. This, for Goldman, represents the continuing aim of anarchism—an insight which allows her claim "Nietzsche was an anarchist."[40]

APPENDIX:
Chronology of Talks Given on Friedrich Nietzsche by Emma Goldman
1913

April 25, 5 PM: the Women's Club, and 8 PM: Howe Hall, Denver. Scheduled to present the opening lecture in a series on Nietzsche.

April 26, 5 PM: Women's Club, and 8 PM: Normal Hall, Denver. Scheduled to give lecture on Nietzsche.

April 28, 5 PM Women's Club, and 8 PM: Howe Hall, Denver. Scheduled to give talk on Nietzsche.

April 25: Women's Club, Denver. Scheduled to give lecture on Nietzsche.

April 30, 5 PM: Women's Club, 8 PM: Howe Hall, Denver. Scheduled to present a paper on Nietzsche.

May 1: Women's Club, Denver. Scheduled to give lecture on Nietzsche.

June 8: Jefferson Square Hall, San Francisco. "The Anti-Christ Friedrich Nietzsche: Powerful Attack Upon Christianity."

June 15: Mammoth Hall, Los Angeles. "Friedrich Nietzsche, The Anti-Governmentalist."

July 20: Jefferson Square Hall, San Francisco. "Friedrich Nietzsche, The Anti-Governmentalist."

November 23: Harlem Masonic Temple, New York City. "Friedrich Nietzsche, The Anti-Governmentalist."

November 30: Harlem Masonic Temple, New York City. "Beyond Good and Evil."

December 21: Harlem Masonic Temple, New York City. "The Anti-Christ: Friedrich Nietzsche's Powerful Attack on Christianity."

1915

March 21: Harlem Masonic Temple, New York City. "Nietzsche, the Intellectual Storm Center of the Great War."

May 30: Marble Hall, Denver. "Friedrich Nietzsche, the Intellectual Storm Center of the European War."

July 25: Averill Hall, San Francisco. "Nietzsche, the Intellectual Storm Center of the War."

August 3: Turn Hall, Portland, Oregon. "Nietzsche and War."

Date unknown, Philadelphia: "Friedrich Nietzsche, the Intellectual Storm

Center of Europe."

November 16: Turner Hall, Detroit, Michigan. "Friedrich Nietzsche, the Intellectual Storm Center of the European War."

December 2: Fine Arts Theatre, Chicago, Illinois. "Nietzsche and the German Kaiser."

1916

February 13: Harlem Masonic Temple, New York City. "Nietzsche and the German Kaiser."

March 23: Arcade Hall, Washington, D.C. "Nietzsche and the German Kaiser."

March 28: Conservatory of Music, Pittsburgh. "Friedrich Nietzsche, the Intellectual Storm Center of the Great War."

June 15: Burbank Hall, Los Angeles. "Friedrich Nietzsche and the German Kaiser."

July 21: Averill Hall, San Francisco. "Friedrich Nietzsche and the German Kaiser."

1917

May 20: Harlem Masonic Temple, New York City. "The State and Its Powerful Opponents: Friedrich Nietzsche, Max Stirner, Ralph Waldo Emerson, David Thoreau and Others"; scheduled to give talk on Nietzsche.

Information provided by Emma Goldman Papers Project, University of California at Berkeley.

Notes

1   See Emma Goldman, *Living My Life* (New York: Dover Publications, 1970).
2   Information provided by Candace Falk, Editor/Director of the Emma Goldman Papers Project, University of California at Berkeley.
3   Goldman, *Living My Life*, p. 172*ff.*
4   Ibid., p. 172.
5   See Roger Cardinal, *Expressionism* (London: Paladin, 1984), passim.
6   Goldman, *Living My Life*, p. 172.
7   Ibid.
8   Ibid.
9   Ibid., pp. 193-94.
10 Ibid., p. 194.
11 Ibid., p. 195.
12 See Appendix.
13 O. Shilling, "Emma Goldman in Philadelphia," *Free Society,* March, 13, 1898.
14 Ibid.
15 Introduction, Alix Kates Shulman, ed., *Red Emma Speaks: Selected Writings and Speeches* (London: Wildwood House, 1979), p. 14.
16 Goldman, Preface, *Anarchism and Other Essays* (New York: Dover Publications, 1969), pp. 41-43.
17 Ibid., p. 44.
18 Ibid.
19 Goldman, 'The Failure of Christianity,' *Red Emma Speaks*, p. 186.

20 Ibid., pp. 186-87.

21 See Appendix.

22 See Appendix.

23 Goldman, Preface, *Anarchism and Other Essays*, pp. 44-45.

24 See Appendix.

25 David Leigh, "Emma Goldman in San Francisco," *Mother Earth*, October, 1915, pp. 278-79.

26 Ibid.

27 The original of this lecture is housed in the Manuscript Division of The New York Public Library, as noted by Alix Kates Shulman in her preface to Part Two of *Red Emma Speaks*, p. 103. Shulman posits this text as circa 1912.

28 Goldman, "Jealousy: Causes and a Possible Cure," *Red Emma Speaks*, pp. 168-69.

29 See Appendix.

30 Harry Boland, "Two Days in Philadelphia" in *Mother Earth*, December, 1915, p 342.

31 Ibid.

32 It is interesting in this context to note that many of Goldman's lectures were given on separate occasions in Yiddish. This would seem to indicate that whilst espousing a Nietzschean project of the transvaluation of all values, including a rejection of tradition and religion, she yet retained a certain sense of cultural continuity. See *Living My Life*, passim.

33 "The Individual, Society and the State" in *Red Emma Speaks*, p. 94.

34 Ibid., p. 89.

35 Ibid.

36 See Appendix.

37 See Linnie Blake, "A Jew, A Whore, A Bomber: Becoming Emma Goldman, Rhizomatic Intellectual" in *Angelaki* 2:3 (1997), pp. 179-90.

38 See Roger Cardinal, passim.

39 Goldman, "Intellectual Proletarians" in *Red Emma Speaks*, p 178.

40 Goldman, *Living My Life*, p. 194.

Revolutionary Seer for a Post-Industrial Age
Ananda Coomaraswamy's Nietzsche

Allan Antliff

On March 5, 1916, the *New York Tribune* published an unsigned article entitled "To India the Great War is a Civil Conflict," which reported the arrival of "Dr. Ananda Coomaraswamy" in New York. "Dr. Coomaraswamy," the reporter noted, "comes under the unusual pledge not to criticize in any way the English government. And he keeps his promise. What he says is not politics—it is a comparison of civilizations and the ebb and flow of Asiatic idealism and Western materialism. But in this comparison there is much unwritten political prophecy."[1]

In early 1916 the *Tribune* described Coomaraswamy as a reserved and congenial "Asiatic idealist," but the reality was more complex. Coomaraswamy had been categorized as a dangerous subversive and this accounts for the unusual conditions under which he arrived in New York. Though a resident of England in 1916, he had lived in India on and off since 1903 and was very active in the Indian independence movement. His response to the British enactment of universal conscription in January 1916 was to register as a conscientious objector on the grounds that Indians had "no imperative call to offer military service."[2] He was finally permitted to emigrate to the United States with the understanding that he would never be allowed back into England and only after a portion of his property had been confiscated.[3] In the United States, Coomaraswamy served as curator of the Asian art collection of the Boston Museum of Fine Arts, and published extensively on Indian art and religion. He also immersed himself in New York City's anarchist movement, where he contributed to several journals and formed a circle at the Sunwise Turn bookstore, whose owners published his most famous book, *The Dance of Siva*, in 1918.[4]

Ananda Coomaraswamy was a child of nineteenth-century British imperialism, born on August 22, 1877 in Colombo, Sri Lanka (Ceylon). His father, Sir Mutu Coomaraswamy, belonged to the island's Tamil nobility and was the first Indian to be called to the bar in England. His mother, Elizabeth Clay Beeby, was a member of the English upper-class. In 1878 Elizabeth returned to England with her son. Ananda's father intended to follow, but fell ill and died. Consequently Coomaraswamy grew up in England, where he received a Bachelor's degree in Geology and Botany in 1900 from the University of London.[5]

He met his first wife, Ethel Partridge, while on a geological expedition in the south of England in 1901. The next year they married and sailed for Sri Lanka, where Coomaraswamy had been appointed Director of the Mineralogical Survey by the British government.[6] Ethel most likely introduced her husband to the writings of William Morris and other arts-and-crafts theorists. Partridge's father was an accomplished artisan and her brother, Fred Partridge, was a craftsman at the Chipping Campden Guild of Handicraft in Gloucestershire, England, run by the arts-and-crafts theorist and architect, C.R. Ashbee.[7] Sometime during their stay in India the Coomaraswamys commissioned Ashbee to refurbish a rundown Norman Chapel in Broad Campden, a village near Ashbee's Guild. This is where they settled after leaving Sri Lanka in 1907.

After two years of residence at the Chapel, Coomaraswamy began traveling again, and between 1909 and 1913 he moved back and forth between India and England. Ethel accompanied him to India in 1910, but returned to Broad Campden alone. Their marriage broke up shortly afterwards. At that point Ashbee took over maintenance of the Chapel and Coomaraswamy's presence grew less and less frequent.[8]

The couple's political activism (and the beginning of Ananda's art criticism) dates from 1905, when they played a key role in founding the "Ceylon Social Reform Society" and a journal, *The Ceylon National Review*, to "encourage and initiate reform in social customs amongst the Ceylonese, and to discourage the thoughtless imitation of unsuitable European habits and customs."[9] Significantly, one of the Society's earliest guest lecturers was Annie Besant, president of the International Theosophical Society, who spoke in November 1907 on "National Reform: A Plea for a Return to the Simpler Eastern Life."[10] Besant, who lived in Calcutta, was a spokesperson for the Indian *swaraj* (self-rule) movement which promoted *swadeshi* (indigenousness) on two fronts: the boycott of English industrial imports and the return to indigenous manufacture.[11] Besant's support for Indian independence can be traced to the theosophical movement's belief that the world was undergoing a universal "awakening" in which humanity's "spiritual" consciousness would overcome all social, cultural, and political-based divisiveness.[12] The theosophists regarded consciousness as the prime force in history, and they found a kindred attitude among Indian anti-colonialists associated with Coomaraswamy, notably the poet Rabindranath Tagore and his nephew, the painter Abanindronath Tagore.

The Tagores were prominent spokespersons in the Indian wing of the early twentieth-century pan-Asian independence movement, which attracted many artists and activists. Other pan-Asians included Coomaraswamy, Besant, the Japanese artist-poet Okarkura Kakuzo, and a loose network of Asian, European, and North American radicals.[13] The pan-Asianists called for pre-colonial cultural revivals among their respective peoples and rejected the European state model of social organization in favor of a "world brotherhood of nations" animated by spiritual values. To this end the Tagores combined resistance to Westernizing trends in the Indian independence movement with calls for the revival of India's traditional arts and culture. Coomaraswamy's contribution to the effort was to develop a sophisticated arts-and-crafts critique of industrial-capitalism and colonialism which linked Indian religious idealism and the country's artistic heritage to concrete social and economic issues.

Coomaraswamy argued India's *swadeshi* depended on the renewal of indige-nous arts and the spiritual idealism that had shaped the sub-continent's pre-industrial, pre-colonial social order. He underlined this point in the foreword to his first important art historical study, *Medieval Sinhalese Art* (1908), where he described conditions in the region of Sri Lanka prior to British occupation. At that time, sculptures and paintings were created by craftsmen to serve a spiri-tual purpose and art was inseparable from the cultural and material life of the community. Working under a social corporate structure "not unlike that of early medieval Europe," craftsmen produced art that was regarded by nobility and peasants alike as an integral feature of the religious practices which were the foundation of Indian society.[14] In *Essays in National Idealism*, a collection of essays that brought him great fame in India, Coomaraswamy expanded on this notion of an interrelationship between art, society, and religiosity.[15] Indian art was an "art of living" created according to the religious ideal that shaped and determined the life of the people, both "spiritually and materially."[16] Artist-craftsmen were intent not on expressing the "external forms of nature," but rather the "idea behind sensuous experience," a concept central to Indian reli-gion.[17] Out of this effort had grown a body of traditional forms "molded imper-ceptibly by successive generations" of craftsmen inspired by the religious ideal-ism animating the country as a whole.[18]

Industrial capitalism was destroying both the religious ideal in Indian art and the modes of production that tied this art to India's economic life. British imperial rule had disrupted the nobility's sponsorship of the artist-craftsman. Worse still, under the imperial capitalist economy machine-made mass-pro-duced goods were introduced to the East. In *Medieval Sinhalese Art* Coomaraswamy lamented the "grim" finality of this process which drove the vil-lage craftsmen from their looms and tools, thus divorcing "art from labor."[19] Each craft's demise entailed the death of another sphere of the community's "means of culture" as imported goods displaced the intellectual, imaginative, ethical and educational force embodied in the artisan.[20]

Imperialism also introduced cultural values that were equally destructive of the arts. As a result of commercialism, modern Europe had become materialis-tic: it placed a premium on appearances, encouraging the artist to create prod-ucts that gave pleasure through the imitation of the beautiful.[21] The "complete divorce between art and life" blinded Europeans to Indian art's organic rela-tionship to the "spiritual and material life of the people who gave it birth."[22] As a result, European art critics compared Indian art to the Western Greek proto-type and found the former wanting.[23] Seeing no worth in India's artistic her-itage, the British taught academic classicism in colonial art academies and neg-lected Indian religions and languages in institutions of higher learning. Thus they compounded the damage wrought by the economic assault on the sub-con-tinent's arts-and-crafts with a cultural program of "civilization" that Coomaraswamy bitterly denounced.[24]

In his 1907 essay, "The Deeper Meaning of the Struggle," Coomaraswamy argued industrial capitalism could only be overthrown through a struggle for independence that would renew the economic, social and religious conditions which had forged the sub-continent's pre-capitalist way of life.[25] Therefore, it was imperative to break the ideological power of industrial-capitalist modernity within the ranks of the independence movement. *Essays in National Idealism* contains a heated polemic against nationalists who argued indigenous industrial capitalism and the adoption of European social practices were paths to independence. Those who pursued "the wrong *swadeshi*," wrote Coomaraswamy, had no appreciation of the interrelation between craft production and social identity. They rejected their own culture and stood indifferently by while the craft industries and hereditary skills which were the key to true independence decayed and perished.[26]

Here, Coomaraswamy's relationship to the revolutionary socialist William Morris, founder of the English arts-and-crafts movement, becomes important. Roger Lipsey and others have pointed out that Coomaraswamy's art criticism was profoundly indebted to the anti-industrial, anti-capitalist writings of Morris.[27] Coomaraswamy even borrowed the title of the "Deeper Meaning of the Struggle" from a pamphlet by Morris. In his tract Morris roundly criticized industrial capitalism and called for a renewal of the "organic" arts-and-crafts of pre-industrial medieval Europe, when artistic expression was realized by the broad mass of the populace through craft production.[28] Morris saw the arts-and-crafts as the foundation for a better social order in which art would be "made by the people and for the people, as a happiness to the maker and the user."[29] And while he worked to realize this vision in England, he also extended it to the non-European world. In 1882, he penned a stinging attack on the introduction of industrial goods to India, claiming that by displacing the traditional crafts British imperialism was impoverishing Indian aesthetics and having a detrimental effect on cultural and religious life.[30] Morris protested, but it was Coomaraswamy and the *swadeshi* movement that gave this protest unprecedented force. Their anti-colonialism placed the arts-and-crafts at the forefront of a total refusal of industrial capitalism.

In England, Coomaraswamy's criticisms were enthusiastically supported by numerous arts-and-crafts radicals, including Arthur J. Penty and A.R. Orage, editor of London's influential journal, *The New Age*.[31] *The New Age* was an important vehicle for those among the British left who were critical of state socialism, a position which led it to champion various causes, including anarchist syndicalism, Nietzschean individualism, and Coomaraswamy's arts-and-crafts anti-colonialism.[32] In fact, Penty and Coomaraswamy were close friends and allies: both wrote for *The New Age*, and Penty repeatedly cited Coomaraswamy's work in his own publications. Penty was a well-known arts-and-crafts activist who promulgated an anarchist form of Guild Socialism in which federations of community-run arts-and-crafts guilds akin to Kropotkin's federated communes would replace both the state and privately-owned industry. And, like Coomaraswamy, Penty lamented the spread of industrial capitalism in the colonies and Europe, but held out the hope that the world could yet turn the tide.[33]

In 1914 Coomaraswamy coined the term "post-industrialism" to character-
ize his program.[34] He used the term to attack the Eurocentric progressivism of
European and non-European "modernizers" who divided the world into the
"advanced" and "backward" and fetishized the Western industrial capitalist experience as the most advanced stage. To speak of *post*-industrialism was to assert
his anti-industrial, anti-capitalist alternative was an immanent form of modernity not only in competition with European industrial capitalism, but destined
to supersede it.[35]

Summarizing the position of himself and Coomaraswamy, Penty wrote that
post-industrialists in both East and West were guided by a renewed "medievalism" which was ideological.[36] "Medievalism" designated the critical attitude of
the post-industrialist, who, in Penty's words, challenged "the concept of
progress with its undiscriminating industrial advance by exalting an age which,
whatever its defects, was at any rate free from the defects of the present and
thus provides something concrete and tangible around which our thinking may
crystallize."[37] Neither Penty nor Coomaraswamy sought a wholesale resuscita-
tion of medieval institutions: the period encapsulated a *model* for the social
organization of the future.[38] The most important feature of medieval society was
the integration of spiritual idealism with the day-to-day activities of the population, primarily through art. Indeed, Coomaraswamy bluntly stated that the "permanent revolution" which post-industrialism represented could "only [be real-
ized] by means of art."[39]

What, then, was Nietzsche's role in this revolution? Coomaraswamy posited
the spiritual revolt against colonialism in the East was being augmented by the
rise of Nietzschean anarchism in the West. This is the message he propagated in
numerous books and articles, including his major publication of the World War
I period, *The Dance of Siva*.

Let us begin with Coomaraswamy's codification of anarchism in *The Dance
of Siva's* closing essay, "Individuality, Autonomy, and Function." The title was a
translation of the Hindu principles of *sva-bhava*, *sva-rajya*, and *sva-dharma*, terms
that indicated Coomaraswamy was plumbing the depths of India's cultural and
spiritual heritage to formulate his interpretation of anarchism.[40] He opened his
essay observing that "the object of government," whether that of a conqueror,
hereditary monarchy, or majority government by representation, "is to make the
governed behave as the governors wish." The repudiation of such tyranny, therefore, necessitated the rejection of all forms of governing in favor of the anarchist
ideal, "individual autonomy."

There were two options. One was to reorder society so as to maximize the
desired independence of the individual. In this arrangement, people would only
cooperate on the basis of the agreement of each individual to submit to majority rule. Coomaraswamy, however, had no faith in the viability of such a system;
dissenters, he argued, would constantly split from the group. The end result
would be a society of autonomous self-ruling individuals, "each, as it were, sit-
ting armed in his own house, prepared to repel the intruder." The flaw of "majority rule" individualism was that it supported a desire to govern on the part of

each individual in which the focus of everyone's activity was self-aggrandizement. The resulting "anarchy of chaos" led to an "unstable [social] equilibrium" that could only be righted by a return to some form of the previous, "tyrannical" order: "the *status quo ante*."[41]

An alternative approach to individual autonomy was self-fulfillment through "renunciation—a repudiation of the will to govern." If this ethos was adopted there was nothing to prevent the recognition of common interests or the cooperation needed to achieve a harmonious society. Alert to the fact that some readers might construe his alternative to the "anarchy of chaos" as a call for state socialism, Coomaraswamy quickly added that "cooperation is not government"—a reiteration of the principle theme of Kropotkin's *Anarchist-Communism* manifesto of 1887. Drawing on Kropotkin, he argued that the ethos of renunciation encouraged the growth of "mutual aid" and allowed each individual to "fulfill his own function." He called this form of social organization a "spontaneous anarchy of renunciation." Spontaneous anarchism eliminated the desire for individuals to rule over each other, thus creating a stable social equilibrium that could bring an end to humanity's social strife and discord.[42]

Spontaneous anarchism was his "ideal." In practice he envisaged the anarchist ethos of renunciation guiding society's reorganization under an "enlightened executive." Though still retaining a semblance of government, this society of "unending love and unending liberty" would be blessed by "the greatest degree of freedom and justice practically possible."[43] In effect, Coomaraswamy recast the ancient Hindu doctrine of "individuality, autonomy, and function" as a form of anarchist individualism for his own time.

In "Individuality, Autonomy, and Function," he referred to the consciousness of the "renunciating anarchist" as a "will-to-power," a will which sought not to govern others, but only itself.[44] A second essay from *The Dance of Siva*, the "Cosmopolitan View of Nietzsche," developed this theme. Here Coomaraswamy brought Eastern religion, anarchism, and Nietzsche together in a bid to give the post-industrialist struggle in the West an individualist and idealist foundation similar to the East, where spiritual renewal along the lines of an "anarchy of renunciation" was a central feature of the coming post-industrial order.

Coomaraswamy opened his essay characterizing Nietzsche's philosophy as "the religion of modern Europe—the religion of Idealistic Individualism."[45] Nietzsche's "superman," he wrote, resembled the Chinese concept of the superior being and the Indian *Purusha, Bodhisattva,* and *Jivan-mukta*. Like its Eastern mystical counterparts, the superman realized the "unity and interdependence of all life and the interpenetration of the spiritual and material." This is why Nietzsche was so hostile towards Christianity—Christians cleaved the sacred off from the secular and divided the world into absolute polar opposites of "good" and "evil."[46] Nietzsche's superman, "whose virtue stands 'beyond good and evil,'" was the Western equivalent of the Indian *Arhat* (adept), *Buddha* (enlightened), *Jina* (conqueror), *Tirthakara* (finder of the ford), the *Bodhisattva* (incarnation of the bestowed virtue), and above all the *Jivan-mukta* (freed in this life), "whose actions are no longer good or bad, but proceed from his freed nature."[47]

The superman strove for "inner harmony" by ceasing to distinguish between "selfish" and "unselfish" actions. Her "supreme and only duty" was to be what she was.[48] Elsewhere Coomaraswamy summed up Nietzsche's philosophy as a process in which the individual gradually moved towards the Real by submitting to the "the artist, the saint, and the philosopher within." "For *that Reality*," he concluded, "*art Thou.*"[49]

Lawrence J. Rosàn has defined Indian religiosity as an "absolute" form of monism in which subjective consciousness is the crucial unifying component. If, as in Indian thought, "the individual is *consciously* to unite with the One Reality," then "that Reality itself," writes Rosàn, "must be a kind of consciousness."[50] Drawing on Nietzsche, Coomaraswamy constructed an individualist bridge between an Eastern religious ethos of enlightenment (Hinduism-Buddhism) and a Western ideal of harmonious social organization (anarchism).

The radicalism of Coomaraswamy's transnational anarchism, however, really comes to the fore when we compare his post-industrial revolution with Marxism. Marxists argue that the prerequisite historical stage in humanity's development toward a liberated society is industrial capitalism. As Marx conceived it, his endorsement of emergent industrialism in the West rendered his revolutionary program modern and "materialist" by virtue of its immanence in world history, as opposed to the supposedly non-immanent "utopianism" of Charles Fourier, Pierre-Joseph Proudhon, and other radicals. Indeed, Marx's followers have since dismissed all manner of "anti-modernists"—from William Blake, William Morris, and Nietzsche to twentieth-century revolutionaries such as Guy Debord and artist-anarchist Barnett Newman—as impractical "romantics" whose criticisms betray a "nostalgia" for pre-capitalist (read pre-modernist) forms of economy and community.[51]

Of course the question arises as to whose "modernity" Marx and his latter-day acolytes are taking about, for industrial capitalism and the train of political and social institutions associated with it has been, first and foremost, a Western affair. In fact, the smug tenacity of Marxists who locate modernity's immanence in industrialism to the exclusion of every other socioeconomic system is remarkable, given that it has brought us to nothing less than an environmental and social catastrophe of planetary proportions.[52]

By way of contrast, the anarchism of Coomaraswamy represents a compelling instance of cross-cultural intermingling in which a European critique of industrial capitalism founded on the arts-and-crafts was turned to anti-colonial ends in a campaign against Eurocentric cultural imperialism and its material corollary, industrial capitalism. As we have seen, Coomaraswamy's Nietzschean "renunciating ethos," which would resolve social conflict in favor of "the bestowing virtue of the superman," was inseparable from his post-industrial economic order.[53] This was an eminently anarchist project in which individualism flourished under an equitable social order that was ecological to the core.

By the time of his death in 1947, post-industrialism was all but forgotten. It represents a road not taken, bypassed after World War I by the capitalist West, the Soviet Empire, and Asia's numerous "modernizers," ranging from Jawaharlal

Nehru's India to China's Communist Party oligarchy. As the consequences become more and more clear, however, Coomaraswamy's critique only gains in force and urgency.

Notes

1   "To India the Great War is a Civil Conflict," *New York Tribune*, March 5, 1916, sec. 5, p. 2.
2   Roger Lipsey, *Coomaraswamy 3: His Life and Work* (Princeton: Princeton University Press, 1977), p. 124.
3   Ibid., p. 123.
4   Allan Antliff, *Anarchist Modernism: Art, Politics, and the First American Avant-Garde* (Chicago: University of Chicago Press, 2001).
5   Lipsey, *Coomaraswamy 3*, pp. 9-11.
6   Ibid., p. 14.
7   S. Durai Raja Singam, ed., *Ananda Coomaraswamy: Remembering and Remembering Again and Again* (Kuala Lumpar: S. Durai Raja, 1974), p. 4.
8   Ibid., pp. 15, 76.
9   Lipsey, *Coomaraswamy 3*, p. 22.
10 Ibid., p. 26.
11 Partha Mitter, *Art and Nationalism in India, 1850-1922* (Cambridge: Cambridge University Press, 1994), p. 235.
12 Ruth L. Bohan, "Katherine Dreier and the Spiritual in Art," *The Spiritual Image in Modern Art*, ed. Kathleen J. Regier (Wheaton: Theosophical Publishing House, 1987), p. 57.
13 Stephen N. Hay, *Asian Ideas of East and West: Tagore and His Critics in Japan, China, and India* (Cambridge: Harvard University Press, 1908), p. v.
14 Coomaraswamy, *Medieval Sinhalese Art* (Broad Campden: Essex House Press, 1908), p. v.
15 Lipsey, *Coomaraswamy 3*, p. 89.
16 Ananda Coomaraswamy, *Essays in National Idealism* (Colombo: Colombo Apothecaries Co. Ltd., 1909), pp. ii-iii.
17 Ibid., p. ii.
18 Ibid., 41. Coomaraswamy's conception of the oppositional import of this religious ethic vis-à-vis industrial capitalism is summed up in the 1916 introduction to *Buddha and the Gospel of Buddhism* where he contrasted the "Asiatic" belief that only a society based on moral order and mutual responsibility can obtain "the fruit of life" with the "laissez-faire competition and self-assertion" of contemporary European society. Ananda Coomaraswamy, *Buddha and the Gospel of Buddhism* (New York: Harper and Row Publishers, 1964), pp. vi-vii.
19 Coomaraswamy, *Medieval Sinhalese Art*, p. vi.
20 Ibid., p. vii.
21 Ibid., p. ix.
22 Coomaraswamy, *Essays in National Idealism*, p. 82.
23 Ibid., p. 84.
24 Ibid., pp. 96-108.
25 Originally published as a separate pamphlet in 1907, "The Deeper Meaning of the Struggle" is the keynote essay in *Essays in National Idealism*. See Coomaraswamy, *Essays in National Idealism*, pp. 1-6.
26 Ibid., pp. 74-75.
27 Lipsey, *Coomaraswamy 3*, pp. 258-64. See, for example, Ananda Coomaraswamy, *The Indian Craftsman*, with a foreword by C.R. Ashbee (London: Longmans, Green and Co., 1950), pp. 355-357.
28 William Morris, "The Deeper Meaning of the Struggle," *The Letters of William Morris to His Family and Friends*, ed. Philip Henderson (London: Longmans, Green and Co., 1950), pp. 355-57. This letter to the *Daily Chronicle* newspaper was later reprinted as a pamphlet by the Hammersmith Socialist Society.
29 Morris, *Hopes and Fears for Art* (London: Longmans, Green and Co., 1882), p. 66.

30 Ibid., p. 52.
31 On Ashbee's support for Coomaraswamy, see C.R. Ashbee, "Foreword," *The Indian Craftsman*, pp. v-xv.
32 Antliff, *Anarchist Modernism*, pp. 77-78.
33 Ibid., pp. 131-32.
34 A.J. Penty, *Post-Industrialism* (New York: The Macmillan Company, 1922), p. 14.
35 Carlo Mongardini has argued that progress, with its notion of a "development route leading from the present to the future," implies a stable social system exists wherein "progress is closely linked with the idea of culture and tradition." Coomaraswamy appropriated this powerful concept to provide a firm historical grounding for the values and social practices of the post-industrial future in Europe's medieval past and India's non-industrial present. This in turn framed the cultural and social practices shaping the progressive continuum from past to present globally, in contrast to the narrow Eurocentric frame of "progress" under nineteenth-century industrial capitalism. See Carlo Mongardini, "The Decadence of Modernity: The Delusions of Progress and the Search for Historical Consciousness," *Rethinking Progress: Movements, Forces, and Ideas at the End of the 20th Century*, eds. Jeffrey C. Alexander and Piotr Sztompka (Boston: Unwin Hyman, 1990), pp. 53-54.
36 Penty, *Post-Industrialism*, p. 16.
37 Ibid., p. 29.
38 Penty's fervent medievalism has been explored in Edward J. Kiernan, *Arthur J. Penty: His Contribution to Social Thought* (Washington, DC: The Catholic University of America Press, 1941).
39 Coomaraswamy, "The Purpose of Art," *The Modern Review* 13 (June, 1913), p. 606.
40 Coomaraswamy, *The Dance of Siva*, p. 137.
41 Ibid.
42 Ibid., 138. Peter Kropotkin, *"Anarchism" and "Anarchist-Communism: Its Basis and Principles"* (London: Freedom Press, 1987), pp. 23-59.
43 In Kropotkin's theory of anarchist communism, spontaneous mutual aid was one of the cornerstones of the future anarchist society. See Peter Kropotkin, *Mutual Aid* (Montreal: Black Rose Books, 1989), pp. 223-24.
44 Coomaraswamy, *The Dance of Siva* (New York: Dover Press, 1972) p. 138.
45 Ibid., p. 115.
46 Ibid., p. 118.
47 Ibid., p. 116.
48 Ibid., p. 120.
49 Coomaraswamy, "Love and Art," *The Modern Review* 17 (May, 1915), p. 581.
50 Lawrence J. Rosán, "Proclus and the Tejobindu Upaisad," *Neo-Platonism and Indian Thought*, ed. R. Baine Harris (Albany: SUNY Press, 1982), p. 45.
51 See, for example, the discussion of romanticism in Micheal Löwry, "Consumed by Night's Fire: The Dark Romanticism of Guy Debord," *Radical Philosophy* 87 (January/February, 1998), pp. 31-34. See also David Craven, *Abstract Expressionism as Cultural Critique: Dissent During the McCarthy Period* (Cambridge: Cambridge University Press, 1999), pp. 151-69. On Marxism and capitalist industrialism see Jean Baudrillard, *The Mirror of Production* (St. Louis: Telos Press, 1975).
52 See Murray Feshbach and Alfred Friendly Jr., *Ecocide in the USSR: Health and Nature Under Siege* (New York: Basic Books, 1992) and Judith Shapiro, *Mao's War Against Nature: Politics and the Environment in Revolutionary China* (Cambridge: Cambridge University Press, 2001).
53 Coomaraswamy, "The Religious Foundation of Life and Art," *Essays in Post-Industrialism: A Symposium and a Prophecy*, eds. Ananda Coomaraswamy and A.J. Penty (London: Foulis, 1914), n.p.

Dionysian Politics
The Anarchistic Implications of Friedrich Nietzsche's Critique of Western Epistemology

Andrew M. Koch

Introduction

Anyone who has more than a passing interest in Friedrich Nietzsche might be surprised to find a discussion of his work in the context of anarchism. Nietzsche repeatedly criticizes anarchism,[1] along with socialism and Christianity, for being naïve and ignoring the natural inequality of human beings. The result, he claims, produced a dysfunctional political order. To Nietzsche, the anarchist, socialist, and Christian are the decadent purveyors of an unnatural and destructive interpretation of the human condition.

However, one must be careful not to jump to a hasty conclusion on the issue of anarchism precisely because of Nietzsche's association of it with socialism and Christianity. When Nietzsche speaks of anarchism, he associates it with the ideals of equality and empowering the powerless discussed by anarchist writers such as Proudhon, Godwin, and Kropotkin. Thus, Nietzsche sees a similar thread to the "blessed are the wretched" ideas contained in Christianity. To him, this form of anarchism, along with socialism, is a "modern" addendum to the slave morality presented in Christianity.

Read literally, it is not difficult to come away from reading Nietzsche with the view that he is seeking a return to an aristocratic ideal.[2] This is the conclusion drawn by Bruce Detwiler's detailed interpretation of Nietzsche's politics.[3] The values of strength and nobility are continually stressed throughout Nietzsche's various works and such a conclusion is quite plausible. Aristocracy is praised for its recognition of the fundamental inequality of human beings. However, aristocracy in the traditional sense implies far more structure than what Nietzsche has in mind.

Democratic politics provides far more openness than aristocracy. In his attempt to construct a Nietzschean defense of democracy, Lawrence Hatab pursues this theme using the concepts of contemporary post-structuralism.[4] However, democracy, as the political manifestation of the slave morality, is denounced repeatedly in Nietzsche's writings. Representative democracy's open structure and implied meritocracy are compatible with Nietzsche's ideas, but to Nietzsche the logic of representative democracy suffers from the same flaw that Plato identified in the *Republic*. How can inferiors be expected to select those that are truly their superiors? One must presuppose "equality" before democra-

cy becomes a logical political prescription. Ultimately, democratic political practice denies the "will to power" and the natural hierarchy among human beings.

Those who claim that Nietzsche had anarchist tendencies can find support in
his undeniable hatred of the modern state. The State is for the "herd," the "superfluous ones."[5] The modern state perpetuates itself through promoting the lies of
"liberty" and "equality," which serve to justify the continual expansion of state
power. However, even considering these attacks on the nation-state, Nietzsche
does not simply fall into the category of "anarchist." The criticisms of the nation-
state, and its democratic ethos in the modern period, do not constitute a critique
of power in general nor a criticism of the use of power. To Nietzsche, the exercise of power is not only strategically useful, but the desire to exercise power is
argued to be part of the essential ontological constitution of all life.

Thus, the critical question: if Nietzsche is not, at least overtly, an anarchist,
and even his criticisms of the nation-state are not critiques of power, per se, but
criticism of the modern configuration of power, then what can Nietzsche possibly have to say that is worthwhile to anarchists? The central point of this paper
will be that it is not what Nietzsche has to say about politics that is important for
a discussion of anarchism, but what he had to say about "truth." The concern
about what validates statements as "true" or "false" is in either the foreground or
the background of all of Nietzsche's texts from *The Birth of Tragedy* to *Ecce Homo*.
When Nietzsche examines the "truth" that lay under the emergence of the modern democratic political order, he finds the old metaphysics in a new guise.

However, the problem is more complex than simply one of rejecting the old
slave morality and its secular and democratic form. If life should be viewed
through an aesthetic rather than a moral lens, and life and art both depend on
illusion,[6] then that aspect of life called the political must also be illusory. Lacking "truth," politics must operate under presuppositions. These presuppositions
have their origins in the Apollonian dream, the will to construct, not in any
essential truth about the world or human beings.

Only when confronted with Dionysus is the illusion revealed and the foundation for fixed structures destroyed. Nietzsche's epistemological critique leads
to a denial of all assertions of foundational validity. The character of the world
is anarchistic, without essential form or specific teleology. Therefore, the illusions by which we live are all transitory and ephemeral.

I. Politics as an Apollonian Enterprise

Following his general genealogical methodology, Nietzsche seeks explana-
tions for the existing social and political order not in the ideas and ideals of
human consciousness, but in the historical necessities that arose as human
beings struggled against nature and against each other for their survival. "Consciousness" has been nothing more than a recognition of that necessity. In the
area of morality, this has led to the revaluation of values coming with Christianity and the rise of the underclass to a position of dominance.[7] In politics,
Nietzsche claims that the nation-state arose out of the material concerns of land-
ed and commercial interests.[8]

The character of the nation-state, and the validity of its foundations, represent another matter. If the nation-state arose out of conditions that are historical and dependent upon the material conditions of life then, obviously, there can be no link between the exercise of power and any transcendental notion of collective essence, human or social teleologies, or moral foundations. There is still a question, however, regarding the "will to structure" as part of the "will to power." What is the origin of the process that initiates the construction of a political structure? The will to any structure is, for Nietzsche, Apollonian will.

Nietzsche's position is that the relationship between human beings and the world of nature was essentially an aesthetic relationship. The world is justified only as an aesthetic phenomenon.[9] This claim has several facets. The world requires interpretation. Human beings do not engage in uncovering any hidden transcendental truths. Science does not uncover truth, but is only a form of interpretation that takes place within a strict syntactical structure. The "objectivity" it seeks to bring to interpretation produces an outcome of a lower order than the artistic.[10] Science's real character is actually the suspension of "will" in its interpretation.[11] The condition of artistic creation is the highest condition for the human being.

The Apollonian and Dionysian are the two forces whose tension produces art. Nietzsche uses the metaphors of "dream" and "intoxication" to indicate what he means by these two concepts.[12] The Apollonian is an aesthetic will to construct an illusion, a fantasy, that brings beauty and order. Through the construction of an image we interpret our place and activities in relation to the world. "If we could imagine an incarnation of dissonance—and what is man if not that?—that dissonance, in order to endure life, would need a marvelous illusion to cover it with a veil of beauty. This is the proper artistic intention of Apollo..."[13] We are redeemed through these illusions.[14] The illusions give us identity, purpose, and connection.

Nietzsche argues that this fantasy has its origins in necessity.[15] Necessity initiates the construction of the illusion, but that alone is insufficient to validate the tentative and contingent outcome as corresponding to the "true." This is important because it establishes the foundationless character of all political structure. If the origin of structure is aesthetic rather than "essential" or even "scientific," then the tentative and contingent nature of any structure is more apparent. As Nietzsche puts it, art is not an imitation of nature but its metaphysical supplement, raised up beside nature to overcome it.[16]

The construction of a political order is precisely the type of product that Nietzsche describes as the outcome of Apollonian will. A political structure is the residue of the "will to power" as it seeks to bring order to the world by constructing an image of its structure. This drive gives rise to the formation of an illusion. The origin of the "political" is the need to create order and structure, to raise human beings out of the dissonance of nature.

In political terms, the will to construction, driven by necessity, has generated the representation of "human nature" as a fixed reference point for a deductive process of political application. Once a definition of the human character can be asserted, a political structure emerges as a logical outcome. This is the case regardless of the content of that representation.

Nietzsche's rejection of the Western philosophic tradition would, therefore, also constitute a rejection of the Western political traditions. From the perspective of genealogy, the characterizations of human nature that have served as the foundation for political prescriptions from Plato to Hobbes, Locke, Kropotkin, and Marx[17] have their origins in specific historical and contextual necessities. Human nature was represented in order to provide a basis for an Apollonian construction, the need to bring order and structure. The practice of politics is the application of that illusion.

II. What Dionysus Knows: Nietzsche's Critique of Western Epistemology

In the tension between Apollo and Dionysus, Nietzsche declares himself a disciple of Dionysus.[18] The metaphor Nietzsche uses to describe the power of Dionysus is "intoxication." However, an important question remains: what is the significance of intoxication within the general construction of art, interpretation, and Western epistemology? Nietzsche describes the condition directly. The world is to be understood as an aesthetic phenomenon. It is the Dionysian energy that is art's original power.[19]

The stirrings of Dionysus represent a condition of ecstasy, an emancipation from all symbolic powers.[20] The Dionysian state suspends the ordinary barriers of existence.[21] Under the influence of Dionysus one is no longer an artist, but a work of art.[22] While Nietzsche presents some self-criticism of his overly metaphysical language in *The Birth of Tragedy*,[23] he never abandons the basic distinction between Apollonian and Dionysian forces in the fabrication of both art and life.

This begs a question. What is it that Dionysus knows? Nietzsche makes the claim that the meaning to life can only be addressed as an aesthetic, interpreted phenomenon, and that any such interpretations are illusions. Dionysus knows that any claim to truth is nothing more than the assertion of an illusion. Truths are illusions that we have forgotten are illusions.[24]

> There exists neither "spirit," nor reason, nor thinking, nor consciousness, nor soul, nor will, nor truth: all are fictions that are of no use. There is no question of "subject and object," but of a particular species of animal that can prosper only through a certain relative rightness; above all, regularity of its perceptions (so that it can accumulate experience)...[25]

The living organism embodies the will to power. The will to power manifests the will to survival. In order to survive, Nietzsche claims that the human being must have some grasp of the regular functions encountered in the environment in order to enhance the chances of survival. Preservation is the motive to knowledge.[26] Thus, Nietzsche claims that it was unlikely that our knowledge would ever extend beyond what is necessary for survival.[27] The species must be able to comprehend enough of the calculable and constant occurrences in the world to base a scheme of behavior on them. However, the character of the world is chaos, with no essential order or beauty.[28] Those Apollonian constructs come as human beings interpret the world.

The human species creates illusions as a means of survival.[29] The criteria for truth is biological utility.[30] Therefore, there can be no *a priori* truths.[31] There are no "facts," only interpretations.[32] There is no single truth, but countless truths, no single meaning but countless interpretations.

Interpretations require language, which is an expression of power.[33] The word is a nerve stimuli.[34] It is an illusive bridge between things that are eternally apart.[35] The properties that words assign, however, are arbitrary.

Nietzsche also describes a sequence by which concepts are formed. First the organism has a sensation, then a word is created, and from the words concepts are built.[36] Concepts are used to designate cases where there are some similar characteristics.[37] But our language is metaphorical; it does not describe the essence of an object. To borrow terminology from semiotics to explain Nietzsche's point, our words refer to other words. They do not connect a sign to a referent, or some essential "thing-in-itself."

From Nietzsche's perspective, language sets the parameters for that which can be conceptualized. We think in the form that language provides for us.[38] This is the case with the rules that connect the words as well. It is grammar that has forced us to imagine that every deed must have a doer and that every result must have a cause. Grammar compels us to distinguish the lightning from its flash, conditioning us to think in terms of cause and effect.[39]

As images and impressions are turned into concepts, they allow for the construction of pyramidal structures, laws, subordination and boundaries, all of which appear to us as more stable than the uniqueness of each impression.[40] Thus, language contains power, not only as the constructs serving survival, but also as a set of structures to manipulate, control, establish hierarchies, and regulate behavior. Nietzsche refers to the product of this process using the metaphor of a "prison."[41]

Nietzsche is not just speaking of the issue of "knowledge" within the realm of social and artistic activity. In contrast to the transcendental tradition in Western epistemology going back to Plato, Nietzsche argues that knowledge is created, not discovered. All knowledge is a human construction. Science builds and rebuilds concepts.[42] Human beings build a conceptual web the way a bee builds a wax structure in order to hold its honey.[43] Nietzsche then gives another example to make his point. If human beings construct a definition of a mammal, and in looking at a camel pronounce, "There is a mammal," Nietzsche asks, "Of what truth value is such a claim?" That the camel is a mammal is not true in itself, but only in relation to the human category created for it. Nietzsche concludes by saying, "At bottom, what the investigator of such truths is seeking is only the metamorphosis of the world into man."[44]

The "truth" of these conceptual schemes does not rely on their capturing what is essential in a object, but only in that we have the will to believe in them as truth. The metaphors congeal and take on a reality of truth just as an eternally repeated dream would appear to be reality.[45] Apollonian dreams now impose themselves as the "real." The strength of these truths comes not from their inherent power, but from their antiquity, the fact that they have been so often repeated that to deny them is regarded as madness.[46]

The outcome of this critique of the dominant trend in Western epistemology is to reduce all speech to rhetoric. However, rhetoric is mastery of speech, not the capturing of "truth." Driven by necessity, all knowledge is interpretive, contingent, and historical. We grasp at fragmentary utilities, we do not construct universals in morals, nor do we capture essence in our search for understanding.

III. Subjectivity and Morality as the Foundational Lies of Politics

The political implications of Nietzsche's critique of epistemology are profound. If every concept exists only as words, and if there is no link between the words and some essential truth about the world, we only really "know" words. Therefore, "[Truth] is a movable host of metaphors, metonymies, and anthropomorphisms; in short, a sum of human relations which have been poetically and rhetorically intensified, transferred, and embellished, and which, after long usage, seem to a people to be fixed, canonical, and binding." Truth is an illusion that we have forgotten is an illusion.[47] The grandest illusion that governs our political lives is a fixed and constant notion of "subjectivity."

The "subject" is an invention.[48] Nietzsche means this in the strictest possible sense. Challenging Descartes, Nietzsche claims that a stable representation of subjectivity is grammatical custom, not fact.[49] What Nietzsche is really questioning is not the ontological certainty of being but the content of any configuration of being as it appears as a construct used in language. The "subject" is the fiction that many similar states in us are the effect of one substratum.[50] Subjectivity is the rhetorical imposition of unity, but it is we who construct that unity.[51] This imposed unity produces an effect, which allows for the assertion that ego has substance.[52] That has allowed the concept of "free will" a place to take up residence.

Like many philosophers before him, Nietzsche understands the link between the assertion of free will and the idea of morality. As Kant describes it, the autonomy of the will is the supreme principle of morals.[53] The reason for this link is simple: if one does not have the freedom to act, then one cannot be accountable for one's actions. To Nietzsche, the declaration that human beings have free will represents a link between religion, especially Christianity, and the transcendental tradition in Western philosophy, and the punitive nature of secular law.

Nietzsche's anti-moralism must be seen in this context. He denies traditional morality because it could not be justified without the assumption of free will. Nietzsche asserts that today free will could no longer be considered a faculty.[54] Free will is a human creation.[55] It holds sway only in half-educated people. In the real world there is no such thing as free will, only strong and weak wills.[56]

If free will is not the natural condition of human kind, where did the idea of morality come from and what is the origin of our contemporary errors about morality? This is a complicated issue because Nietzsche must confront different configurations that have justified moral prescriptions. In answering this question Nietzsche contrasts his own view to that of the explanation offered by the British empiricist tradition, even while acknowledging the importance of their non-theological approach to the issue of morality. British "psychology" is problematic in that it has an atomistic explanation that ignores the role of will, as will to power, and it assumes that morality is linked to unegoistic deeds.[57]

Nietzsche is interested in how morality has come to exercise power over individuals, especially in light of his critique of Western epistemology. Denying the "truth" of any definitions of a transcendental subject, Nietzsche concludes that there must be another method by which an analysis of our present condition must proceed. Hence, his genealogical exploration of the origins of morality links the exercise of power and the construction of subjectivity. The genealogical method represents a materialist approach to the study of social phenomena that seeks to explain the origins of constructs without reference to a transcendental subject as an explanatory basis for existing or past practices. If moral practice cannot be grounded in the "truth" of subjectivity, then it must be grounded in the exercise of power. There are no moral facts. Morality must be read as a symptom.[58] Because morality does not reflect universal truth or divine commandments, the real question of morality is what it tells us about its creators.[59]

Thus, when Nietzsche analyzes the transvaluations of values that occurs between antiquity and the rise of Christianity, he is looking for an explanation in the competition among differing classes from which a definition of subjectivity would emerge. Nietzsche assumes that different classes would have different experiences and, therefore, different outlooks on life. The concept of "good" has it origins in the actions of a noble class. To Nietzsche, the Greek concept of "noble" embodied values of strength, activity, happiness, health and vigor.[60] The noble person creates an image of "good" from itself and is so secure in that image that it can even see it in enemies.

The coming of Christianity brought about the first transvaluation of values. In itself, Nietzsche claims that religion has nothing to do with morality. It is simply a way of life backed up by a system of rewards and punishments.[61] Morality and religion are simply the means by which human beings seek to gain control over others. Encouraged by a class of priest that craved power over human beings, the great masses of people began to believe that their superior numbers gave them superior virtue. The values of strength, vigor, and happiness were replaced by guilt, blame, and revenge, personified by the Old Testament god of vengeance. The New Testament brought the "seducer of the poor"[62] who could entice ears hungry to hear that the wretched, ugly, depraved, and stupid are really the blessed of the earth. Armed with such a morality, the "herd" can now storm the castle and replace the noble values with the doctrine of equality and engage democratic political practice.

This transvaluation moved from what Nietzsche considered a more "naturalistic" morality to one that is "anti-natural." Natural morality is dominated by the instincts of life.[63] What is natural embraces the "will to power." The will to power is a "pathos," an event or activity in which life seeks to extend its force.[64] Anti-natural morality turns against the instincts of life.[65] It turns human beings into despisers of life, as it demands that they turn their energies against what is instinctual.

This transvaluation was largely carried out by a class of priests armed with a message of debt owed to their doctrine. The Christian priests asserted that one is bound to a creditor who has sacrificed himself to a debtor.[66] These priests are "the poisoners of life."[67] The priests invented sin in order to make the people subservient to them.[68]

The practical side of "free will" now emerges. The doctrine of "free will" has utility for the existing order of power. Nietzsche claims that free will was invented by theologians in order to make people "responsible" and, therefore, allow them to be punished.[69] Human beings are told they are free and responsible in order to justify subjugation and punishment as transgressors and sinners. Through the process of creating sinners, the church both legitimates its existence and extends its power, as the ability to punish. To Nietzsche, this is where Christian morality has taken Western culture.

While Nietzsche's target generally remains the exercise of church power, the imposition of "responsibility" has a parallel within the state. Morality and religion can shape men if it shapes legislation.[70] Given that claim, the myth of "free will" also serves the interest of the state as it is embodied in the structure of the judicial system. Using the concept of free will, the state can invent criminality and moral responsibility. This serves a very important function, because the more it can extend the idea of criminality, the more the state can extend its power. The more it can punish, the more it can justify its existence. In a time of peace, observes Nietzsche, the human being turns its aggression back on itself.[71]

The state has no claims to moral standing. It is an organization of power that protects a particular mode of existence. "The state organized immorality—internally: as police, penal law, classes, commerce, and family; externally: as will to power, to war, to conquest, to revenge."[72] By dividing responsibility and making virtues of patriotism and duty, the state can do things that no human being would ever consider. The state is a powerful entity, particularly in its ability to shape beliefs, but it has no intrinsic moral character.

This is particularly evident in the state's judicial function. Nietzsche claims that while the meaning of punishment is uncertain, its effects are not. The attempts of punishment to instill guilt are continually hindered as the practice of brutalization, lies, and violence against criminals by the state only makes prisoners hard and cold, strengthening their resistance.[73] Punishment is, therefore, only vengeance carried out by a collective power.

The impact of such a system extends beyond those labeled as the criminal.[74] As the "slave morality" has imposed its power on society, it has promoted ideals that Nietzsche identifies as being contrary to life. Weakness is seen as meritorious, impotence is called virtue, and misery is asserted as a sign of being chosen by god. In this "workshop where ideals are manufactured" the great mass comes to believe that they have to lick the "spittle" of the lords of the earth because their god had commanded them to obey authority. Nietzsche says of this workshop, "it stinks of so many lies."[75]

Nietzsche claims that what was needed was a new type of human being.[76] This person understands the world beyond the concepts of good and evil inherited from an age of decadence. They must be able to inhabit a culture in which there is no special purpose bestowed upon humanity, and understand that no one is responsible for being here.[77] Mankind has no special mission to fulfill, no purpose to realize. No one is to blame for us being who we are.[78]

To Nietzsche, human beings have the will and the ability to construct illusions. Life cannot be lived without them. Subjectivity and morality constitute the residue of Apollonian will. Apollo is the deity of self control.[79] Apollonian illusions direct life activity. Thus, it is the Apollonian will that also directs the production of morality. This 'will to construct' establishes a fabrication of subjectivity, from which it can impose a particular order of life on the world. This process is natural. The problem is that the current set of illusions are destructive to life, to people, and to the superior individual, who is not just the carrier of culture, but is its creator. What Apollo creates, Dionysus must destroy.

IV. Dionysian Politics

In his work, *A Nietzschean Defense of Democracy*, Lawrence J. Hatab makes the claim that given Nietzsche's critique of Western moral and epistemological foundations, democracy wins by default.[80] Democracy, Hatab asserts, is the only form of government that can accommodate an "ungrounded" politics, embrace the idea of political struggle, and still remain compatible with the kind of meritocracy that Nietzsche implied in his writings.[81] Representative democracy constitutes a temporary aristocracy, chosen by the citizens, securing that the best will rule.[82] The proceduralist approach of democratic practice secures that the mechanism will adjust to any change in the configuration of forces between the competing interests in the political arena.

While Hatab's work is a strong defense of democracy, it is open to question how strong a case he makes for involving Nietzsche in the discussion. One is left with the impression that Nietzsche either has to be pacified and turned into a democrat or dismissed as too radical and dangerous. Hence, Hatab discusses the "danger of the aesthetic approach" as requiring too grand a refashioning of society,[83] disassociating Nietzsche from the scope of his observations and the depth of his insights. This final section of this paper will try to bring together Nietzsche's critique of epistemology and morality and argue that the only political stance that can be consistent with these anti-foundational claims is anarchism.

Thus far, it has been argued that the "will to construct" is essentially an Apollonian activity. But Nietzsche claims to be a disciple of Dionysus. As such, Nietzsche asserts that these constructions are products of context, language, biological need, and historical circumstance. The structures produced are the result of circumstances, not reflections of any essential truths, universal conditions, or absolute knowledge. Our problem, according to Nietzsche, is that we have invented a myth about who and what we are, and then have taken it to be universal truth. That has led us to cultural, philosophic, religious, and political errors.

To say that Nietzsche had a dislike for the nation-state would be a gross understatement. "Fatherlandishness" is irrational "soil addiction."[84] In *Thus Spoke Zarathustra* he refers to the state as "the coldest of all cold monsters." It is the "New Idol,"[85] now that god has died. Nationalism is a swindle, perpetrated by politicians.[86] It is "insanity."[87] Perhaps, most importantly, Nietzsche claimed that nationalism is a "fiction," something that has been made.[88]

From these, and many other passages, it is clear that Nietzsche abhors the nation-state. But there is still a question about whether or not this disgust is the result of the current configuration of the state around a democratic ethos, or whether the configuration of any organized power within a collective would likely result in the same response. Simply put, it is both.

Nietzsche's venom toward democracy is expressed in places too numerous to mention. Democracy represents a decline in the way in which the state organizes power.[89] It puts power in the hands of the "herd."[90] In democracy all are equal, as with cattle.[91] The idea of "equal rights" is a "superstition that turns everyone into part of the "mob."[92]

Socialism and anarchism, along with liberal democracy, are caught in the web of criticism. Socialism is the doctrine of the most stupid of the herd animals. It represents the rebirth of the Christian idea of a "social instinct," in a secular form.[93] In asserting a "social instinct," socialism denies the uniqueness and differences among human beings. Therefore, Nietzsche concludes that socialism is opposed to life.

Anarchism is associated with socialism in Nietzsche's writings. Anarchism is a means, a form of agitation, in the service of socialist ideals.[94] According to Nietzsche, anarchism demands equality for a declining social strata.[95] The "last judgment" and "the revolution" both constitute otherworldly escapes.[96] They are both symptoms of decadence.

Liberalism, with its democratic ethos, also relies on a the metaphysics of equality. It seeks to make men small.[97] The liberal notion of a social contract does not change the basic problem of democratic politics. The contract simply constructs the idea of community around the invention that everyone is a debtor, owing allegiance to the state as their creditor.[98]

Socialism, anarchism (as associated with socialism), and liberalism are all rejected. What Nietzsche embraces is aristocracy. But what does he mean by aristocracy, and how can this vision be made compatible with the epistemological critique offered by Dionysus? In *The Will to Power*, Nietzsche states, "...I defend aristocracy." What he is defending against is extremely important. His target is the "herd animal ideals."[99]

Nietzsche is defending an aristocracy, but an aristocracy of merit, not of structure. Dionysus is opposed to structure. It interferes with the passion and spontaneous joy that Dionysus represents. Everything in the state is contrary to man's nature.[100] The legal structure in the state represents a partial restriction on the "will to life."[101] Human beings do not realize their creative force as part of the collective, but only as individuals.

However, there are only a few of these truly great individuals. People and races exist for the production and maintenance of the few of value in any civilization.[102] The rest are "superfluous."[103] The masses exist to serve great human beings and to emulate them.[104] Thus, power is not rejected as a part of social life. Power is necessary to order the mass. Even this age in which human beings are increasingly turned into "cogs in a machine"[105] may have its advantages. The turning of the masses into machines may provide a precondition for the invention of a "higher man."[106]

The arena of social life must be open to the influence of great individuals. Nietzsche's ideal is expressed in the *Use and Abuse of History*:

> The time will come when we shall wisely keep away from all constructions of the world-process, or even of the history of man—a time when we shall no more look at the masses but at individuals who form a sort of bridge over the wan stream of becoming.... One giant calls to the other across the waste space of time, and the high spirit-talk goes on, undisturbed by the wanton, noisy dwarfs who creep among them. The task of history is to be the mediator between these, and even to give motive and power to produce the great man.[107]

Nietzsche's defense of the individual is not the result of the types of transcendental assertion that arose from some Enlightenment thought. This is not humanism. All "constructions of the world-process" are to be rejected as Apollonian fictions that contain no truth, no essential representations of human nature, political, or social life. Such representations are fictions created out of fear and circumstance. They have no intrinsic validity and are arbitrary in nature. One cannot construct a political edifice where there is no place on which to build a foundation. Hence, Nietzsche rejects much of the Western tradition in philosophy, since it has sought to fabricate an image of the human being and of consciousness as the basis for social and political life.

Nietzsche's connection to anarchism stems, therefore, from his critique of Western epistemology. The representation of the human character that provides the foundation for political prescriptions is, to Nietzsche, nothing more that an image used to justify a particular configuration of power. The schematization of experience follows from arbitrarily assigned categories, the basis of which cannot be validated in any essential way. The products of this process of knowledge creation serve only to maintain and extend the arbitrary character of structure.

In place of truth, there is only language and power. In the absence of truth, there is no form of political life that can be given priority. Given the absence of epistemological validity for any moral or structural underpinnings to a particular form of political life, the superior individual emerges as the "default" condition. Where there is no possibility of constructing *a prioris* about human nature, there can be no universals regarding politics.[108] The superior individual is given primacy in Nietzsche's political thinking only because of the essential anarchistic character of the world.

Conclusion: Anarchism and the Overman

With every structure open to Dionysian deconstruction, the essentially anarchistic nature of life is revealed. Nietzsche does not perceive this in negative terms, but as opening up the possibilities for human achievement. The human task is to interpret, to live and reflect life in creative achievements. It is the anarchistic nature of the world that makes this both possible and necessary.

In Nietzsche's claim that a tension exists between Apollo and Dionysus which is essential to art and life, he introduces a question for political life that cannot be ignored. If politics is grounded in presuppositions that cannot be validated, then the order of life manifested by those presuppositions is open to challenge. To put it simply, there can be no moral or ethical grounds for obedience. Further, since any practical-utilitarian justification for obedience can always be superseded by another order of life, another set of illusory goals, the order of the state remains foundationless. With "truth" deconstructed, all that remains is power.

Anarchism emerges from Nietzsche's philosophy not as a political prescription but as an underlying condition to social and political existence. The world is anarchistic, devoid of any specific content and meaning. Since representation of the human character is possible, any politics constructed on a characterization of human nature must be false. Owing to this epistemological void, the aspirations of the superior individual, an individual who is bound to a particular historically determined condition of necessity, becomes paramount. Only individuals in the process of life are real. All else is illusion.

Nietzsche's critique of existing morality and of politics is oriented to the present, but his understanding of political possibilities is oriented toward the future. Nietzsche claims that his politics is for an age not yet born.[109] Politics, as it is presently conceived, must come to an end. Does this mean that Nietzsche is a utopian? He never claims that the age of the overman would end conflict, bring the reign of "truth," or end suffering. He simply argues that it would function better than an age in which human beings are taught to despise themselves.

The overman is an ideal, but it is a concept devoid of any particular content, of any particular image. The overman comes after the anarchistic nature of the world is understood, after a recognition that the world does not contain a singular truth or a teleologically destined way of life. The overman embodies creativity and is capable of self-sacrifice, and as such, love, but Nietzsche adds little that is specific. To do so would be to suggest the content of a future before we get there. In the light of his critique of such sorcery, Nietzsche cannot justify the assertion of any specific character, except the overman's recognition that it must create itself in a world without structure. It is a world in which there is power, but a world in which all knowledge and meaning are recognized as human inventions.

The overman can be a future for mankind only after the historical and contingent nature of Apollonian illusions are revealed. With the death of that collective illusion called "god," human beings must have a new goal in order to be able to soar. "...[T]his is what the will to truth should mean to you: that everything be changed into what is thinkable for man, visible for man, feelable by man."[110] Our new knowledge expresses praise and a justification for "impermanence."[111]

The overman is created from the Dionysian. It is the activity of creating and recreating ourselves, the hammer chipping away at the stone until the image is revealed.[112] The overman is in mankind's future only in a context free from structure, free from a predetermined image to which the future and human kind must conform.

Notes

1 See, for example *Twilight of the Idols*, in Walter Kaufmann, trans. and ed., *The Portable Nietzsche* (New York: Viking Press, 1968), p. 534; *The Antichrist* in Kaufmann, *The Portable Nietzsche*, pp. 647-48.

2 It should be noted that this is not a Burkian type of aristocracy, with the strong component of tradition, but an open notion of aristocracy, more consistent with a deontologized Plato.

3 Bruce Detwiler, *Nietzsche and the Politics of Aristocratic Radicalism* (Chicago: University of Chicago Press, 1990).

4 Lawrence J. Hatab, *A Nietzschean Defense of Democracy* (Chicago: Open Court, 1995).

5 Friedrich Nietzsche, *Thus Spoke Zarathustra*, in Kaufmann, *The Portable Nietzsche*, p. 161.

6 Nietzsche, *The Birth of Tragedy and the Genealogy of Morals*, trans. Francis Golffing (New York: Doubleday Anchor, 1956), p. 10.

7 Nietzsche, *On the Genealogy of Morals and Ecce Homo*, trans. Walter Kaufmann (New York: Vintage, 1989).

8 Nietzsche also recognized that there were forces at work eroding the continued existence of the nation-state; see *Human all too Human*, pp. 61-62.

9 Nietzsche, *The Birth of Tragedy and the Genealogy of Morals*, §24.

10 Nietzsche, *The Will to Power*, trans. Walter Kaufmann (New York: Vintage Press, 1968), §816.

11 Nietzsche, *The Will to Power*, §812.

12 Nietzsche, *The Birth of Tragedy and the Genealogy of Morals*; Nietzsche, *The Will to Power*, §798.

13 Nietzsche, *The Birth of Tragedy and the Genealogy of Morals*, §25.

14 Ibid., §§4, 16.

15 Ibid., §1.

16 Ibid., §24.

17 See the critique of Marx in Jacques Derrida's *Positions* (Chicago: University of Chicago Press, 1981).

18 Nietzsche, *Beyond Good and Evil*, trans. Walter Kaufmann (New York: Vintage, 1966), §295.

19 Nietzsche, *The Birth of Tragedy and the Genealogy of Morals*, §25.

20 Ibid., §2.

21 Ibid., §7.

22 Ibid., §1.

23 See the 1886 Preface to *The Birth of Tragedy*, entitled "Backward Glance."

24 "On Truth and Lies in a Nonmoral Sense," in *Nietzsche Selections*, ed. Richard Schacht (New

York: Macmillan, 1993), p. 49.

25 Nietzsche, *The Will to Power*, §480.

26 Ibid., §480.

27 Ibid., §494.

28 Nietzsche, *Joyful Wisdom*, trans. Thomas Common (New York: Frederick Ungar, 1960), §109.

29 Ibid., §110.

30 Nietzsche, *The Will to Power*, §584.

31 Ibid., §862.

32 Ibid., §481.

33 Nietzsche, *On the Genealogy of Morals and Ecce Homo*, p. 26.

34 Nietzsche, "On Truth and Lies in a Nonmoral Sense," p. 47.

35 Nietzsche, *Thus Spoke Zarathustra*, p. 328.

36 Nietzsche, *The Will to Power*, §506.

37 Nietzsche, "On Truth and Lies in a Nonmoral Sense," p. 48.

38 Nietzsche, *The Will to Power*, §522.

39 Nietzsche, *On the Genealogy of Morals and Ecce Homo*, p. 45.

40 Nietzsche, "On Truth and Lies in a Nonmoral Sense," p. 49.

41 Ibid., p. 52.

42 Ibid.

43 Ibid., p. 50.

44 Ibid.

45 Ibid., p. 51.

46 Nietzsche, *Joyful Wisdom*, §110.

47 Nietzsche, "On Truth and Lies in a Nonmoral Sense," p. 49.

48 Nietzsche, *Joyful Wisdom*, §481.

49 Ibid., §484.

50 Ibid., §485.

51 Ibid.

52 Ibid., §488.

53 Immanuel Kant, "Metaphysical Foundations of Morals," in *The Philosophy of Kant*, ed. Carl Friedrich, (New York: Random House, 1977), p. 187.

54 Nietzsche, *The Antichrist*, §14.

55 Nietzsche, *On the Genealogy of Morals and Ecce Homo*, p. 69.

56 Nietzsche, *Beyond Good and Evil*, §21.

57 Nietzsche, *On the Genealogy of Morals and Ecce Homo*, pp. 24–26.

58 Nietzsche, *Twilight of the Idols*, in Schacht, *Nietzsche Selections*, p. 315.

59 Nietzsche, *Beyond Good and Evil*, §187.

60 Nietzsche, *On the Genealogy of Morals and Ecce Homo*, pp. 28-38.

61 Nietzsche, *The Will to Power*, §146.

62 Nietzsche, *On the Genealogy of Morals and Ecce Homo*, p. 35.

63 Nietzsche, *Twilight of the Idols*, in Schacht, *Nietzsche Selections*, p. 311.

64 Nietzsche, *The Will to Power*, §§635–36.

65 Nietzsche, *Twilight of the Idols*, in Schacht, *Nietzsche Selections*, p. 311.

66 Nietzsche, *On the Genealogy of Morals and Ecce Homo*, pp. 90-92.

67 Nietzsche, *The Antichrist*, §8.

68 Nietzsche, *The Antichrist*, §26.

69 Nietzsche, *Joyful Wisdom*, p. 314, and in *The Antichrist*, p. 598.

70 Nietzsche, *The Will to Power*, §144.

71 Nietzsche, *On the Genealogy of Morals and Ecce Homo*, pp. 84-85.

72 Nietzsche, *The Will to Power*, §717.

73 Nietzsche, *On the Genealogy of Morals and Ecce Homo*, pp. 80-82.

74 Although, it should be noted that Nietzsche asserted that all great men were criminals in relation to their time. See Nietzsche, *The Will to Power*, §736.

75 Nietzsche, *On the Genealogy of Morals and Ecce Homo*, p. 46-47.
76 Ibid., p. 96.
77 Nietzsche, *Joyful Wisdom*, p. 315.
78 Nietzsche, *The Will to Power*, §765.
79 Nietzsche, *The Birth of Tragedy and the Genealogy of Morals*, §4.
80 Hatab, *A Nietzschean Defense of Democracy*, p. 4.
81 Ibid., p. 117.
82 Ibid., p. 125.
83 Ibid., p. 232.
84 Nietzsche, *Beyond Good and Evil*, §241.
85 Nietzsche, *Thus Spoke Zarathustra*, p. 160.
86 Nietzsche, *The Will to Power*, §78.
87 Ibid., §256.
88 Ibid., §251.
89 Nietzsche, *Twilight of the Idols*, in Kaufmann, *The Portable Nietzsche*, p. 543.
90 Nietzsche, *The Will to Power*, §156.
91 Ibid., §752.
92 Ibid., §864.
93 Ibid., §§20, 30.
94 Ibid., §784.
95 Nietzsche, *Twilight of the Idols*, in Kaufmann, *The Portable Nietzsche*, p. 534.
96 Ibid., p. 534.
97 Nietzsche, *Twilight of the Idols*, in Schacht, *Nietzsche Selections*, p. 317.
98 Nietzsche, *On the Genealogy of Morals and Ecce Homo*, pp. 71-72.
99 Nietzsche, *The Will to Power*, §936.
100 Ibid., §383.
101 Nietzsche, *On the Genealogy of Morals and Ecce Homo*, p. 76.
102 Nietzsche, *The Will to Power*, §679.
103 Nietzsche, *Thus Spoke Zarathustra*, pp. 161-62.
104 Nietzsche, *The Use and Abuse of History*, trans. Adrian Collins (New York: Macmillan, 1988), p. 61.
105 Ibid., p. 44.
106 Nietzsche, *The Will to Power*, §866.
107 Nietzsche, *The Use and Abuse of History*, p. 59.
108 Andrew M. Koch, "Poststructuralism and the Epistemological Basis of Anarchism," in *Philosophy of the Social Sciences*. 23 (3) 327-51, 1993, p. 339.
109 Nietzsche, *The Will to Power*, §958.
110 Nietzsche, *Thus Spoke Zarathustra*, p. 198.
111 Ibid., p. 199.
112 Ibid.

The "Death of God"

Index of Possibilities for 'Moving Beyond' Without Horror

Franco Riccio

1. The death of God as a metaphor. The style of Nietzsche. Deleuze points out a method of approach, one among many possible ones, without claiming exclusive rights to it. Singularity of style. One which reclaims the 'right to antisense,' legitimating a philological evasion of the text and exercises of literature, because at its core, as Deleuze observes, moves 'something which does not and will not let itself be codified.' These are observations to take into favorable consideration, since they move to the heart of the Nietzschean corpus which, in the form of aphorism and metaphor, sets the conditions for a new approach, a movement of 'derive' which Deleuze describes with the expression 'to be embarked with.' In Deleuze's writing we are confronted with a book 'in movement' so-to-speak, whose inputs are given by the immediate contact between the pages and the outside; this contact allows a relation of co-involvement through which energy fluxes cross and distribute themselves according to the specificity of the contact with which the inputs manifest themselves. This movement legitimizes 'antisense' and establishes the 'being embarked with.'

This kind of movement is not without risk. On this body lines of actualization can cross in different directions and find themselves mixed together in every possible synthesis, specters of a recoding under the sign of the Law, the Contract, and the Institution: the principal means of codification of all societies.

Convergence of Deleuze and Foucault

An inevitable risk. However, not inscribeable as a limit of the written word, totalizing a break with the *logos*, prelude to irrationalism. To the contrary, despite all the possible deformations which could conceal themselves in this co-involvement, it expresses the intrinsic element in the attempt of radical decoding—an attempt which goes beyond old and new codes in order to propose itself as a dynamic movement, through which thought and writing allow the flow toward the 'outside,' and there temporalization inscribes the encounter on temporal scales which fix the angle of encounter itself.

This piece originally appeared in *Mille Piani* #14, 1998. Translated from the Italian by Jeffrey Bussolini and Laura Fantone, City University of New York (Center for the Study of Culture, Technology, and Work).

From the textual grammar to the temporal fluctuations of a writing which takes shape through the immediate encounter with the fluctuating variables of the 'outside,' in relation to which it can verify itself (as is possible in face of its opposite) in an evolution of the Nietzschean deconstituting work, deciphered in the readiness to listen to the multiple messages which the fragmentary character of writing and the metaphorical style subtract from the unity of interpretation.

Deleuze is explicit. Nietzsche not only "founds a thought and writing on an immediate relation with the outside," as has been claimed, but since "an aphorism is a state of force," it is necessary "to find an actual external force" able to run a "stream of energy" through Nietzsche's texts.[1]

2. Deleuze's reading, the one that is re-encountered in Klossowski and Foucault, gives motion to multiple developments of Nietzsche's thought. Out of line with the interpretive thread promoted by Heidegger, it is possible to undertake an experiment as abandonment of interpretation, re-proposing the matter of the hegemony of the signifier, and on the contrary surveying indications, promoting further articulations. An experiment whose aim is not to verify, but to open 'inactual' spaces of becoming beyond the grid of representational thinking. Clearly, such experimentation proposes a new way of thinking and, consequently, of taking positions. A new way of thinking because it calls for "thinking through inactuality" of its "not-yet being," and as such is a digression from the institutional use of thought that reinforces identity. A nomadic thinking abandons this paradigm's certainty and its axiomatic definitions, in an interruption of 'historical memory,' to move towards paths without horizons in a disjunctive inclusion of the various emergent differences passing through them.[2]

The new positioning actualizes the choice of non-neutral exploration aware of the impossibility of an objective criterion, able to situate itself outside of any controversy about unobtainable objectivity. And this not as a limit, but as a scientific title to a thinking through the possible options between different paths. New emergences of an 'outside,' always more unobjectifiable due to their dynamics of movement, open to the sciences and philosophy, "an approach from a perspective which strips them of the ideal of purity and disinterestedness with which their path has usually been adorned," an experimental perspective which "promotes vectors of innovation, catalyzing cultural and intellectual inventions. However, to be understood and appreciated at their right value, that is as adventure and not revealing universal truth, this calls for the same type of critical spirit necessary in all other debates of cultural, social and political ideas."[3] Far from Nietzsche, contemporary epistemology rediscovers by various paths the 'other' dimension of the subjective, anthropomorphic representation of modernity and that the 'announcement' of the 'death of God' entails the vanishing of the 'apparent' world,[4] pointing out the experimentation of a becoming nomad, involving thinking and nature, humans and society in the coextensivity of the same process which, in constant relation between thinking and the outside, develops, in a surprising recalling of Prigogine, by *stochastic* paths and *sections of the movement of scattering*.[5]

3. There is no theme more literally Nietzschean than that of 'power,' associated with the 'inactual' constant relation between 'thinking' and 'the outside'—themes to which are tied a unanimous recognition of the various interpretations, and at the same time source of irremediable differences. Differences are the 'natural state' of Nietzsche's work, as we have seen previously. The singularity of Nietzsche's work neutralizes the criterion of objectivity and urges that taking of position the critical value of which has already been underlined and discovered in the new epistemology.

This taking of position is as much authorized as it is intent to liberate from the text fluxes of energy, 'lines of flight,' as Deleuze and Guattari would call them, in the actions of 'striation' worked by dominating Reason, promoting creative acts—not only artistic-literary, but philosophical-political.

This positioning is, consequently, a choice. It is built on the assent to the 'being-embarked-with' to acquire an experimental valence of approach to the themes indicated and to bring them back to the Nietzschean announcement of the 'death of God,' holding onto indices of a 'rejuvenating entropy' outside of the syntax and the grammar which formalize the written word, the function of which is to seduce the subjective angle to a hermeneutics of the univocal sense, thus pushing the possibility of thinking the death of God toward that which has already been (given to) thought. Undoubtedly this is an 'arbitrary' position. All the same it is an 'inactual' exercise of opening toward the internal fold of the announcement of the death of God which promotes it, and in relation to which the following are possible:

—a line of flight from dialectical thinking and, even more so, from a thinking of the power of identity, for which 'power,' 'thinking,' and 'the outside' assume either contradictory values or a stroke of reciprocal exclusion;

—working a disjunctive connection of the three terms as part of the announcement of the death of God, temporalizing the complex dynamic of movement and of connection in relation to an external 'power' which promotes 'antisense' and which finds singular attention in contemporary scientific experiments;

—searching for an adequate language, not reducible to the various modalities of 'discourse.'

4. The Nietzschean announcement of the death of God and the implosion of meaning gives space to the game of interpretations from which the taking of positions distracts attention, in order to direct attention instead toward that which is definitively, notwithstanding the proclamation of faith, revealed in the Christian-bourgeois use of the name of God: the attribution of a finite mode of thinking born in the city and articulated through its historical transformations.

An operation tangential to the others, in the attempt at an 'antisense' suggested by Deleuze, is made possible through a force emerging from the outside, defigured in the microprocesses of its stochastic fluctuations and involving both life time and thinking time. An operation without the ambition for an exhaustive and definitive result, aware of the limiting spiral of the 'unfaithful' approach, spurred by an unpredictable present in its emergences to imprint the syntactic-grammatical fixity of the announcement. In its immediate relation to an 'outside' which is non-structurable, and therefore non-formalizable and non-historicizable, an index of the decodifying movement of a style of thought whose de-axiomatic and axiomatic functions have always returned and return still today, as Deleuze would say, to the transhistorical activity of the Greco-European valence.

This methodological prolegomenon is indispensable for the passage from the rather indecipherable indications of the 'announcement' to a mode of thinking in the quality taken from the 'name.' This cannot be done without underlining the two ways of dealing with such a question: subtraction and generalization.

—Subtraction from the echoes of the 'ante,' so common in the literature on Nietzsche, which seems so unaware of the fact that that 'ante' for Nietzsche always comes from *ressentiment*.

> I know you well... you are the assassin of God... You do not support
> the one that you see—since you see always from part to part, you,
> the ugliest of men! You have won out against this evidence.[6]

At the same time, it is the reactive condition through which the ancient perpetuates itself:

> Those who battle against monsters must be careful not to become,
> in doing so, monsters.[7]

It is worth noting here the neutralizing of every discourse on the Antichrist and on the problem of the Nietzsche-Christ relation. The latter was documented by the fact that Nietzsche signed his last letters as Dionysus or the Crucifix alternately.[8]

—Generalization because the 'announcement' gives to the name the peculiarity of thought, a memory assembled by the various theoretical and practical machines, smoothing their apparently irreducible differences and channeling innovation into 'molar instances'[9] traceable not only in the classic and modern rationalism, but in contemporary problems in informatics and in cybernetic machines 'to the degree in which they give power to a central memory or organ.'[10]

5. God is identity, centrality: Trinity taken from the name and given to finite thinking, subtracted to the internal dynamic of the earth, even though the earth is its condition of existence and development. For such an appropriation, finite thinking imposed itself as an infinite thinking; thinking outside of any temporalization of space, through which it gives to humanity a 'planetary and biospheric' becoming, even if this becoming is limited to the modernization of its power of administering contingency, and as such separated from the complex totality (physical-biological-anthropological) of the earth, in which life is an

emergence of its history, as Morin says.[11]

The consequence of the attribution of an indeterminable form of thinking, which in the very logical processes of formation and functioning does not quite conform itself to its origin, the temporalization of the earth, the morphogenetic geographic space: it becomes the memory of an infinite positive, able to reconcile absence and presence of meaning in the emergence of events, through substraction to the game of causality, temporality and truth.

It is not a divine truth, an historical moment, defined by the "childhood of modernity" in which the conjuncture of economic, social, expansionist political elements, all substracted to the risk of uncontrolled transformation, become granted not by reason, but by God, who gives truths to the operations on the plane of the finite. It is rather the historical constitution of a logical form of thinking (genealogically defined) into a *'imperium del pensare vero'*[12] (domination of truth thinking), based on an unfair self-attributed appropriation of an intrinsic quality of interiority and foundational efficacy, so as to create a form, a central model of organization of multiplicity according to exclusive and bivocal relations, based on centers of significance and subjectivations.[13]

This model delineated the not-accidental possibility of historical discontinuities in the multicultural West, marking differences in the attribution of improper qualities, affirming itself across different projects, strengthened by its elevating itself to memory. A memory rejuvenating its organizational strength in the physiological and biological necessity to determine an order, a structural reduction, able to redirect all lines of escape into identity and stable institutions.[14]

This can be seen as a typical project of philosophy, especially its Greek element.[15] Certainly true, but this project renews itself in the crisis of philosophy, and in the same real antagonism,[16] to become the project of science, and revive itself paradoxically in the very project of cybernetics, whose notions of information as negative entropy (negentropy) are combined in the equation of knowledge acquisition and organizational capacity.[17]

Paradox of difference. In its historical possibility, difference discovers its positive function by memory and the remembering of its condition, the condition of having taken a quality expressed by the name of God: infinite thinking, determined and to be studied outside of its temporal and spatial origin. A self-centered thinking, proceeding from its self-affirmation as the central acting presence and place of consistency from which emergence can affirm itself, produced by the interaction of interdependent and random variables, in a spatial and temporal game, so as to become positive and institutionalized in a "regime of truth."

Thinking, however, *which is* as much as *for is*,[18] where the is reaffirms the originary identity of this thinking with itself,[19] so that an order is created in which multiplicity is inserted by the exclusive logic of the being. Infinite thinking as such does not allow itself to be saturated by any finite model. On the contrary, it gives meaning to finite models, configuring their sense. This configuration duplicates that which with Artaud it is possible to affirm as "the fragile and restless nucleus" of the forces of life, "elusive to form" and which the earth lets

emerge[20] in the real world and the apparent world:
—The real world inasmuch as it is organized around the existence of a center (the point of measurement), and the subsequent prospective image of a total horizon.
—The apparent world, inasmuch as it is not organized, is uncertain and chaotic.

In conclusion, the meaning of the name is not very important per se. The history of the West, not only as a philosophical project, but as a scientific, technological, economic, political, social, real or virtual project temporally tied to limited forms of sovereignty, provided a variety of names to substitute, like a chameleon skin. All the names share the same familiarity with the process of "appropriation," so we can state with Derrida that "the history of metaphysics and the history of the West could be seen as the history (of these different names)"[21]—through which the effraction of the earth has taken and is still taking place, as is the domination of humans over other humans. This implies a renewal of memory of the name in its changing forms, while "the entire earth is brilliantly illuminated by the sign of a triumphal misfortune."[22]

"God is dead." This announcement dies in the continuing repropositions of that quality, stolen from a name, which memory actualizes, denaturalizing humans and nature, in order to reduce to identity and institutional stability what is always unstructured and emergent.

"God is dead: but given the way of men, there may still be caves for thousands of years in which his shadow will be shown"[23] impeding in this way the arrival of the event "to the ears of humans."[24]

6. 'The Shadow of God,' as a masked political question:
—On the philosophical plane, the persistence of an ontological need as an interdiction to the *errancy* of the world.
—On the scientific-technological plane, the exigence of a criterion axiomatizing experiences as linked to the chaos of the world either in the form of 'realism' or in the form of derealization of the real in *virtual reality*, both responding to the necessity of the market.
—On the individual and collective plane, the persistence of a need indebted to a reassuring certainty as a subtraction of the risk of being implicated in the game of the futures and consequences predisposed to the *delegation* of confrontations to the administrators of order.

Evocation of *memory* in the moment when unifying, totalizing, and subjectivizing dispositives come from 'sovereign formations,' which, in fact, serve the positive function of normativizing factuality, which is otherwise irreducible to this schema, and redefining the social-economic-political organization on the basis of one or more global models, acts of inscribing in a stable context, buttressing the economic-political hegemony of 'subjected groups,' the productive oscillation of the dynamic of individual and collective comportments.[25]

Here the advice of Nietzsche is salutary:

"We still have to vanquish his shadow, too."[26]

A shadow always more persistent the more the reactivity of the oedipo-cap-italist organization tends to reroute, with methods tied to the conquest of liber-atory chances through subjectivation, the desire for liberation to the inside of a linear space, attenuating and fragmenting its force in so many new institutions of control.[27]

The advice, all the same, does not stop at the enunciation or limit itself to stimulating the adoption of a frank conscience of every center of identity which ties humans to the Earth. Finding a method of chance which reveals profundi-ty, more than a *logic* of life, a *style*, located in the 'enunciation' and built on the *inactual* becoming of the Earth, in co-participation with which humans make themselves 'more than human.'[28]

The metamorphosis of the 'lion' into the 'child' converts the advice into a single instance of chance. Still a metaphor. The style of Nietzsche is precise. However, the possibility of deciphering the message, foreclosed in metaphor, is to search in historical experiences for the breaking actions of critique and of chance which verify the convertibility of desire into qualities of life in a 'spec-trum of refraction' in the works of 'striation,' at work in force.[29]

The actions of force need fertile spaces which Deleuze and Guattari, in Niet-zschean terms, define as 'the subterranean forms of Dionysian becoming.' Risk of ontologizing the differences. Undoubtedly the analyses are true to history, but in the measure to which the actions of thought and of chance recuperate the *his-torical memory* which offers logic, means, and language for the affirmation of *dif-ference*.

Derrida and Adorno mark this return. In his particular way, Adorno sees more than in language (Derrida), in the attempt to guide the co-active character of the logic of force with the same means ending up falling into the same co-activity (or real antagonism) or by furnishing new arms of disciplinary power for society (as in May '68).

The 'child' expresses the subtraction to the logic of power through the breaking of historical memory as condition of qualitative [salto]. I have already analyzed this theme in my work *Verso un pensare nomade* [*Towards Nomadic Thinking*], to which one can refer to avoid repetition here.

A brief consideration here already expressed in my work: the 'child' "is the indication of the potential which puts into short-circuit the flow of *memory* to conscience, interrupting in this way the circuit to carry it to a continuity in which the 'differences' emphasize themselves in profundity."[30]

7. The 'outside,' today, verifies the pressure of the eruptions of new emergences on the patterns of historical determination and of spatio-temporal localization proper to a thought related to identity, provoking, in the flattening, the implo-sion of historical memory. The lines of actualization of the various knowledges are in the practices of movement, indeed in their irregular unwinding toward the fractures of history, allowing to circulate, as detailed in *Towards Nomadic Thinking*, "a microphysics of circuits, through which pass, braiding, influencing, relating, yields of denotative scientific enunciations, together with prescriptive

rules and diachronic fluxes of social movement" provoking thereby the implosion of memory.

Given the emergence of a *today*, unique in its perfunctory effects, through which 'the announcement' carves out the 'unheard' message, this short-circuits the chronology of the *post*, on the basis of a rupture of the temporal symmetry, re-raising thus a dynamic internal to the microscopic level which, in provoking an instability of movement, manifests an absence of signification, which gives play to the multiplicitous concatenations and thwarts the return to an anterior unity (Prigogine).

In such an emergence *today* changes physiognomy. *Today, our present,* indeed, cannot define the dimension of *that which we are*—repetition of the simplifying model to organize thought[31]—but *that which we are becoming,* according to the indications of Deleuze.

Given that on which we are reflecting, we should give to the 'announcement' a legibility outside of the orthodoxy. Observing the underlined fact, we come to upset the punctual organization of memory, in which functional concept *the present* comes to inscribe itself along the horizontal/synchronic line of time and along the vertical/diachronic line of the order of time, remodeling the asymmetric becoming according to aims and ends which are not for becoming.

Coming to appear differently is an 'inactual' becoming, without origin and without prearranged direction, evoking *place* as principle and as destination, subtracting to time and refracting in the *name* of God the molar instance of certain victory; and this 'announcement' discloses the inexistent: announcement of an inexistent death, if not in the predation of *name* on the function of 'striation' and which, in relation to the experimentation of Prigogine, confirms such inexistent individuation of the complexity of the microscopic level, which temporal dynamic shows combinatory models of complex elements and not relations predicated on the One and the multiplicity.

Instrumental blindness to an appropriation which *renders real all that which is thinkable* (Parmenides) and which the announcement converts into "*all that which is thinkable and irreal*"[32] infringing like this on *the principle of reality* and letting fibrillate a dynamic of casual concatenations, and which the thermodynamics of processes far from equilibrium discovers on the basis of the spontaneity of materials and their self-organization.

From *being* to *becoming,* the 'announcement' brings light to the dynamic nature of the physical universe and the elementary particles. A becoming not explicative, but constructive. A becoming, therefore, which engineers new combinations of instability and fluctuation, new modes of capturing energy, new modalities of evolution, belonging in intensive spaces which temporalize themselves and whose stages of interruption of memory give coextensivity to its recuperation of actions of 'striation' on the part of sovereign formations.

As for the nature of the casual fluctuations, which, not obeying a law inherent in things—*God is dead*—renders unstable the becoming 'without foundations,' up to the level in fact of the elementary particles. This pertains to the element of interruption, and, like all singularities, asks for the time to affirm itself and be recognized thus as the 'announcement' which precedes it and in which such an external force lets delineate a world "for us once again infinite,"[33] existing "behind every cavern a still more profound cavern—a world more vast, more strange, more rich than the superficial one, an abyss under every base, under every foundation."[34]

Aphorisms for this force are explainable as indices of the complex level of the microscopic, that which lets subsist a dynamic of movement, tied to the existence of irreversible temporal processes which, making up a rupture of the symmetry of space and time, lets circulate, across the production of dissipative structures (Prigogine), entropy and information which co-involves the times of life and the times of thought.

The 'death of the inexistent God' itself liberates us thus from metaphor and leaves visible an *earth* which shows its constructive elemental particles of history as intensive forces which insinuate themselves between things, taking thousands of paths, pouring from non-unitary transformations.

The 'announcement,' more than giving us a cosmology and a hermeneutics,[35] delineates, through the Prigoginean revisitation of the second principle of thermodynamics, in the language of time, a temporalization of the spaces and a spacialization of times through which the *earth is itself made to become* and in which fibrillations, in the asymmetry of their fluctuations, make possible all the crystallizations (Apollo and the recuperation of memory) as much as their fluid motions, originating new Dionysian-child processes and the interruption of memory.

The earth, free from mortgages, appears multiform, multiplicity in the infinite entities under the force of time, that of the three-dimensional rupture, in consequence of which the past comes to separate itself from the future and this does not come to be the present in that, letting emerge mutations and innovations, it persists in the generation of 'new types' and of 'new ideas.'[36]

The earth liberated like this, all the same, "is not an automaton nor chaos. It is [an earth] of uncertainty, but also [an earth] in which individual actions are not necessarily condemned to insignificance. It is [an earth] which is not drawn from a single truth."[37]

8. If there is a way under suggestion in Deleuze: search for such an 'external actual force' both able to draw the 'announcement' from the indications for an 'other' sense of horror, perpetuating the *empire of true thinking* pertaining to the diachronic/synchronic proposal of *representative models*, and which found and finds, fertilized by innovation, promise in science, now technological and digital, and in political battles, its experiential fringe in the society of consumption and of 'ecumenicalism' de-axiomatizing/axiomatizing Capital and the apparatuses of the State.

Individuating this external force in the Prigoginean discovery of the role of time at the level of the microscopic, by which it is made complex, is the stochastic process putting in motion states of continual variation, through which collect the singularities of matter, irreducible to a model, the 'cartography' of the 'announcement,'[38] the relation with being verifying the stochastic nature (Diony-sus in the metaphor) of becoming at all levels, starting from the *earth*.

By this relation the 'announcement' lets emerge an *earth* restored to its processes and springing up in diverse horizontal planes, different in grade of complexity and not in quality, on which they themselves produce variable con-catenations in relation to the role played by time, and, as such, making possible both the formation of territories (Apollo and the recuperation of memory) and the opening of new mobile spaces.

We come, therefore, to delineate an *exteriority of the accident*, made possible by subtracting to the selective pressure which this *name*, in all of its variations, exerts and coinvolves in its geographical spaces, traversed by the 'bolts of biospeheric time' and thinking activity.

In fact, each plane, in exteriorizing an earth universe in mobile expansion, manifests:

—the constitutive character of *instability*, provoking irreversible processes, in relation to which come to be formed 'dissipative structures' (Prigogine) through which the rupture of spatio-temporal symmetry lets the entropy of information circulate;

—the same provenance delineated by *fluctuations of order* which draw attention to the non-existence of *Law* and the *name* of God evoked as centralized instance, formalizing the order of the world;

—-the belonging of the same universe to nonduplicative or multiplicative coex-tensive levels which molecular biology justifies in the reencounter between matter and living beings. A different level integration and not a qualitative difference.[39]

The political implication is important. With the fall of every preordained 'centrality,' in letting emerge a singular geographic space, in which humans and nature, civil society and political society, are no longer opposed figures, tied to a hierarchic and causal account, but a singular reality, transversed by the 'bolts of time,'[40] the action of humans *could* become incisive for the promotion of spaces of liberty, for which "our old earth would become more amenable to being inhabited by that which we haven't seen up until now."[41]

A difficult task that only a liberatory action can attempt lies before us, if being is to be brought in line with the earth recuperating its ownmost process-es in a mode of actualization, as being, to vectors of deterritorialization of its own territoriality.

However, 'inactuality' of action, in which stochastic effects are found in syn-thesis with those of the earth, lets open always new spaces, going by lines of flight more than codifying new orders, producing interruptions in memory which Apollo always re-establishes as a trap in the moment of uncertainty:

"Apollo would like to give peace to his own individual beings in mapping out the area between their lines of confinement and passage and calling them always back again to memory, by means of their precepts of conscience of them-selves or of misery, as the most sacred laws of the world."[42]

Notes

1   Gilles Deleuze, *Pensiero Nomade* [*Nomadic Thinking*], It. trans. in *Aut-Aut* no. 226, 1996.
2   Cf. Franco Riccio, *Verso un pensare nomade* [*Towards Nomadic Thinking*] (Milan: Franco Angeli, 1997).
3   Isabelle Stengers, *Da una sciencza all'altra. Concetti nomadi* [*From One Science to Another: Nomadic Concepts*] (Firenze: Hopefulmonster, 1988).
4   Cf. Friedrich Nietzsche, "How the Real World at Last Became a Myth" in *Twilight of the Idols*, It. trans. in G. Colli & M. Montanari, eds., *Opere* (Milano: Adelphi), vol. VI, tomo III, pp. 75-76. English trans. (New York: Penguin, 1968).
5   Cf. Ilya Prigogine, *From Being to Becoming*, It. trans. (Torino: Einaudi, 1986). Originally in English (New York: W.H. Freeman, 1980).
6   Nietzsche, *Thus Spoke Zarathustra*, It. trans. in *Opere*, vol. VI, tomo 1, p. 320. English trans. (New York: Penguin, 1954).
7   Nietzsche, *Beyond Good and Evil*, §. 146, It. trans. in *Opere*, vol. VI, tomo II, p. 79. English trans. (New York: Vintage, 1989).
8   Cf. Nietzsche, *Sämtliche Briefe* [*Collected Letters*], G. Colli & M. Montinari, eds. (München, Berlin: Walter de Gruyter, 1986), pp. 571-77. For the literature on Nietzsche see H.W. Reichert & K. Schlechta, *International Nietzsche Bibliography* (Chapel Hill: UNC Press, 1968), the same updated to 1971 in M. A. Stefani, *Nietzsche in Italia. Rassegna bibliografica (1893-1970)* [*Nietzsche in Italian: Collected Bibliography*] (Roma: Ca, 1975); G. Vattimo, *Introduzione a Nietzsche* (Bari: Laterza, 1985).
9   Cf. Gilles Deleuze & Felix Guattari, *A Thousand Plateaus*, It. trans. (Roma: Istituto Enciclopedia Italiana, 1987), pp. 80-81. English trans. (Minneapolis, London: University of Minnesota Press, 1987); originally *Mille Plateaux* (Paris: Editions de Minuit, 1980).
10 Ibid, p. 23.
11 See E. Morin, "Una politica per l'éta planetaria" ["A Politics for the Planetary Age"], in *Pluriverso*, no. 1, December 1995, p. 13.
12 Deleuze & Guattari, *A Thousand Plateaus*, vol. II, pp. 547-49.
13 Ibid, in particular vol. I, the first part.
14 Cf. Gilles Deleuze & Claire Parnet, *Dialogues*, It. trans. (Milano: Feltrinelli, 1980), p. 16. English trans. (New York: Columbia University Press, 1987); originally *Dialogues* (Paris: Flammarion, 1977).
15 Cf. Martin Heidegger, *Was ist das—die Philosophie* (Pfullingen: Günther Neske, 1956). English trans. *What is Philosophy* (New York: Twayne Publishers, 1958).
16 See Theodor Adorno, "Eredità" in *Minima moralia*, It. trans. (Torino: Einaudi, 1954), p. 154. English trans. (London: New Left Books, 1974); originally *Minima moralia* (Berlin: Suhrkamp Verlag, 1951).
17 Cf., in addition to what Deleuze has cited, O. Costa de Beauregard, *Le second principe de la science du temps* [*The Second Principle of the Science of Time*] (Paris: Seuil, 1963).
18 A combinatory act from my wanderings between the folds of the formulations of Heidegger (*cf.*, Heidegger, *What is Philosophy*) and of Deleuze in *Logique du sens* (Paris: Editions de Minuit, 1968); English trans. *The Logic of Sense* (New York: Columbia University Press, 1990).
19 Cf. Heidegger, *Identitat und Differenz* (Pfullingen: Günther Neske, 1957). English trans. *Identity and Difference* (New York: Harper and Row, 1968).
20 Antonin Artaud, "The Theater and Culture" in *The Theatre and Its Double*, It. trans. (Torino: Einaudi, 1968), p. 113. English trans. (New York: Grove Press, 1958); originally *Le Théâtre et son double* (Paris: Gallimard, 1938).
21 Jacques Derrida, *Writing and Difference*, It. trans. (Torino: Einaudi, 1982), p. 360. English trans. (Chicago: University of Chicago Press, 1978); originally *l'écriture et difference* (Paris: Seuil, 1967).
22 Max Horkheimer & Theodor Adorno, *Dialectic of the Enlightenment*, It. trans. (Torino: Einaudi, 1966), p. 3. English trans. (New York: Continuum, 1973; Stanford: Stanford Univer-

sity Press, 2002); originally *Dialektik der Aufklärung* (New York: Social Studies Association, 1944).

23 Nietzsche, *The Gay Science*, §108, III, in *Opere*, vol. V, tomo II, p. 117. English trans. (New York: Vintage, 1974).

24 Ibid, §125, "The Madman," p. 130.

25 For a further treatment of this point see Riccio, ibid.,, starting on p. 51.

26 Nietzsche, *The Gay Science*, §108.

27 Cf. Deleuze, "Post-scriptum sur les societés de contrôle" in *Pourparlers 1972-1990* (Paris: Editions de Minuit, 1990), pp. 240-47. English trans. "Postscript on Societies of Control" in *Negotiations* (New York: Columbia University Press, 1995).

28 An indication of the sense in which it is possible to come to by putting in relation *Human All Too Human* and *Inactual Consideration*.

29 Cf. Deleuze & Guattari, *A Thousand Plateaus*, where the distinction between 'smooth space' of desire and 'striated space' of power is analyzed, together with their particular ties to reciprocal convertibility.

30 Riccio, ibid., p. 14.

31 Cf. Stephen Jay Gould, *Time's Arrow: Myth and Metaphor in the Discovery of Geological Time*, It. trans. (Milano: Feltrinelli, 1989), p. 21. Originally in English (Cambridge: Harvard University Press, 1987).

32 Pierre Klossowski, *Nietzsche and the Vicious Circle*, It. trans. (Milano: Adelphi, 1981), p. 121. English trans. (Chicago: University of Chicago Press, 1997); originally *Nietzsche et le cercle vicieux* (Paris: Mercure de France, 1969).

33 Nietzsche, *The Gay Science*, §374, in *Opere*, p. 253. English trans. (New York: Vintage, 1989).

34 Nietzsche, *Beyond Good and Evil*, §289, in *Opere*, pp. 200-201.

35 Cf. Carlo Sini, *Semiotica e filosofia* [*Semiotics and Philosophy*] (Bologna: Il Mulino, 1991).

36 Cf. Prigogine, *From Being to Becoming*, pp. 120, 225.

37 Ibid., p. 227. In Prigogine's text the end is the world.

38 Terminology introduced by Deleuze & Guattari in *A Thousand Plateaus*, starting on p. 10, to designate the directions taken by multiplicities entering and exiting the *rhizome* of the real, diversifying the representative model which functions by re-emphasizing that which is already formed and constructed.

39 Cf. Francois Jacob, *The Logic of Life: A History of Heredity*, It. trans. (Torino: Einaudi, 1970), p. 215. English trans. (Princeton: Princeton University Press, 1993); originally *La logique du vivant, une histoire de l'hérédité* (Paris: Gallimard, 1970).

40 "We are not in general the bolt of time, but on the contrary we are its children." Ilya Prigogine, *The End of Certainty: Time, Chaos, and the New Laws of Nature*, It. trans. (Torino: Bollati Boringhieri, 1997), pp. 12-13. English trans. (New York: Free Press, 1997); originally *La fin des certitudes* (Paris: Odile Jacob, 1996).

41 Nietzsche, "The 'Humaneness' of the Future," §337, *The Gay Science*, in *Opere*, p. 196.

42 Nietzsche, *The Birth of Tragedy*, in *Opere*, vol. III, tomo I, p. 70. English trans. (New York: Vintage, 1967).

Horror Vacui:
Between Anomie and Anarchy

Salvo Vaccaro

In the context of the philosophy of modernity in general, and of political philosophy in particular, the idea of the practice of freedom gives rise above all to a sense of panic. Freedom's infinite expansion and absolute intensity have provoked a reaction which expresses itself in the bipolarity *discipline/punishment* (to evoke Michel Foucault). The irreconcilable divide between liberalism and anarchism turns on this ground: the first feels the necessity of building freedom in order to better designate it *through* limits, while anarchy underlines the importance of *subtracting* freedom from foundational limits *through* the valorization of its unlimited potential/power (if not, indeed, of its own intensive rhythm). In a way, then, modernity has never thought freedom in itself, but only its metaphysics: freedom is always an attribute which is adjunct or attached to a base which renders it certain, stable, and predictable.

Politics, religion, morality, and philosophy of nature: all of these constitute external obstacles that guide freedom toward a transcendental path. Its disciplinary constriction comes from outside and aims to interiorize itself to the point of becoming second nature, as if it were inconceivable to think a freedom without limits, a freedom which gives itself its own planes of immanence, without founding them on well-established certitudes, on truths pre-constituted by the same strategic operations which *place value* on it. This has proven inconceivable for all except for anarchism and for Nietzsche, who rid themselves of every transcendence: politics, religion, morality, and philosophy of nature.

Western thought has given meaning to the world through an *order of fullness*. The semiotic sphere is full of meanings which are distributed along a vertical axis on which runs in a double sense the political theology which characterizes Western civility, in one direction, and its *cruelty* (as Artaud said), in the other. The double movement of the *divine* (high) and of the *foundation* (low) entrusts the fullness of things to a language shaped by a transcendental grammar in which, namely, sense is *given as full*, in which stands guard the prejudice of wholeness, and in which signification assumes sense only if it is entrusted to

This piece originally appeared, with some changes, in *Anarchismo e Modernità* (Pisa: BFS, 2004). Translated from the Italian by Laura Fantone and Jeffrey Bussolini, City University of New York (Center for the Study of Culture, Technology, and Work).

raised or rooted entities which fill up the world of words and things, according to one joint double-identity movement of *assignation* (from on high) or of *rooting* (from below).

From this perspective, the West has always been both modern and pre-secular at the same time, that is of one part created and invented, even when appearing in the powerful and elusive nature of Greek mythology (Zeus's lightning, Volcano's tempests), of a *natura naturans*; and of another part, at the same time, not fully emancipated from a destinal mortgage which inscribed the difficult passage of freedom into the theological regime of signification (the *deus sive natura* of Spinoza, which was in turn criticized by Nietzsche). It is almost irrelevant, in fact, as the Greeks teach, that the gods or a monocratic God inhabit the unfathomable peaks of the sky or the inscrutable abysses of a dark foundation from which everything originates and on which everything stands.

The regulation of the world is set along a vertical double-axis, ascending and descending, onto which are then distributed vectors of hierarchization of peoples, whose symbolic and cultural practices (in the anthropological sense) must be trained and disciplined to the point of being held by invisible strings descending from above (transcendence), or standing upon heavy bases (foundation) which sustain burdens and evolutionary trajectories compatible with the regime of signification.

To stay in the world means already to be weighed down by the burden of transcendence which directs from above, or on the other hand to be already anchored to a foundation, in both cases binding foreseeable freedom in diverse forms of life to a *fullness* which ritually and rationally lends obedience. It is not by chance if the enigma of political philosophy—an auto-suspended point in the chain of sense, something in between Münchhausen's paradox, the *Grundnorm* taboo, and Kelsen's paradox—is itself the reason of voluntary servitude. This philosophy converges to augment the sense, that is, which binds the contingent polyformity of social ties that unite us to the world with their institutions of stability that administer freedom by rendering it a slave from the outset. Not even the master/slave dialectic adequately renders the idea of the complex contrivances that turn freedom into its opposite: "Kant, as after him the idealists, could not tolerate freedom without constriction. Already in him the explicit conception itself produced such fear of anarchy that it then persuaded the bourgeois conscience to the liquidation of its own freedom."[1]

Whole, stable, certain, Western thought has tied the world to strategies of truth which play by our rules—"to establish and order a world *which for us can be called true*"[2]—fishing in the currents of the passions, feeding the metamorphosis of the agonistic game (free, casual, voluntary, autonomous) into competitive conflict dominated by the rules of the victor, even though both roles interchange.

The figurative language of the grammar of truth expresses only one meaning, that of the *whole*, of *total fullness* as an emblem of words and things, inside of which the plural proliferation of chains of concurrent signification is allowed. Each one of these sediments a specific stratum which is designated as a relatively autonomous subsphere with its own specific jargon: politics, science, aes-

thetics, morality, religion. Within each sphere a unipolar grammar, characterized by the transcendental fullness of sense, generates polyarchies which con-
verge, even in their disjunction, to reinforce the stability of their hold on the
world: existence in the world coincides with the sense given to it now by history, now by theology, now by the truth of science (bio-physics).[3] Even that which
seems to be a language less based on a primary substrate, whether high or low,
in the last analysis shows itself as a remnant of an operation of the excessive giving of sense, of an over-determination in the positive sense.

But this posture of affirmation has not completely settled accounts with the
nihilism of the senseless origin of the world, of the casual arbitrariness of our
existence associated with the world ("a hiatus between two abysses"),[4] and therefore it betrays the heteronomy which marks its very origin and destiny. This pos-
itivity is tied, in fact, to a sense which comes from a magic circle outside of
nihilistic arbitrariness, negating the immanence of planes of insistence in order
to entrust itself to the vertical fracture of the molar plane of consistency—a hard
fullness which Nietzsche's nihilism resists. "The idea of a beyond, of a suprasen-
sible world and of all of its forms (God, essence, the good, the true), of values
superior to life... is the constitutive element of every fiction. Values beyond life
always bring a devaluation of life and a negation of the earthly world, as a result
they cannot be separated from how much the desire to negate and slander the
world really constitutes their principle.... The value of life is nothing, the fiction
of the higher values which give this value and this will to nothingness to life
constitute the origin and the foundation of nihilism."[5]

Nietzsche poses the radical interrogation, questioning the fullness of sense:
why does Western thought feel the *physiological* need of *assimilating* itself to that
which it builds, projecting and positioning the affirmation of sense on a transcendental ontological plane, to which it regresses as if it were an originally-given
datum rather than a fragile invention lying on nothingness, on the void? Nihilism
is the outcome of the subtraction of words and things from the 'special effect' of
reality—a reality created by transcendental simulation—so that the concepts
behind words no longer match the linguistic and grammatical consistency that
selects and disciplines them. That which sense fills up with reality escapes on all
sides from the 'supposed *aim of becoming*,'[6] eluding both the seductive paths: the
fascinating lights of transcendental sacredness (shining from above) and the dark
shadows that evoke the deep *arcana imperii* (from below).

Nietzsche reclaims the absolute infinity of the earth subtracted from its
reducibility to the sensible world (a re-territorialized de-territorialization, as
Deleuze and Guattari would put it), overflowing with good sense (nature, history, God, law, morality). Nietzsche does this by placing the *arbitrary, non-rule oriented* nature of worldliness, which does not have the chance of escaping every
transcendental plane, at the center of his argument. The *arbitrary*, 'boundless
and bottomless chaos,' marks uncertainty as the permanent condition in which
bodies and brains move in their game of contacts and interactions with which
they build the changeable and revocable social ties that allow for a combined
existence without necessarily giving place to a social unity which would repre-

sent a mythical place from which associative processes are derived, a sort of original matrix of inscription. "The eternal return does not assent to any establishment of a fundamental foundation, and on the contrary destroys and absorbs every foundation as an instance which sets down the difference between the original and the derived, the thing and simulacra, posing us in front of a universal breakthrough. By breakthrough we mean the freedom of the unmediated foundation, immediate reflection of the informal and of the superior form which constitutes the eternal return."[7]

Without destination, without pre-ordained and pre-assigned destiny, without certain location, the *arbitrary* characterizes the earth as crossed by multiple world fluxes which transmute and intersect in various forms of contingent and revocable life, outside of the social contracts armored and protected by the blackmail of force (Hobbes), combinations subject to the agony of bodies and minds. We don't have the least reason to think that we need transcendental values to compare and select modes of existence, or to decide that one is better than another. On the contrary, there are none but immanent criteria and the possibility of life valued in itself, based on tracing movements and intensities which create on a plane of immanence. But, on a new plane, the problem could concern the existence of those who believe in the world, not as existent but as possibility of movement and intensity, acts which generate new and novel modes of existence.[8]

The *arbitrary* of anarcho-Nietzschean nihilism is not the *arbitrariness* of the winning power, as Deleuze tells us, inviting us to reflect and to avoid the trap of conceiving the *Wille zür Macht* as the will to domination. Reason and passion, instances of body and mind reflecting, merge in the empty space of the absolute arbitrary, becoming finite vectors through which we can reach infinity or multiplicity, becoming pluralities which spread themselves horizontally in the molecular flow of minor becoming. In fact, it is only in the subtraction of minor becoming that it is possible to find provisional senses which contingently take account of social ties, evading transcendental grids through a multi-stratified plane of immanence, "a different space than that of Power and Domination."[9]

Nietzsche's nihilism erases all conceptual constructs that push toward the high, which want to be reunited with the transcendental in order to legitimate themselves through this fortunate contact or through ecstatic vision itself; but Nietzsche also cleans up the mythical illusions of "things hidden since the beginning of the world" (René Girard's expression), which veil the search for origins— sacred founts of legitimacy—that presuppose a transcendental schema in which the thinker is put into a tautological spin in searching for stable certainties. While declaring to reflect upon what we are searching for, we search for what we already thought.

Nietzsche's nihilism is disenchanting in a radical fashion because it does not allow itself to be lured into any re-enchantment. The world full of misfortune is also full of values which reproduce them; it is impossible to erase them unless other values replace them, fulfilling the same function, new inhabitants which live in the same mythical place from which meanings continue to originate directly and indirectly. "How can we remember the time when God lived on the earth and united humans and nature, or the time when the founding word was a direct, face to face dialogue with God? And, vice versa, how can we forget that time, if it is indeed made up of time, on the earth abandoned by God, knowing precisely that this communion is gone, and this face to face dialogue is improbable. Exactly this double movement of memory constitutes disenchantment."[10]

Zarathustra escapes from Medusa, whose smile reflects the wit of a re-enchanting reason that petrifies bodies and minds through an incessant division of labor, assigning roles, distinguishing spheres of competence and responsibility, setting limits, adopting linguistic processes obedient to the old grammatical principle.

The movement of nihilism desubstantiates words and things, 'opening only the void,'[11] recalling nothingness, a perpetual fluctuation in the void where thousands of planes of immanence lie, radically hostile to any transcendental re-enchantment, radically estranged from any dialectical process, retrieving a law of movement, a variation tinged with the immobility of the *semper aequalis* (always equal). Nietzsche outlines a "thought as affirmation of chance, affirmation in which his thought necessarily refers to itself—infinitely—through the aleatory (non-fortuitous); in this relation Nietzsche's thought becomes plural."[12]

The bonds of freedom possible in an absolute void of existence do not, in fact, obey the spectacular overturning of the dialectical cut, according to which freedom can only emerge from subjugation as a necessary reversal, as "abstract permutations" of a "game of oppositions."[13] The results would be fatal: the renewing of an old mechanism under a new mask, the updating of a care-worn grid. "The changing of values does not give us a new scale of values from the negation of every absolute value, but it makes us arrive at an order in which the notions of value cease to apply."[14]

Senses and bonds appear freely on planes of immanence which do not offer any guarantee of success and stability, but that are constantly re-invented, created and experienced as joyful research (gay science), similar to an artistic creation or an erotic gaze. The plane of immanence sparkles with experiments and experiences, improvising nomadic practices and becoming multiple. The void becomes populated but does not fill up, never being saturated by axiomatic institutions. "We are deserts, but populated by tribes, flora, and fauna... The desert, experimentation on our selves, is our only identity, our only possibility, due to all the combinations which inhabit us."[15]

Western thought has always had a blind terror of this: it is hostile to the freedom of anarchist lifestyles (without origin, without aim), to the "*enjoyment* of every sort of uncertainty, to the faculty of experimentation"[16]—it has always felt a horror full of rancor against the promise of a 'gay freedom.' Western thought always aimed at chaining the plane of immanence to a heavy anchor that would drag it down, weighing it down with transcendental instances which striate it with codes and axioms. "Modernity was a continuous and uncompromising effort to fill or to cover up the void; the modern mentality held a stern belief that the job can be done—if not today then tomorrow. The sin of postmodernity is to abandon the effort and to deny the belief... once one remembers that abandoning effort and denying belief does not, by itself, neutralize the awesome propelling force of the fear of the void."[17]

The *void* following from the arbitrary condition of existence assumes three possible forms which have always haunted western thought. One of the forms is *horror vacui*, it saturates images giving them a disquieting meaning with the goal of neutralizing the seductive nature of nihilism and substituting a fatal power that fills with sense that which would not otherwise have it. The strategy of containment of the forms of *the infinitely arbitrary—the height of the peaks, the depth of the ocean, the crossing of the desert—* has searched to fill up the sense of horror without mitigating its effect. Despite their goal, they do not reduce the fear and the effects of the *horror vacui*, but double it, increasing the terroristic tones of the images, without selective censors, and thus accentuating fear and horror and making them unbearable. Such containment strategies did not so much neutralize the fear, as much as the possibility of thinking other ways of coexistence, tolerant ways, different dimensions in which the inevitable and unbearable weight of humanity (both individual and collective), is manipulated and externalized in a transcendental function of salvation, an external refuge. This is similar to the fiction invented by Hobbes in political philosophy: the state of nature, the war of all against all (*bellum omnium contra omnes*), the social contract, the surrender of sovereignty in exchange for security.

Heteronomy is rooted in the assumption that one, *alone*, cannot be autonomous, cannot venture into inaccessible heights, into unfathomable depths and onto imperceptible paths: without a predefined destination beyond the goal of following our path, as we wish, as each one desires. Undoubtedly, a sort of compass is needed to guide the traveler through the voyage, which would serve above all to avoid losing bearings in the face of *vertigo, fear,* and the *uneasiness* in front of the unknown which the nomad is formed to know how to encounter.

For Adorno, it is the *Abgrund*, the sense of a bottomless abyss at whose edge we stand, *alone and without outside help*, too high up, or of plunging down, *alone and without help*, too far down for assistance. But the sensation of being without a foundation that philosophically characterizes Nietzsche's nihilism—that which, in saying '*no*' to the tutors of existence who constrain it to remain minor, notwithstanding Kant's call for a major reason, says a vigorous '*yes*' to life as it is, without adjectives and hypothetical supports which, to the end of helping us to face the indeterminate insensibility of the world, end up entrusting life to godfathers who take away one's immanence and transform it into voluntary servitude to a transcendental destiny—is similar to the wavy plate of the desert, whose effect of dis-identification erodes the ground below the feet where one builds every identity as forced individuation that in turn becomes stable, secure, and predictable, strongly guided by a superior authority that renders them legitimate.

Yet, the human condition is solitary by definition, and each person's singularity can acquire enough strength to be able to confront life on the edge of the abyss of nonsense, of the constitutive arbitrariness, and of the void to be crossed without being voided on the inside. Humans without God "stand by themselves as on a rope over an abyss of nothingness, suspended in the void."[18] Such a singularity is constructed through *experimentation of styles*, starting from Nietzsche's aesthetics and continuing with Derrida, Foucault and Deleuze, in their reciprocal differences. It is precisely human finitude which succeeds in reclaiming a unique style capable of confronting the infinitely irreducible: the nomadism of a practice of thought and action freed from sovereign authority, including that internalized into the dogma of the 'I' (contrary to Stirner's view).

The void will not be *dominated*, but only *domesticated*, anesthetized, or plowed, neutralizing its perverse and distortive effects. The goal is not to cross the line between anomie and anarchy, risking a precipice, shipwreck, or madness, but rather to follow that line in a unique way.

Free style: that of a rock climber who, paradoxically, does not fight against vertigo to reach the top, but searches for the top to be able to look out at infinite horizons, not to found abysmal verticalities; it is the style of a desert nomad, who can roam vast territories and measure their contingent intensities, now mobile, now static;[19] the style of the sailor on the open seas, with no aim but that of meeting the challenge of the water and the waves[20] (involuntarily, he might even succeed in making out the northwest passage, but this is another story, as Michel Serres would say); the style of the swimmer who does not look down to the deep bottom of the ocean but, in need of oxygen, moves holding his breath to strengthen the possibility of movement in the void of air, in the friction of the water, in a finitude that does not reduce the infinity but rather exalts it.[21]

It is the *style* that traces a plane of immanence, that proposes a horizontal dimension that, before all, evades the transcendental mortgage that has ruled the law *up until now*. The style innovates because it is singular despite its repetition, giving itself its own rhythm and tracing its own differential routes, overcoming unexpected obstacles, inhospitable seas, and sudden storms. "We are free only in becoming free and we become free only by our own will."[22]

Such a style also depicts the emblem of the *overman*, able to endure vertiginous heights and the *horror vacui*, able to find his way in the desert and to navigate the open seas. For Nietzsche, "it is not a matter of escaping the Dionysian as a world of fear and insecurity, but to find it beyond fear as a world of freedom, creativity, and, that which is most important, of the elimination of barriers, social and otherwise."[23] The *Übermensch* does not designate a superior quality, but a different one, an *other* one, one that is mutated through deliriously construing limits and positions of value, through getting rid of all signification through sentimental and stylized experimentation. Foucault re-elaborated this *askesis* in order to de-individualize the subject (*déprendre de soi-même*), to the point of constructing a variety of figures of the self whose multiple identities do not recombine into yet another selective, immovable identity of the 'I.' *All the names of history are me...*

The opposition between the self and the I denotes what the style emphasizes: as Nietzsche would say, the will to power, the resistance to the vertigo of the *Abgrund*, the strength to go on in the terror of the void without losing our singularity, but striving to proliferate stratified planes of immanence through which we pass nomadically (from Leibniz's monadology to Deleuze's nomadology).

Anarchist thought activates a power of resistance. But at the same time it traces a projecting horizon which is articulated through practices of liberation and freedom, of destruction and construction (Bakunin), of subtraction and multiplication. There is no difference in nature of the two moments, but a difference of degree: two folds of a single becoming, two paths bifurcating and rejoining, two movements of one unwinding similar to a Moebius strip as in a drawing by M.C. Escher.

Anarchist thought encompasses the power of immanence combined with a powerful evoking of the outside. Liberation is freedom in the coherence of means and ends, method and content, while freedom is already liberation in action because it does not call for any final, eschatological end towards which the process of transformation is drawn. Anarchist revolution is infinite, impossible to stabilize in a society identified as anarchist. Instead, it could devote itself to a libertarian society in becoming-anarchic, always expanding and never becoming saturated; a society in which the chances of freedom that women and men will be able to invent historically would reject any authoritarian instances, without guarantee of success, but also with no fatalism attending to the assumption that the world is immovable in its essence.

Notes

1   Theodor W. Adorno, *Negative Dialectics*, It. trans. (Torino: Einaudi, 1970), p. 208. English trans. (New York: Continuum, 1973); originally *Negative Dialektik* (Frankfurt: Suhrkamp Verlag, 1966).

2   Friedrich Nietzsche, *The Will to Power*, §516, It. trans. (Milano: Bompiani, 1992), p. 284. English trans. (New York: Vintage, 1967).

3   "The internal apparatus of consciousness is an apparatus to abstract and simplify—not oriented toward consciousness, but toward *domination* over things: 'ends' and 'means' are very far from essence according to 'concepts.' With the 'end' and with 'means' we seize the concepts (or invent a process which can catch them), but, with 'concepts' we seize the 'things' which form the process." (Ibid., §503).

4   Ibid., §303.

5   Gilles Deleuze, *Nietzsche and Philosophy*, It. trans. (Milano: Feltrinelli, 1992), p. 175. English trans. (New York: Columbia University Press, 1983); originally *Nietzsche et la philosophie* (Paris: Presses Universitaires de France, 1962).

6   Nietzsche, ibid., §12.

7   Deleuze, *Difference and Repetition*, It. trans. (Bologna: Il Mulino, 1971), p. 114. English trans. (New York: Columbia University Press, 1994); originally *Différence et répetition* (Paris: Presses Universitaires de France, 1976). "The world of the eternal return is a world in a state of intensity, a world of differences, which does not suppose either the One or the Identical, but which builds on the tomb of the one God just as on the ruins of the 'I' of identity."—Gilles Deleuze, "The Conclusions on the Will to Power and the Eternal Return," It. trans. *il Verri*, no. 39/40, 1972, p. 77. English trans. in *Desert Islands and Other Texts: 1953-1974*, ed. David Lapoujade (New York, Los Angeles: Semiotext[e], 2004); originally, "Sur la volonté de puissance et l'éternel retour," in *Cahiers de Royaumont, no. VI; Nietzsche* (Paris: Editions de Minuit, 1967).

8   Gilles Deleuze & Felix Guattari, *What is Philosophy?*, It. trans. (Torino: Einaudi, 1996), pp. 64-65. English trans. (London: Verso, 1994); originally, *Qu'est-ce que la philosophie?* (Paris: Editions de Minuit, 1991). "La libertà deriva dall'alea"—Georges Bataille, *On Nietzsche*, It. trans. (Bologna: Cappelli, 1980), p. 145. English trans. (New York: Paragon House, 1992);

originally *Sur Nietzsche* (Paris: Gallimard, 1945).

9   Deleuze & Guattari, *A Thousand Plateaus*, It. trans. (Roma: Istituto Enciclopedia Italiana, 1987), p. 154. English trans. (Minneapolis, London: University of Minnesota Press, 1987); originally *Mille Plateaux* (Paris: Editions de Minuit, 1980). "Only the innocence of becoming can give the *maximum courage* and the *maximum liberty!*"—Friedrich Nietzsche, ibid., §787.

10 Sergio Givone, *Disincanto del mondo e pensiero tragico* [*The Disenchantment of the World and Tragic Thought*] (Milano: Il Saggiatore, 1988), p. 4. "As much as enchantment is impenetrable, it is just enchantment"—Theodor W. Adorno, "Introduction" to *The Positivist Dispute in German Sociology*, ed. Frank Benseler, It. trans. in *Scritti sociologici* (Torino: Einaudi, 1976). English trans. (New York: Harper and Row, 1976), originally *Der Positivismusstreit in der deutschen Soziologie* (Neuwied, Berlin: Luchterhand, 1969).

11 Bataille, ibid., p. 32.

12 Maurice Blanchot, "Reflections on Nihilism" in *The Infinite Conversation*, It. trans. (Torino: Einaudi, 1977), p. 211. English trans. (Minneapolis, London: University of Minnesota Press, 1993); originally *L'Entretien infini* (Paris: Gallimard, 1969). "In other terms, we could call eternal return only becoming, multiplicity. This is the law of a world without essence, without unity, without identity. Far from presupposing the One and the Identical, this builds the only unity of multiplicity inasmuch as the only identity which is is difference." —Gilles Deleuze, "The Conclusions on the Will to Power and the Eternal Return," pp. 78-79.

13 Deleuze, *Nietzsche and Philosophy*, p. 185. On the significance of contra, see Theodor W. Adorno, *Negative Dialectics*, p. 29: "A dialectic which will not remain glued to identity, which will provoke, if not the charge of not having earth under one's feet..., that of bringing dizziness."

14 Blanchot, ibid., p. 204.

15 Gilles Deleuze and Claire Parnet, *Dialogues*, It. trans. (Milano: Feltrinelli, 1980), p. 16. English trans. (New York: Columbia University Press, 1987); originally *Dialogues* (Paris: Flammarion, 1977).

16 Nietzsche, ibid., §§1060, 1067.

17 Zygmunt Bauman, *Intimations of Postmodernity* (London, New York: Routledge, 1992), p. xvii.

18 Karl Löwith, *Nietzsche's Philosophy of the Eternal Return*, It. trans. (Bari: Laterza, 1996), p. 44. English trans. (Berkeley: University of California Press, 1997); originally *Nietzsches Philosophie der ewigen Wiederkehr des Gleichen* (Berlin: Verlag Die Runde, 1935).

19 "The nomadic distribution is much different, a nomadic *nomos*, without propriety, confines, or measure, where there are no longer partitions of a distribution, but rather repartitions of forces distributing themselves in an open space, unlimited, or at the least without precise limits."—Gilles Deleuze, *Difference and Repetition*, p. 67.

20 "Our force compels us to take the sea towards the widest point, down there where up until now the sun has set: we *come to know* a new world..."—Friedrich Nietzsche, ibid., §405.

21 "When the body [in swimming] combines certain of its singular points with the moving principles of the wave, tied to the principle of a repetition which is no longer that of the Same, but which includes the Other, which implicates difference, giving a wave and a gesture to the other, and which transports each difference into the repetitive space which is constructed thus. To learn is to properly build this space of the encounter with signs, which determinative points reverberate with the ones and the others, and where repetition is formed in the same moment in which it is masked."—Gilles Deleuze, ibid., p. 44-45.

22 Martin Heidegger, *Nietzsche*, It. trans. (Milano: Adelphi, 1994), p. 334. English trans. (New York: Harper and Row, 1979 and 1984), vols. I and II; originally *Nietzsche* (Pfüllingen: Verlag Gunther Neske, 1961).

23 Gianni Vattimo, *Il soggetto e la maschera* [*The Subject and the Mask*] (Milano: Bompiani, 1983), p. 33. "...superior humans: bear *the heaviest responsibility without breaking*"—Friedrich Nietzsche, ibid. §975.

Nietzschean Anarchy and the Post-Mortem Condition

Max Cafard

"In a friend one should have one's best enemy," says Zarathustra,[1] and Nietzsche certainly proves himself to be the best friend and the best enemy of anarchism.

Even a cursory survey of Nietzsche's works reveals that the term "anarchist" is for him invariably a term of abuse. He does not hide his boundless contempt for this "sickly" and "decadent" "slanderer" who is an "underminer" and a "destroyer." For Nietzsche, anarchism is one of the most baneful expressions of that psychic malaise he calls *ressentiment*. It is a symptom of modern society's grave and perhaps terminal illness—destructive nihilism. What better friend could anarchists possibly wish for than this brilliant and uncompromising enemy?

Yet there is beyond, and indeed beneath, Nietzsche's anarchophobia a Nietzschean Anarchy that is infinitely more anarchistic than the anarchism he assails.

It is nothing like the Nietzschean Anarchy that some recent observers have discovered. We will call these observers "Post-Mortemists" and their view from the crypt "Post-Mortemism." We will call these Post-Mortemists the "Waking Dead," because of their peculiar celebration of death. They find themselves to be "in the wake" of death. They consider their morbid celebration to be "a wake" for the dead. I say none of this in accusation: I only recount what they repeat endlessly about themselves. *Ces revenants*.

Endlessly. For the spirit of Post-Mortemism is pervaded by a certain kind of repetition compulsion, a fixation on certain images, certain figures of speech, even certain catch phrases (though in fact they catch little). For Nietzsche, "the scholar is the herd animal in the realm of knowledge," one who speaks and thinks as he does "because others have done so before him."[2] The Post-Mortemists, these sheep in wolves' clothing, are just such herd animals, despite their ferocious exterior, despite their howling, wild enough to wake the dead.

Nietzschean Anarchy is not the Anarchy of Post-Mortem wakes, but rather the Anarchy of the Awakened Mind (a pre-Ancientist idea). The Post-Mortemist wake is the Party of Death. The Nietzschean Anarchist Party is the Party of Life.

This piece originally appeared in *Exquisite Corpse* #62 (online edition: www.corpse.org/issue_1) and in *The Surre(gion)alist Manifesto and Other Writings* (Baton Rouge: Exquisite Corpse, 2003).

We will call the Post-Mortemists the "Anarcho-Cynicalists." Cynicism is the disease of preference of our age, and Nietzsche has the distinction of being one of the first to diagnose its onset. Post-Mortemism is one of the most exotic growths to blossom in the decaying social body. It attacks the reigning cynicism on behalf of a more radical cynicism. The uncharitable Nietzsche would reserve a special contempt for those Post-Mortemists "who lost their high hope" and then "slandered all high hopes"[3] using a borrowed tongue—often, ironically, a tongue borrowed from Nietzsche himself.

For many, Nietzsche is a Post-Mortemist anarchist who inspires the somber celebration of the Death of God. But for us—Pre-Ancientists and Surre(gion)alists—Nietzsche is a Pre-Ancientist anarchist who celebrates the eternal Rebirth of the Gods.

"For us," I say. But what right do we have to claim "Nietzsche" as our own? None at all, and we will not raise a hand if you attempt to carry off this rotten corpse to put it in some museum or reliquary.

Yet we will claim him anyway, justifying this outrage by our full recognition of the multiplicity of Nietzsches. Of course, it is a commonplace that there are as many Nietzsches as there are readers of Nietzsche. But beyond this, there are many Nietzsches within Nietzsche, and within the many Nietzsches. As the philosopher himself comments, there is a chaos within the creative self. And as the philosophical joker Zhuangzi told in his Pre-Ancient story, brutal interference, however well intended, causes the Body of Chaos (Hun-Tun) to die. We recognize then that we must refrain from violence against the chaotic body—the Body of Nature, the Social Body, the Spiritual Body. We recognize that we can have no knowledge of "self," except as we explore the regions of self, regions that have no clear boundaries of selfhood, which extend deeply beneath the surface of selfhood, and outward beyond the borders of selfhood.

So our present surre(gion)al journey will explore, not "Nietzsche," but rather, certain Nietzschean regions. Regions that we might call, collectively, Anarchica. You are invited along on this voyage: "Travel to Anarchica and stalk the Cold Monster!"

In our exploration we will be guided by the strict science of Psychogeography. The earliest Psychogeographers discovered that not only does one never step into the same river twice, but that one never arrives at a single source. Whether this be the Source of the Nile, or the Source of Nihilism.

For this reason, nothing would be more pointless than to seek some true Nietzsche who "is" or "is not" an anarchist. A Prof. Basinski (under the influence of Martin "Dr. Death" Heidegger),[4] assures us that Nietzsche never believed in the Will to Power, Eternal Recurrence, and the *Übermensch*. These were, we are told, no more than metaphysical illusions he created to hide his own nihilism.[5]

Of course Nietzsche didn't believe in any of it! And the good Prof. Basinski cannot possibly believe any of these silly rumors he's spreading about Nietzsche.

So we forsake the quest for the Promised Land of Nietzsche. There is no compass that could direct us to such a destination. Here as everywhere, Nagarjuna's radical Awakened-Mind dialectic must be our guide. As we cross the nonexistent borders of the Nietzschean regions, we find that we might explore the Nietzsche who is an anarchist, the Nietzsche who is not an anarchist, the Nietzsche who both is and is not an anarchist, and the Nietzsche who neither is nor is not an anarchist. Or more accurately, we might explore the ways in which the many Nietzsches are and are not all of these.

In what follows, we will hear from some of these Nietzsches.[6]

The Antichrist versus The Anarchist

Bakunin said, "the urge to destroy is also a creative urge." But as Nietzsche pointed out, sometimes the urge to destroy is—let's face it—an Urge to Destroy.

Of course, Nietzsche is well aware of the truth in Bakunin's insight. In fact he expressed the same idea much more eloquently than did Bakunin: "The desire for *destruction*, change and becoming can be an expression of an over-flowing energy that is pregnant with future..."[7] So, yes, it can be creative.

"But," he adds, "it can also be the hatred of the ill-constituted, disinherited, and underprivileged, who destroy, *must* destroy, because what exists, indeed all existence, all being, outrages and provokes them. To understand this feeling, consider our anarchists closely."[8] This is almost touching: "our anarchists." How many philosophers have been willing to claim as their own these oft-scorned stepchildren of politics? Nietzsche does, and even seeks to understand their feelings! What he discovers is that "our anarchists," poor souls that they are, are in the grips of a nihilistic rage against reality.

When he speaks of "our anarchists," Nietzsche has in mind a certain kind of anarchist. His model is not the anarchist who is a fanatic for freedom, but rather the one who is obsessed with injustice. For him, this anarchist is just the extreme type of a certain kind of revolutionary, one who expresses viscerally the revolt of the masses, of the downtrodden, of the "underprivileged." The anarchist is thus the purest and most spiritually contaminated expression of a certain kind of reactivity, the perfect embodiment of *reactive revolt*. Nietzsche's stinging charge against such an anarchism is that it is, at its deepest level, *reactionary*. Reaction is not the exclusive preserve of the right, in Nietzsche's perceptive analysis.

Though Nietzsche doesn't hesitate to cast aspersions on the "underprivileged" and their self-ordained champions, his critique is no simplistic defense of "privilege." He can as well as anyone attack and demolish the smug pretensions of the privileged. After all, it is those very "privileged" who overturned the old order of privilege to create the mass society and herd morality that Nietzsche detests so fervently. He sides neither with the established order nor with those who struggle to topple it. For Nietzsche, to paraphrase Bierce, conservatives are those who heroically defend the old absurdities, while "our anarchists" are those who strive mightily to replace them with new ones. His critique is thus a diagnosis of a sensibility rooted in reactivity, ressentiment, and one-sided negativity. Those of "our anarchists" who fall prey to such an insidious sensibility become obsessed with the injustices of the existing world and with their own powerlessness in the face of such evil. They are in effect, the mirror image of

those slavish souls who are entranced and corrupted by the awe-inspiring spectacle of power, wealth and privilege. But in the case of our rebellious little anarchists, the spirit is poisoned by an impotent, reactive rage.

It is Nietzsche the Antichrist who savagely attacks the Anarchist, since anarchism for him is a kind of Christianity. He does not, by the way, mean by "Christianity" the spiritually and socially inflammatory teachings of Jesus, which he
shows to be ironically negated by the entire history of the Church. He means,
rather, the reactive institutional Christianity that retreats into pessimism and
nihilism in its utter dissatisfaction with the world. Nietzsche's indictment of
Christianity and anarchism resembles Hegel's dissection of the "Beautiful Soul."
For Hegel, the moral idealist creates a dream world with little connection to ethical reality, the embodiment of good in the actual world. But Nietzsche is much
more scathing in his assault on such idealism. The "Beautiful Soul" is for him a
quite "Ugly Soul," corrupted by its narrowness and alienation from the truths of
experience and the virtues of the world.

If the higher person, the *Übermensch*, is like a vast sea in which immense evil
is diluted and dissolved, then the moral purist is a small stagnant puddle, in
which the most exalted goodness putrefies. "The Christian and the anarchist:
both decadents, both incapable of having any effect other than disintegrating,
poisoning, withering, bloodsucking; both the instinct of mortal hatred against
everything that stands, that stands in greatness, that has duration, that promises
life a future."[9] The tragic flaw in both these character-structures results from an
identification of the self with an ungrounded, ahistorical ideal. The result is a
rage against the real, in which the most authentic achievements evoke the most
intense reactive hostility, since they threaten the necessity of the absolute break
with what exists, *l'ecart absolu*, that has become a psychological necessity.

Nietzsche's image of the anarchist is inspired by the classical anarchist revolutionary who was the reactive response to the industrializing, accumulative
capitalism and the centralizing, bureaucratically expanding nation-state of the
19th century. Yet much of what he says also characterizes—perhaps even better—
various strands of Western anarchism that emerged in the 1960s and which
linger on in certain subcultures. Such an anarchism defines itself practically by
what it is against. It fumes and fulminates against "all forms of domination," by
which it means every one of this fallen world's institutions and social practices,
none of which has any liberatory potential.

This is the anarchism of permanent protest. The anarchism of militant mar-
ginality. The anarchism of sectarian theoretical purity. The anarchism of grand
gestures that become increasingly petty and indeed meaningless as they are dissolved in the vast Post-Mortem Ocean of Signifiers. As sophisticated surrealism
becomes the stuff of advertising and music videos, and the entire culture lapses
into brutal cynicism tinged with irony, all homely gestures of resistance, all sighs
on behalf of the oppressed, all "critiques of all forms of domination," all this
becomes low-level noise, lost in a din of background noise (The High Deci-Bel
Epoque). Though if any of it happens to be mildly interesting, it can be recycled
as bits and pieces of style.

Nietzsche once pointed out that the interesting question for Kantian ethics is not what actions are necessary according to the Categorical Imperative, but why belief in a Categorical Imperative was so goddamn necessary for Kant. Similarly, we might ask why for certain classical anarchists cataclysmic revolution was an absolute necessity, and for certain contemporary anarchists sectarian dogmatism and the politics of permanent protest are a psychological necessity. Why does their spirit (and perhaps their nervous system) crave it so intensely? I have heard certain anarchists proclaim, with evident satisfaction, that "everything our enemies say about us is true" (and many more have entertained such thoughts, whether with pride or guilt). According to their Manichean worldview, everything these enemies think to be so horrifying is in reality quite wonderful, and to be accused of it should be a source of boundless pride. Such anarchists thus recreate themselves in the reactive image of the reactive image that reactionaries have of them. Rather than negating the negation, they affirm the negation, achieving the bliss of some rather incoherent sort of pure negativity.

The particular anarchists that Nietzsche targets are only one variety of a nihilistic species that includes all kinds of "slanderers, underminers, doubters, destroyers." It is for this reason that he places "anarchism" in a seemingly bizarre list that includes such other symptoms as "celibacy," "sterility," "hystericism," and "alcoholism."[10] Such an anarchism sees nothing but the negative in what is, yearns for revolutionary destruction, and finds hope (or perhaps merely a "principle of hope") only in a post-revolutionary Utopia bearing little connection to anything that actually exists. Such an anarchism is a kind of Left Platonism, taking refuge not in Plato's Realm of Eternal Forms, but in an equally ghostly and disembodied Realm of Eternal Forms of Freedom.

The critique of anarchism is merely a minor variation on Nietzsche's major theme of the destructive nature of all varieties of ressentiment. "This plant," he tells us, "blooms best today among anarchists and anti-Semites," who seek "to sanctify *revenge* under the name of *justice*—as if justice were at bottom merely a further development of the feeling of being aggrieved—and to rehabilitate not only revenge but all the *reactive* affects in general."[11] The wisest old anarchist I ever met once said to me (summing up his philosophy of life): "We deserve the best!" His entire life has been a celebration of as much of this *best* as we (all of us—no one is excluded from his Anarchist Party) have experienced and created. Yet for every anarchist with such a spirit, I have found many whose whole being proclaims the question, "Why have they done this to me?" Such an anarchist is a walking complaint.

In the 19th century this ressentiment of revolt was embodied above all in Sergi Nechaev's fanatical and murderous nihilism. But it also found expression in the side of Bakunin's character that drew him so powerfully to Nechaev, the lumpenproletariat, and the brigands, and led him to fantasize vast revolutionary potential in every poorly-organized insurrection. In recent anarchist sectarianism ressentiment reemerges ("with a vengeance," needless to say) in Bookchin's anarcho-negativism, in which political theory and practice deteriorates into the politics of spleen. Social ecology becomes anti-social egology. The cult of negativity finds its *déraison d'être* in ressentiment—not only against "all forms of domination," but against every existing reality. Every practical attempt to transform the conditions of life is condemned as irrelevant, simpleminded, or else some sort of devious reactionary plot. And the more insidious it is, the more seriously it threatens to accomplish some good deemed unattainable according to the dictates of abstract dogmatism.

Post-Mortemists have depicted Nietzsche as the enemy of dialectical thinking. They presume that merely because he demolishes the sophistries and self-delusions of dialecticians that he is somehow anti-dialectical. Yet no one has ever put more teeth into a biting dialectical logic. "Whoever fights monsters should see to it that in the process he does not become a monster. And when you look long into an abyss, the abyss also looks into you."[12] How many anarchists in their struggle against the state have reproduced a little state within themselves? How many leftists in their crusades against domination have turned themselves into domineering, power-hungry dogmatists? The monster signifies violence, fanaticism in ideas, rigidity of character, contempt for persons—all of which have been reproduced in abundance, even in more extreme forms, in the monster-slayers themselves. The warriors of being fall into the abyss of nihilism. "We are nothing but we shall be all." But out of nothing comes nothing!

Such an affirmation of nothingness (a Bad Infinity, to be distinguished from the Nothingness of Affirmation of Gautama, Böhme, etc.) arises from the propensity to define oneself in relation to that which one is not; in this case the system of power and domination. By defining oneself as powerless, or merely subject to power, one overlooks the marvelous powers that are slumbering within one's own creative spirit. Just as "power corrupts and absolute power corrupts absolutely," powerlessness corrupts and absolute powerlessness corrupts absolutely. In the case of the oppressed, or, rather those who allow themselves to be defined by the conditions of their oppression, their souls are poisoned by their reactive will to power. Their oppositional perspective comes to absorb their entire being. They are lions—occasionally dangerous, but always tiresome. The spirit of the child has been entirely extinguished in them. Their creativity, spontaneity, playfulness, and vitality are destroyed.

Nietzsche's message concerning such anarchist sectarians is the same as his message about all dogmatists, all who wield their truth like a weapon. "Avoid all such unconditional people! They are a poor sick sort, a sort of mob: they look sourly at this life, they have the evil eye for this earth. Avoid all such unconditional people! They have heavy feet and sultry hearts: they do not know how to dance. How should the earth be light for them?"[13] In effect, Nietzsche says to the "unconditional" anarchists, "If I can't dance, I don't want your anarchism!" Despite all their ideological purity, despite their incessant talk of "humanity" and "ecology," such anarchists cannot love actual human beings, nor can they love the earth.

On Monsters Hot and Cold

So Nietzsche proves himself to be anarchism's best friend and enemy. But his gift to anarchism goes far beyond his amicable hatred. For despite his scathing attacks on anarchists, he shows himself to be not only a good friend and a good enemy of all anarchists, but also to be a good anarchist.

One of the most distinctive characteristics of anarchism is its voluntarism— its opposition to the imposition of the will of one upon another through force and coercion. And no anarchist has stated the case against coercion more perceptively than has Nietzsche. Coercion is corruptive force, he says. But contrary to the conventional anarchic complaint, its most significant corrupting effect is on the victims, not the perpetrators. "Every power that forbids, that knows how to arouse fear in those to whom something is forbidden, creates a 'bad conscience' (that is, the desire for something combined with the consciousness of danger in satisfying it, with the necessity for secrecy, for underhandedness, for caution). Every prohibition worsens the character of those who do not submit to it willingly, but only because they are compelled."[14] No wonder some anarchist rhetoricians become discouraged when their ringing condemnation of "all forms of domination" falls on deaf ears. They pay far too much attention to the injustices of the oppressors and too little to the ways in which power has transformed those who are coerced and dominated.

Nietzsche's imperious questioning of *techne* also betrays his deeply anarchistic spirit. His critique of technical rationality and technological domination is prophetic. Despite his well-known admiration for some varieties of "will to power," the will to dominate and manipulate nature is the object of his most scornful derision. "Our whole attitude toward nature, the way we violate her with the aid of machines and the heedless inventiveness of our technicians and engineers, is *hubris*."[15] He sees that our will to dominate nature inevitably produces a will to dominate human nature also. "[O]ur attitude toward *ourselves* is *hubris*, for we experiment with ourselves in a way we would never permit ourselves to experiment with animals and, carried away by curiosity, we cheerfully vivisect our souls..."[16] Certain impeccably anarchistic but nonetheless simplistic theories onesidedly trace the quest to dominate nature in the actual domination of "human by human," but dogmatically dismiss the roots of social domination in the urge to conquer nature. In reality the relationship between the two dominations is—as Nietzsche, that great anti-dialectical dialectician, grasped quite well—dialectical.

Nietzsche is not only one of the most devastating *critics* of the state, but also one of the most accurately perceptive *analysts* of that institution. Few before him were quite so indiscrete in divulging the origins of the state in force, violence and domination. The state, he says, "organized immorality—internally: as police, penal law, classes, commerce, family; externally: as will to power, to war, to conquest, to revenge."[17] He grasps the ironic truth that "law and order" as carried out by the state is in fundamental contradiction with the nature of its subjects. The masses on whose subservience it depends are incapable of either the banal cruelties or the paroxysms of horror that define the monster. "How does it happen that the state will do a host of things that the individual would never countenance?—Through division of responsibility, of command, and of execution.

Through the interposition of the virtues of obedience, duty, patriotism, and loyalty. Through upholding pride, severity, strength, hatred, revenge—in short, all typical characteristics that contradict the herd type."[18] Its ability to do that which would terrify the individual is not for Nietzsche a reproach against the state, however, but merely a statement of the brutal truth that the mass of state-worshippers refuse to recognize. "None of you has the courage to kill a man, or even to whip him, or even to—but the tremendous machine of the state over-powers the individual, so he repudiates responsibility for what he does (obedience, oath, etc.)—Everything a man does in the service of the state is contrary to his nature."[19] Here he does no more than taunt the good citizen with the blatant self-deception and hypocrisy on which every state is founded.

There is perhaps no more powerful assault on the state in Western philosophical thought than Zarathustra's vilification of "The New Idol." There Nietzsche indicts the state for its artificial, coercive, technical-bureaucratic reality that contradicts and undermines what is most valuable in any culture. "State is the name of the coldest of all cold monsters. Coldly it tells lies too, and this lie crawls out of its mouth: 'I, the state, am the people.'"[20] Not only is the state not "the people," it devours the people and all that they have created. State versus people is one of the crucial chapters in the epochal story of the battle between mechanism and organism, between the machine and life. The Artificial Monster ("that great *Leviathan*... that *mortal god*") consumes any organic culture:

> The state tells lies in all the tongues of good and evil; and whatever
> it says it lies—and whatever it has it has stolen. Everything about it
> is false; it bites with stolen teeth, and bites easily. Even its entrails
> are false. Confusion of tongues of good and evil: this sign I give you
> as the sign of the state.[21]

All vitality is drained from the living social organism so that the Cold Creature might live. The Monster is a grotesque parasite, a strange Gargantuan vampire, and the people understand this. "Where there is still a people, it does not understand the state and hates it as the evil eye and the sin against customs and rights."[22]

Nietzsche's diagnosis of the state was still prophetic in the 1880s, since the then triumphant Monster still had a century to fulfill its deadly destiny before beginning its precipitous decline and decay. His strident indictment sounds rather dated, however, in the era of the new Monster, the corporate Global Golem. "'On earth there is nothing greater than I: the ordering finger of God am I'—thus roars the monster,"[23] according to Zarathustra. Today such a roar would be met with laughter, except possibly in some Third World dictatorship in which the secret police might be watching. For as Nietzsche himself had quite presciently begun to realize, in mass society nothing really seems so "great," and cynicism reigns supreme. The state as "the ordering finger of God?" Ha! In this sad Post-Mortem world, God has given everything the finger.

So the state may be, as Nietzsche says, the Coldest Monster. But now there are cold, hot and even lukewarm Monsters at large. The late modern state, that Post-Mortem Monster, we are coming to discover, is no more than a Lukewarm Monster. Thus it lies only lukewarmly. It could not with a straight face say, "I the State am the People." It can, however, half-heartedly tell us that it feels our pain.

The dominion of the great Monster Leviathan has been superseded not by that of the Lukewarm Monster, but by the ascendancy of another Beast, one that is neither cold nor lukewarm. It has a rather dark, satanic, and hot interior, but a radiant, divine, and above all *cool* exterior. It is Moloch, the Monster that eats its young—the Consuming Monster.

Nietzsche in fact realized that mass society would have little place for the old authoritarian state. "Who still wants to rule? Who obey? Both require too much exertion." He is slightly less prophetic on the topic of work, observing that "One still works, for work is a form of entertainment."[24] Under the reign of Moloch few would confuse the two. Today, few work for amusement, though many do so because work is for them a means toward entertainment. On the other hand, in an ironic reversal of Nietzsche's aphorism, entertainment has increasingly become a form of work. Just as producers were once taught to feel shame if their work was not up to par, consumers now feel suitably guilty if they are not entertained in the correct manner.

Furthermore, Nietzsche's true object of attack in his assault on the state is not one particular historical institution but all the forces that are destructive of life. "State I call it where all drink poison, the good and the wicked; state, where all lose themselves, the good and the wicked; state, where the slow suicide of all is called 'life.'"[25] Nietzsche's primary target is often statist political conformity—the dissolution of individuality into good citizenship, the homogenization of cultural diversity into official state *Kultur*, the mechanization of life in a techno-bureaucratic world. But he also had strong intimations of where the corporate state was going, that the accent was to fall more on the *corporate*, the economistic, and less on the *state*, the political.

What is the color of power today? "Behold the superfluous! They gather riches and become poorer with them. They want power and first the lever of power, much money—the impotent paupers!" says Zarathustra.[26] As I read this passage late one night, I heard someone passing by outside my window, speaking these precise words (for I wrote them down immediately): "It's not about black and white anymore. It's about power and domination, and it has no color except..." At this point the voice faded out and I could not hear the final word. I rushed to the door but found no trace of the passerby. I'll call the voice, "The Ghost of Nietzsche."

Zarathustra was already on to the message of this Ghost. The progression in his successive tirades against "The New Idol" and "The Flies In The Market Place" prefigures a real historical movement. After warning us about the dangers of the state, Nietzsche cautions us concerning the threat of the developing economistic society. "Where solitude ceases the market place begins; and where the market place begins the noise of the great actors and the buzzing of the poisonous flies begins too." Nietzsche foresees the coming of the society of the spectacle, a world of illusion in which "even the best things amount to nothing without someone to make a show of them."[27] He heralds the coming of those swarms of poisonous flies that now overrun the earth, spreading poison everywhere. They are poisonous indeed! Nietzsche sounds the tocsin for the rising flood of toxins that inundate the world. If we poison the spirit can the corruption of the body be far behind (or vice versa)? As Nietzsche predicted, the masses may have a long life of slow death to look forward to in this poisonous, Post-Mortem world. Perhaps God was lucky to die early and avoid the crowds. Or did he?

Nietzsche may have written the obituary for a certain ancient psychopath who sometimes goes under the alias "God."[28] Yet this same Nietzsche heralds the coming of a new Post-Mortem God. "Verily he [the actor] believes only in gods who make a big noise in the world."[29] The culture of noise, the society of the image, gets the God it needs and deserves. Nietzsche had a prophetic insight into the coming domination of spirit and psyche by what has with suitable irony been called "the culture industry" (presumably because it produces bacteria). Nietzsche understood with Blake that "All deities reside in the human breast." But he also foresaw the day in which the gods of pandering and publicizing, the gods of spectacle and sensationalism would supplant the old psychic Pantheon, the divinities of creative energy and wild imaginings.

Nietzsche is quite explicit in his judgment of the market and the society of the image. "Far from the market place and far from fame happens all that is great..."[30] The free market frees the masses from such burdens as creative imagination, spontaneity, depth of the spirit, solitude, playfulness, the joy of the present moment—all that is "great" and good according to the Nietzschean valuation. Freed from these, one is free to pay for everything else.

According to Nietzsche, culture and the state are "antagonists." "One lives off the other, one thrives at the expense of the other. All great ages of culture are ages of political decline: what is great culturally has always been unpolitical, even *anti*-political."[31] What Nietzsche means, what he perceived so acutely under the Reich, was that culture is the enemy of the "political" in a quite specific sense—it is the enemy of empire and all that is imperial. Greatness of culture is annihilated by empire, whether this empire be political or economic.

Nietzsche is thus once again more anarchistic than the anarchists. It is true that he sounds rather authoritarian in his suggestion that "*Genuine philosophers... are commanders and legislators*" who say "*this shall it be!*"[32] Yet what he intends is as anarchic as the dictum of the anarchist poet Shelley in his "Defense of Poetry" that poets are "the unacknowledged legislators of the world." For Nietzsche's philosophers also rule through their power of creativity. "Their 'knowing' is *creating*, their creating is a legislation..."[33] And he does not mean the philosophers of the academy, but rather the philosopher-poets of the spirit. The question for Nietzschean Anarchy is who shall rule: either the masters of the state and of the market, with their heroic will to plunder and destroy, or the creators with their generous will to give birth, their gift-giving virtue.

We shall return to this anarchic Nietzschean question, but first another question concerning another Nietzschean Anarchy.

Post-Mortemist Nietzsche

"What is Post-Mortemism?" Above all, the "Post-Mortem" is a nihilistic form of consciousness emerging from forces of decline, separation, disintegration, negation, and, in short, Thanatos. Post-Mortemism, can thus, as the expression of an absolute spirit of negation, validly present itself as the most radical form of theoretical Anarchy. But despite attempts by Post-Mortemists to claim Nietzsche as one of their prophets, Post-Mortemism itself falls victim to Nietzsche's anti-anarchist critique.

Nietzsche distinguishes between an "active nihilism" which is "a sign of increased power of the spirit" and a "passive nihilism" which is "decline and recession of the power of the spirit."[34] While Nietzsche's most passionate anarchic dimension expresses his active nihilism, his destruction for the sake of creation, Post-Mortemist Nietzsche becomes the passionless prophet of passive nihilism.

Let us consider a favorite proof-text, much beloved by certain Nietzschean Post-Mortemists:

> What then is truth? A mobile army of metaphors, metonyms, and anthropomorphisms—in short, a sum of human relations, which have been enhanced, transposed, and embellished poetically and rhetorically, and which after long use seem firm, canonical and obligatory to a people: truths are illusions about which one has forgotten that this is what they are; metaphors which are worn out and without sensuous power; coins which have lost their pictures and now matter only as metal, no longer as coins.[35]

Post-Mortemists read Nietzsche as if this were all ever said about truth, as if he had no concern for the truth of the body and the truth of worldly experience.

According to such a view, "truths are illusions" for Nietzsche, mere perspectives on reality. There is no "transcendental signified," for we are bound by our chains of illusion, or perhaps, better, our chains of allusion, our chains of signification.

And indeed, Nietzsche did recognize the inescapably perspectival nature of knowledge. Nietzschean perspectivism is the insight that all perception, all knowing, all valuing come from some*where*. They are arise out of, and are rooted in, some perspective, some position, some *place*. But unlike Nietzschean perspectivism, the Post-Mortem variety is deracinated, *à la dérive*. It is the annihilation of place, the view from nowhere.

Nietzsche's view of truth cannot be reduced to a Post-Mortem nihilism, for it always retains a naturalistic core of pragmatic realism. Signification arises in the midst of a continuum of experience. "The feeling of strength, struggle, of resistance convinces us that there is something that is here being resisted."[36] Nietzsche would dismiss our contemporary Post-Mortemist theoretical Anarchy as the latest form of escape to the dream world of ideas, the terrorism of pure theory, in which comic revolutionaries fantasize heroic conquests of idea by idea, yet remain out of *touch* with a reality that *resists* their control.[37]

Post-Mortemist Nietzsche, we are told, is an enemy of the whole. And quite appropriately (and ironically) this Nietzsche emerges precisely through the dismembering of the Nietzschean corpus. A dissected Nietzsche-part does indeed tell us that "Nihilism as a psychological state is reached... when one has posited a totality, a systemization, indeed any organization in all events, and underneath all events," etc. Nietzsche attacks the "positing" of a fictitious Totality that can give value to one who feels valueless "when no infinitely valuable whole works through him."[38] Yet Nietzsche also shows that when the creative, gift-giving whole (as opposed to any fictitious Totality) does indeed work through the person, there is no need for such a "positing."

Post-Mortemists ignore the Nietzsche who speaks of unity-in-diversity and the dynamic whole. This is the Dionysian Nietzsche:

> The word *'Dionysian'* means: an urge to unity, a reaching out beyond personality, the everyday, society, reality, across the abyss of transitoriness: a passionate-painful overflowing into darker, fuller, more floating states; an ecstatic affirmation of the total character of life as that which remains the same, just as powerful, just as blissful, through all change; the great pantheistic sharing of joy and sorrow that sanctifies and calls good even the most terrible and questionable qualities of life; the eternal will to procreation, to fruitfulness, to recurrence; the feeling of the necessary unity of creation and destruction.[39]

Nietzsche's attack on "decadence" as "the anarchy of atoms" is aimed at those forces that produce a disintegration of the living whole. "The whole no longer lives at all: it is composite, calculated, artificial, and artifact."[40] In other words, it is state, spectacle, and megamachine. In opposition to such a spirit, Nietzsche's Dionysian is based on an affirmation of one's place in the living whole:

> Such a spirit who has *become free* stands amid the cosmos with a joyous and trusting fatalism, in the *faith* that only the particular is loathsome, and that all is redeemed and affirmed in the whole—*he does not negate any more.* Such a faith, however, is the highest of all possible faiths: I have baptized it with the name of *Dionysus.*[41]

Nietzsche is quite prophetic concerning the developing spiritual illness of Post-Mortemism. In fact, he helps us grasp the fact that the "Post-Mortem" is in fact nothing but the "Late Modern."[42] Long before Post-Mortemism emerged as a seemingly revolutionary social transformation, Nietzsche saw the accelerating development of many of its salient themes. Eclecticism, diversification, style, discontinuity, artifice, speed, superficiality, coolness. An:

> abundance of disparate impressions greater than ever: cosmopolitanism in foods, literatures, newspapers, forms, tastes, even land-

scapes. The tempo of this influx *prestissimo*; the impressions erase each other; one instinctively resists taking in anything; a weakening of the power to digest results from this. A kind of adaptation to this flood of impressions takes place: men unlearn spontaneous action, they merely react to stimuli from outside.[43]

An apt diagnosis of the Post-Mortem Condition: in sum, an "artificial change of one's nature into a 'mirror'; interested but, as it were, merely epidermically interested..."[44]

And what of the universal will to power? Does this not lend support to Anarcho-Cynicalism? Does not Nietzsche proclaim: "Where I found the living, there I found will to power; and even in the will of those who serve I found the will to be master"?[45] Post-Mortemists often find in Nietzsche nothing but affirmation of the will and discovery of power-seeking everywhere. He is of course a "master of suspicion." But is not suspiciousness a mark of the slave mentality that he detests? Is not an obsession with power a mark of the inferior sensibility? The highest metamorphosis of the spirit is the child, and only the most neurotic child wastes much time on suspicion. Nietzsche exalts the will *only to forget it*. "He must still discard his heroic will; he shall be elevated, not merely sublime: the ether itself should elevate him, the will-less one."[46] The will attains its greatest power through its own disappearance.

And what about "difference"? Nietzsche, living at the height of productionist industrial society, thought that the great threat to individuality and creativity was the imposition of sameness. "No shepherd and one herd! Everybody wants the same, everybody is the same: whoever feels different goes voluntarily into a madhouse."[47] History's dialectic of absurdity has moved one step beyond Nietzsche, so that the rage for sameness now takes the form of an obsession with difference. The consumptionist mind reaches new levels of brilliance in its sensitivity to difference, which has little to do with excellence, as Nietzsche might once have assumed. The code of commodity consumption creates a minute sensitivity to differences of symbolic import, connotation, image and style. Though sameness is alive and well, huge profits are to be made from the growing quest to "feel different" by means of an infinite variety of modes of consumption. Even "going voluntarily into a madhouse" becomes a form of commodity consumption that can be marketed as a distinctive (and quite profitable) mode of being different. And in academia, that zoo for Nietzsche's "herd animals of the intellect," stupidity finds a refuge in difference. Mediocre intellects pursue their quest for tenure and then fulfill their publication quotas through mindlessly mouthing the slogans and mimicking the jargon of Post-Mortemism. And one is subjected to the tortuous spectacle of Anglo-Saxons, or even more depressingly, Saxons, engaging in an unintentional parody of Gallic wit. The result has all the brilliance of a joke translated by a computer program.

But as much as we might wish to bury Post-Mortemist Nietzsche, his Specter remains very much alive. It has terrified more than one ill-informed anarchist. Murray Bookchin, certainly the most *authoritative* voice in contemporary anarchology, once opposed the idea of a seminar on Nietzsche at his Institute for Social Ecology on the grounds that it might undermine his pupils' values. He was terrified that the philosopher might corrupt the youth of his little polis. In a recent work, Bookchin undertakes the theoretical demolition of Nietzsche's supposedly pernicious influence. It turns out that Bookchin's Nietzsche is no more than a parody of Post-Mortem Nietzsche. At the hands of Bookchin, this genealogist of culture becomes a zany literary type who sees all of history as merely "a disjointed, variable, and free-floating collection of narratives."[48]

Yet Nietzsche went to some lengths to show that realities like "narratives" are symptoms of realities that are far from "free-floating"—realities such as systems of power and cultural institutions that interact with fundamental biological drives and psychological impulses in shaping the self. Bookchin, in his frenzied attack on the evils of Post-Mortemism, discovers a Nietzsche that reflects his own aversion to Post-Mortem textualism more than it reveals anything particularly Nietzschean. Bookchin's Post-Mortemism is an incoherent jumble in which A: Derrida says that there's nothing outside the text, and B: Nietzsche influenced Post-Mortemism, ergo C: Nietzsche must have believed that history is nothing but textuality.

Anyone who is willing to take the plunge into the murky waters of Post-Mortemality will search vainly for a Nietzschean view of history in Derridean textualism. As Nietzsche states in the "preface" to *The Genealogy of Morals*, "our ideas, our values, our yeas and nays, our ifs and buts, grow out of us with the necessity with which a tree bears fruit—related and each with an affinity to each, and evidence of one will, one health, one soil, one sun."[49] Nietzsche would never say that *"il n'y a pas de dehors du texte."* He would say that there is no life that is without perspective. But every perspective is rooted deeply in life, in the body, in the earth, in the great *"dehors."*

We might apply Nietzsche's naturalistic-imaginistic mode of critique to Bookchin himself. Nietzsche would never dismiss Bookchin's creation of his own fictitious character "Nietzsche" as a mere "free-floating narrative." Rather, he would situate the Bookchinite imaginary Nietzsche within Bookchin's own peculiar narrative will to power, his creation of an authoritative theoretical edifice on behalf of which he must do battle with, and attempt to annihilate all theoretical (and intensely emotion-charged) threats. He would also explore the foundations of this edifice in Bookchin's own seething ressentiment, and indeed the foundations of this ressentiment itself—the forces that shaped an imperious will, the underlying states of health and malaise, the qualities of the soil in which it developed, the nature of that sun that infused it with energy, or which perhaps hid its face at crucial moments. Finally, Nietzsche might reflect on why such a marvelous example of the reactive character structure should have found its place of refuge and its field for raging self-assertion in *anarchism*, that most convenient utopia of self-justifying ressentiment.

Literary Anarchy: Forgetting Nietzsche's Umbrella

"It is the habitual carriage of the umbrella that is the stamp of respectability."—Stevenson, "The Philosophy of Umbrellas"

"i forgot my umbrella"—Nietzsche

"Jacques' umbrella is alive and well and living in Paris."—seen somewhere

"Sometimes [an umbrella] is just [an umbrella]."—Freud

There is an Anarchy of the Text. Yet Nietzsche would have no trouble diagnosing Post-Mortem textual Anarchy as a form of what he calls "literary decadence." For Nietzsche "the mark" of such decadence is that "life no longer resides in the whole." Though he would no doubt admire the brilliant sense of multiplicity that it sometimes achieves, he would certainly conclude that its focus on diversity comes "at the expense of the whole" so that "the whole is no longer a whole." Its Anarchy is not the Anarchy of life, of the organic, of the dynamic whole, but rather "the anarchy of atoms."[50]

Post-Mortemist Literary Anarchy is a rebellion against the absurd concept that texts are autonomous totalities, textual organisms in which subtexts are textual organs, textual cells, textual organelles. But in their haste to murder the textual organism in order to dissect it, the Post-Mortemist anarchists ignore the larger ecology of the text. Their urge to deconstruct is an ecocidal urge also.

Derrida exhibits this impulse, the urge to deconstruct totality transmuted into an impulse to murder the whole, to deconstruct that which defies construction. He directs this ecocidal impulse toward a "whole" that he calls "Nietzsche's text," quite appropriately invoking a Monster. Referring to a seemingly cryptic "fragment" found among Nietzsche's papers, Derrida proposes:

> To whatever lengths one might carry a conscientious interpretation, the hypothesis that the totality of Nietzsche's text, in some monstrous way, might well be of the type, 'I have forgotten my umbrella' cannot be denied. Which is tantamount to saying that there is no 'totality to Nietzsche's text,' not even a fragmentary or aphoristic one.[51]

Is it possible that a crucial difference between Nietzsche and Derrida consists in the fact that the former, when he has forgotten his umbrella, knows that it is in fact an umbrella that he, chaos that he is, has forgotten. Derrida on the other hand, might think that *"il s'agit d'un texte, d'un texte en restance, voire oublié, peut-être d'un parapluie. Qu'on ne tient plus dans la main."*[52] Or, as Derrida's English translator renders this idea, those who seek meaning in Nietzsche's aphorism "must have forgotten that it is a text that is in question, the remains of a text, indeed a forgotten text. An umbrella perhaps. That one no longer has in hand."[53]

Here we come face to face with the Anarchy of undecidability. We peer into an anarchic abyss. We are perhaps about to be devoured by the Monster of Post-Mortemism.

It is striking that Derrida chooses as an example of undecidability a text that alludes to the forces of nature, and, indirectly, to protection from the forces of nature. For textualism is itself a metaphysical umbrella that protects one from those very forces. Such strange Anarchy has lost touch with the atmosphere. We are dealing here with *l'oubli de l'atmosphère*.[54]

According to Derrida's English translator, " < <I have forgotten my umbrella. > > "[55] is *"[f]ragment classified no. 12,175 in the French translation of* Joyful Wisdom, *p. 457."*[56]

According to Derrida, " < <J'ai oublié mon parapluie > >."[57] is *"[f]ragment classé avec la cote 12,175, tr. fr. du* Gai savoir, *p. 457."*[58]

According to the original German:[59]

ich habe meinen Regenschirm vergessen

is a note classified "Herbst 1881 12[62]" in Nietzsche's collected works.[60]

On examining this "fragment," we find that Nietzsche not only "forgot his umbrella," he also forgot his punctuation. In this, he is unlike Derrida and Derrida's English translator, both of whom not only remembered this punctuation, but decided to give it back to Nietzsche:

> < <*J'ai oublié mon paraplui* > >
> < <J'ai oublié mon paraplui > >.
>   Derrida, *Eperons/Spurs*, p. 122.

> *"I have forgotten my umbrella"*
> < <I have forgotten my umbrella. > >
>   Derrida, *Eperons/Spurs*, p. 123.

Interestingly, they appear to be incompetent to give him back his forsaken umbrella (no matter how severe the weather may be), yet they are perfectly capable of giving him back these little bits of forgotten text.

Furthermore, in view of Derrida's case for undecidability, the nature of his (and his translator's) restoration of Nietzsche's text seems highly ironic. First, he helps restore Nietzsche's ego, for Nietzsche seemingly defied the laws of punctuation in order to mark his *"ich,"* even though it begins the statement, with a humble lower case "i." However, Derrida bestows on Nietzsche a majescule "J," reversing this self-effacement. Secondly, by restoring the initial capitalization, Derrida helps anchor the case of the umbrella firmly in time. Our floating forgotten umbrella affair now has a point of origination or initiation. And finally, in restoring the "period" he "puts a point" to the whole affair, as if the forgetting were previously held in suspension, but the umbrella is now, once and for all, and quite decisively, "forgotten."

Perhaps Derrida is right and this passage is undecidable, that is, in so far as it *is* a forgotten text, and therefore perhaps *not* about a forgotten umbrella. But how can it be nothing more than a forgotten text? Only in so far as we make a Derridean decision, a decision not to decide.

Jacques, you need to decide!

So we decide that it is *une parapluie*. We decide that it is *un parasol*. We decide that it is a shield against the domineering light of the Sun, that image of hierarchical power and domination. We decide that it is *une ombrelle*. We decide that it is *un nombril*. We decide that it is *le nombril du monde*. We decide that it is the axis of imagination around which turns the wheel of fate. We decide that it is the vast Nietzschean umbrella, which points to the heavens, to the heights, to the lightness of Dionysus, and which opens up to infinity.

We decide, on the other hand, that it is a sad little text signifying that poor Nietzsche forgot his umbrella.

Nietzsche As Prophet Of Pre-Ancientism

As we have seen, Nietzsche is not much of a Post-Mortemist (though he may be the Post-Mortemist's best friend!). And we have begun to discover that he is, at least in his best moments, a Pre-Ancientist. Let us call this Nietzsche "Pre-Ancientist Nietzsche" or PAN. The allusion to the pagan god is appropriately Nietzschean. For Pan, "this dangerous presence dwelling just beyond the protected zone of the village boundary" is the Arcadian counterpart to the Thracian god Dionysus, Nietzsche's favorite deity.[61] And as Bulfinch points out concerning Pan, "the name of the god signifies *all*," and Pan "came to be considered a symbol of the universe and personification of Nature," and later to be regarded as "a representative of all the gods and of heathenism itself."[62] PAN is the Nietzsche of pagan celebration, the Nietzsche of love of the Earth, the Nietzsche of life-affirmation, the Nietzsche of generosity and gift-giving.

PAN celebrates and endows with eternity that which appears. He "saves the phenomena" or "saves appearances" ("*sauve les dehors*") so to speak.

> A certain emperor always bore in mind the transitoriness of all things so as not to take them too seriously and to live at peace among them. To me, on the contrary, everything seems far too valuable to be so fleeting: I seek an eternity for everything: ought one to pour the most precious salves and wines into the sea?[63]

His vision reminds us of another great Pre-Ancientist and anarchist, William Blake, who famously "held infinity in the palm of his hand" and saw "Eternity in an hour." Exactly such an affirmation of being becoming in all its diversity and particularity is the core of PAN's enigmatic doctrine of the Eternal Recurrence. It signifies the infinite depth and richness of the present moment valued for its own being, not for any end beyond itself.[64]

Accordingly, PAN excludes only one philosopher from his general condemnation of the history of Western philosophy.

With the highest respect, I except the name of *Heraclitus*. When the rest of the philosophic folk rejected the testimony of the senses because they showed multiplicity and change, he rejected their testimony because they showed things as if they had permanence and unity. Heraclitus too did the senses an injustice. They lie neither in the way the Eleatics believed, nor as he believed—they do not lie at all... But Heraclitus will remain eternally right with his assertion that being is an empty fiction. The 'apparent' world is the only one: the 'true' world is merely added by a lie.[65]

PAN gives his fellow Pre-Ancientist Heraclitus well-deserved recognition, but does the latter an injustice in regard to his view of the senses. For Heraclitus the senses do and do not lie. And if they lie it is only to reveal truth through their lies. Heraclitus did the senses complete justice when he said "he prefers things that can be seen, heard and perceived."

Pre-Ancientism is a critique of the illusions of centrism. And Nietzsche is one of the great critics of all centrisms, including anthropocentrism. "If we could communicate with the mosquito, then we would learn that it floats through the air with the same self-importance, feeling within itself the flying center of the world."[66] This is the message of Laozi also: the universe does not revolve around us (unless we adopt a metaphysics worthy of a mosquito). "Heaven and Earth are not humane. They regard all things as straw dogs. The sage is not humane. He regards all people as straw dogs."[67] PAN directs us back to pre-Ancient times, before the blockheads carved nature up, geometricized the world and prepared it for domination. The crucial step was the replacement of the multitude of spiritual centers with a centering of power in the ego.

Yet Nietzsche has been seen as a kind of philosophical egoist. One of the great Nietzschean ironies is that this critic of the heroic has so often been reduced to a rather adolescent sort of hero-worshiper. His reflections on the will point in a quite different direction. According to Zarathustra, "all 'it was' is a fragment, a riddle, a dreadful accident—until the creative will says to it, 'But thus I willed it.' Until the creative will says to it, 'But thus I will it; thus shall I will it.'"[68] One might ask who this self is that can be said to have willed all things, wills all things, and shall will all things. The small self with its small will seems to become a great self with a vast will. What is the meaning of this riddle that Zarathustra poses to us?

We find that this person with "creative will" is one who rejects another sort of will—the *heroic* will—and renounces the rebellion against nature. Such a person is, as that most anarchic of Pre-Ancientists, Zhuangzi, calls her, the "man without desire," who "does not disturb his inner well-being with likes and dislikes," the "true man of old," who "accepted what he was given with delight, and when it was gone,... gave it no thought."[69] Whoever possesses a "creative will" accepts life, experience, and the flow of being, the appearance of phenomena, as a gift, and realizes that one can never have a proprietary claim on any gift.[70]

While Heroic will is bound to the Spirit of Gravity and takes everything seriously, the creative will expresses the Spirit of Levity, and takes everything lightly.

Nietzschean Anarchy knows the anarchic power of laughter.[71] "Learn to laugh at yourselves as one must laugh!" says Zarathustra.[72] Elsewhere he explains that it is through laughter that we kill monsters. So as we learn to laugh we learn to kill the self. We slay the Dragon of the Ego. As I-Hsüan said, "if you seek after the Buddha, you will be taken over by the Devil of the Buddha, and if you seek after the Patriarch, you will be taken over by the Devil of the Patriarch." So:

> Kill anything that you happen on. Kill the Buddha if you happen to meet him. Kill a Patriarch or an Arhat if you happen to meet him. Kill your parents or relatives if you happen to meet them. Only then can you be free, not bound by material things, and absolutely free and at ease... I have no trick to give people. I merely cure disease and set people free.[73]

When one laughs at the self one becomes other than the self that is laughed at. One finally gets the joke that is the ego.

> Listen to PAN's diagnosis of the causes of the awful ego-sickness of ressentiment: For every sufferer instinctively seeks a cause for his suffering; more exactly, an agent; still more specifically, a *guilty* agent who is susceptible to suffering—in short, some living thing upon which he can, on some pretext or other, vent his affects, actually or in effigy: for the venting of his affects represents the greatest attempt on the part of the suffering to win relief, *anaesthesia*—the narcotic he cannot help desiring to deaden the pain of any kind.[74]

PAN comes to much the same conclusion as does Gautama concerning this subject: our mental disturbances are rooted in suffering, a false view of causality, and the illusion of the separate ego. Our constructed ego cuts us off from the whole, we resist the flow of energies, we fight against the movement, we seek to step into the same river of selfhood again and again, we blame reality and time, we seek revenge through whatever convenient target presents itself.

PAN might have become an even more skilled physician of culture had he followed Gautama further in exploring the connection between ego, suffering, and compassion. He travels part of the way on this path as he reflects on eternal recurrence and *amor fati*. Just as he goes part of the way down the path of that other great old Anarchic Doctor, Laozi, PAN tears away ruthlessly at some of our most deeply-rooted illusions about ourselves. "Beyond your thoughts and feelings, my brother, there stands a mighty ruler, and unknown sage—whose name is self. In your body he dwells; he is your body."[75] It is true that he here describes the body as the true self, the "great reason," that acts though the ego and the "little reason." But he shows also that he sometimes thinks beyond this body. Zarathustra slips and gives away PAN's more profound view when he says that "the mighty ruler" not only "is your body," but is also greater than the body and "dwells in your body."[76] This is the self of the self of the ego-self, the great reason of the great reason of the little reason. For PAN, our embodiedness carries us not only beyond our little self toward a larger self, but beyond our little body toward a larger body. As Laozi says, "He who loves the world as his body may be entrusted with the empire."[77]

It is this wisdom of the body that is at the heart of PAN's anarchic critique of the domineering ego and its heroic will. Domination has always rested on the hierarchical exaltation of the "world of man"—the human world—over the world of nature, and of the "world of man"—the masculine world—over all that is feminine or childlike. PAN is in accord with Laozi's anti-hierarchical prioritizing of the childlike and feminine aspects of the psyche. Zarathustra praises the child as "innocence and forgetting, a new beginning, a game, a self-propelled wheel, a first movement, a sacred 'Yes.'"[78] Laozi goes one step further, asserting that "he who possesses virtue in abundance may be compared to an infant."[79] Zarathustra surpasses even this, urging us to "to be the child who is newly born," and noting that to do this, "the creator must also want to be the mother who gives birth and the pangs of the birth-giver."[80] An image that Laozi also evokes when he asks, "can you play the role of the female in the opening and closing of the gates of Heaven?"[81] This is the secret of Nietzschean Anarchy—the opening of oneself to these forces of spontaneity, creativity, generosity, affirmation.

Nietzschean Anarchy is PAN's Dionysian dance. It is child's play. It is beginner's mind.

Notes

1   Friedrich Nietzsche, *Thus Spoke Zarathustra*, in *The Portable Nietzsche*, ed. and trans. Walter Kaufmann (New York: Penguin, 1976), p. 168.

2   Nietzsche, *The Will to Power*, ed. Walter Kaufmann, trans. Kaufmann and R. J. Hollingdale (New York: Penguin, 1976), p. 226.

3   Nietzsche, *Thus Spoke Zarathustra*, p. 156.

4   God(is-Dead)Father of Post-Mortemism.

5   Paul A. Basinski, "Nihilism and the Impossibility of Political Philosophy," *Journal of Value Inquiry*, 24 (1990), p. 271.

6   The many Nietzsches are often brilliant, witty, satirical, ironic, incisive, analytical, subtle, intelligent, and profound, but not infrequently also superficial, pretentious, heavy-handed, pathetic, spiteful, petty, fatuous, and buffoonish. It would be tempting to turn our surre(gion)al travelogue into "A Tale of Two Nietzsches." However, we will limit our visit for the most part to "The Best of Nietzsches." There is, however, "The Worst of Nietzsches," and this worst can be indeed abysmal. The abysmal Nietzsche emerges for example in a statement, quite appropriately, on the topic of "depth." A man, he says, "who has depth, in his spirit as well as in his desires... must always think about women as Orientals do; he must conceive of woman as a possession, as property that can be locked, as something predestined for service and achieving her perfection in that." Friedrich Nietzsche, *Beyond Good and Evil*, in Walter Kaufmann, trans. and ed., *Basic Writings of Nietzsche* (New York: Modern Library, 1968), p. 357. And savor the exquisite odor of this statement: "We would no more choose the 'first Christians' to associate with than Polish Jews—not that one even required any objection to them: they both do not smell good." Friedrich Nietzsche, *The Antichrist*, in Kaufmann, *The Portable Nietzsche*, p. 625. On Nietzsche as a pretentious buffoon, see Friedrich Nietzsche, *Ecce Homo*, part two, "Why I Am So Clever," and part five, "Why I Am Such An Asshole."

7   Nietzsche, *The Gay Science*, trans. Walter Kaufmann (New York: Vintage Books, 1974), p. 329.

8 Nietzsche, *The Gay Science*, p. 329.
9 Nietzsche, *The Antichrist*, p. 648.
10 Nietzsche, *The Will to Power*, p. 26. Bizarre, though to be honest, has there ever been a careful study of anarchist groups to see what proportion of their members are hysterical celibates or sterile alcoholics? Perhaps there is grant money somewhere.
11 Nietzsche, *Beyond Good and Evil*, pp. 509-10.
12 Ibid., 279.
13 Nietzsche, *Thus Spoke Zarathustra*, pp. 405-6.
14 Nietzsche, *The Will to Power*, p. 391.
15 Nietzsche, *Beyond Good and Evil*, p. 549.
16 Ibid.
17 Nietzsche, *The Will to Power*, p. 382.
18 Nietzsche, *The Will to Power*, pp. 382-83.
19 Ibid., 383.
20 Nietzsche, *Thus Spoke Zarathustra*, p. 160.
21 Ibid., 161.
22 Ibid.
23 Ibid.
24 Ibid., 130.
25 Ibid., 162.
26 Ibid.
27 Ibid., 163.
28 Though this still redoubtable personage, apparently thinking that rumors of his demise have been greatly exaggerated, lives on in certain circles in a state of indefinitely suspended senility. Some have accused the devotees of the patriarchal authoritarian God with worshipping a "white male God." But their God really is a white male. How do we know? As criminologists have pointed out, that's the exact profile for a serial killer.
29 Nietzsche, *Thus Spoke Zarathustra*, p. 164.
30 Ibid.
31 Nietzsche, *Twilight of the Idols*, in Kaufmann, *The Portable Nietzsche*, p. 509.
32 Nietzsche, *Beyond Good and Evil*, p. 326.
33 Ibid.
34 Nietzsche, *The Will to Power*, p. 17.
35 Nietzsche, "On Truth and Lies," in Kaufmann, *The Portable Nietzsche*, pp. 46-47.
36 Nietzsche, *The Will to Power*, p. 290.
37 Despite all their anarchic pretensions, the failure of Post-Mortemists to join in this resistance constitutes a de facto collaborationism.
38 Nietzsche, *The Will to Power*, p. 12.
39 Ibid., 539
40 Nietzsche, *The Case of Wagner*, in Kaufmann, *Basic Writings of Nietzsche*, p. 466.
41 Nietzsche, *Twilight of the Idols*, p. 554.
42 PM = late.
43 Nietzsche, *The Will to Power*, p. 47.
44 Ibid.
45 Nietzsche, *Thus Spoke Zarathustra*, p. 226.
46 Ibid., 230.
47 Ibid., 130.
48 Murray Bookchin, *Re-enchanting Humanity: A Defense of the Human Spirit Against Anti-Humanism, Misanthropy, Mysticism and Primitivism* (London: Cassell, 1995), p. 179.
49 *Morals*, in Kaufmann, *Basic Writings of Nietzsche*, p. 452. Yes, Nietzsche did indeed say that "our buts grow out of us with the necessity with which a tree bears fruit"—another comment on the decadent life of the scholar, perhaps.
50 Nietzsche, *The Case of Wagner*, p. 626.
51 Jacques Derrida, *Spurs: Nietzsche's Styles* (Chicago: University of Chicago Press), pp. 133, 135.

52 Ibid., p. 130.

53 Ibid., p. 131.

54 See Max Cafard, "Derrida's Secret Name: Or, What Transpired in the Auditorium of Gaea and Logos" in *Exquisite Corpse* 38 (1992): 2-3.

55 Derrida, p. 123. Guillemets in the original.

56 Ibid., p. 159. Reversed italics in the original.

57 Ibid., p. 123.

58 Ibid., p. 159. Reversed italics in the original.

59 N.B.: "the original," that is, as it is represented in a book, and herewith re-represented. We feel compelled to admit that the following is not actually Nietzsche's scrap of paper.

60 Nietzsche, *Sämtliche Werke* [*Collected Works*] (München, Berlin: Deutscher Taschenbuch Verlag and Walter de Gruyter, 1980), Band 9, p. 587.

61 Joseph Campbell, *The Hero With A Thousand Faces* (Princeton: Princeton University Press, 1968), p. 81.

62 Thomas Bulfinch, *Bulfinch's Mythology* (New York: Modern Library, nd), p. 136.

63 Nietzsche, *The Will to Power*, pp. 547-48.

64 Though some humorists say that it means that everything occurs over and over and over and... We will call this the Twilight Zone interpretation.

65 Nietzsche, *Twilight of the Idols*, pp. 480-81.

66 Nietzsche, "On Truth and Lies," p. 42.

67 Laozi [Lao Tzu], *Tao te Ching* [*Daodejing*] in Wing-Tsit Chan, *A Sourcebook in Chinese Philosophy* (Princeton: Princeton Univ. Press, 1963), p. 141.

68 Nietzsche, *Thus Spoke Zarathustra*, p. 253.

69 Chuang-Tzu [Zhangzi], *Inner Chapters* (New York: Vintage Books, 1974), pp. 108, 114.

70 As Nietzsche states it with unusual eloquence, "no one is free to be a crab." *Twilight of the Idols*, p. 547. His point is that we must always go "forward"—even if "downward" into decadence. A crab (in Nietzsche's particular imaginary zoology) backs away from and rejects this gift of life, growth, change, transformation.

71 This does not mean, however, that Nietzsche was funny, for unfortunately he was not. I once attended a lecture in which a philosophy professor spoke at great length on the topic of "Nietzsche and Humor." His thesis was that Nietzsche was a member of that rare species—the funny philosopher! The Professor assured the audience that Nietzsche's works were replete with humorous discussions, funny one-liners and hilarious episodes. Indeed, he revealed that when he reads Nietzsche he is often moved to smile, and even to laugh out loud! What he did not reveal was one single hilarious line from the entire collected works of Nietzsche, though this did not prevent many members of the audience from smiling broadly and even chuckling a bit. Apparently, the highly-developed sense of humor cultivated by certain professors of philosophy allows them to extract a certain quantum of hilarity from statements like "Nietzsche is funny." Or did they get the other joke?

72 Nietzsche, *Thus Spoke Zarathustra*, p. 253.

73 "The Recorded Conversations of Zen Master I-Hsüan" in Chan, p. 447.

74 Nietzsche, *Beyond Good and Evil*, p. 563.

75 Nietzsche, *Thus Spoke Zarathustra*, p. 146.

76 Ibid.

77 Laozi, in Chan, p. 145.

78 Nietzsche, *Thus Spoke Zarathustra*, p. 139.

79 Laozi, in Chan, p. 165.

80 Nietzsche, *Thus Spoke Zarathustra*, p. 199.

81 Laozi, in Chan, p. 144.

Anarchism and the Politics of Ressentiment

Saul Newman

> "A word in the ear of the psychologists, assuming they are inclined to study ressentiment close up for once: this plant thrives best amongst anarchists..."[1]

1. Of all the nineteenth century political movements that Nietzsche decries—from socialism to liberalism—he reserves his most venomous words for the anarchists. He calls them the "anarchist dogs" that are roaming the streets of European culture, the epitome of the "herd-animal morality" that characterizes modern democratic politics.[2] Nietzsche sees anarchism as poisoned at the root by the pestiferous weed of *ressentiment*—the spiteful politics of the weak and pitiful, the morality of the slave. Is Nietzsche here merely venting his conservative wrath against radical politics, or is he diagnosing a real sickness that has infected our radical political imaginary? Despite Nietzsche's obvious prejudice towards radical politics, this paper will take seriously his charge against anarchism. It will explore this cunning logic of ressentiment in relation to radical politics, particularly anarchism. It will attempt to unmask the hidden strains of ressentiment in the Manichean political thinking of classical anarchists like Bakunin, Kropotkin, and Proudhon. This is not with the intention of dismissing anarchism as a political theory. On the contrary, one might argue that anarchism could become more relevant to contemporary political struggles if it were made aware of the ressentiment logic of its own discourse, particularly in the essentialist identities and structures that inhabit it.

Slave Morality and *Ressentiment*

2. Ressentiment is diagnosed by Nietzsche as our modern condition. In order to understand ressentiment, however, it is necessary to understand the relationship between master morality and slave morality in which ressentiment is generated. Nietzsche's work *On the Genealogy of Morality* is a study of the origins of morality. For Nietzsche, the way we interpret and impose values on the world has a history—its origins are often brutal and far removed from the val-

This piece originally appeared in *Theory & Event* 4:3, 2000.

ues they produce. The value of 'good,' for instance, was invented by the noble and high-placed to apply to themselves, in contrast to common, low-placed and plebeian.[3] It was the value of the master—'good'—as opposed to that of the slave—'bad.' Thus, according to Nietzsche, it was in this pathos of distance, between the high-born and the low-born, this absolute sense of superiority, that values were created.[4]

However, this equation of good and aristocratic began to be undermined by a slave revolt in values. This slave revolt, according to Nietzsche, began with the Jews who instigated a revaluation of values:

3. "It was the Jews who, rejecting the aristocratic value equation (good = noble = powerful = beautiful = happy = blessed) ventured with awe-inspiring consistency, to bring about a reversal and held it in the teeth of their unfathomable hatred (the hatred of the powerless), saying, 'Only those who suffer are good, only the poor, the powerless, the lowly are good; the suffering, the deprived, the sick, the ugly, are the only pious people, the only ones, salvation is for them alone, whereas you rich, the noble, the powerful, you are eternally wicked, cruel, lustful, insatiate, godless, you will also be eternally wretched, cursed and damned!'"[5]

4. In this way the slave revolt in morality inverted the noble system of values and began to equate good with the lowly, the powerless—the slave. This inversion introduced the pernicious spirit of revenge and hatred into the creation of values. Therefore morality, as we understand it, had its roots in this vengeful will to power of the powerless over the powerful—the revolt of the slave against the master. It was from this imperceptible, subterranean hatred that grew the values subsequently associated with the good—pity, altruism, meekness, etc.

5. Political values also grew from this poisonous root. For Nietzsche, values of equality and democracy, which form the cornerstone of radical political theory, arose out of the slave revolt in morality. They are generated by the same spirit of revenge and hatred of the powerful. Nietzsche therefore condemns political movements like liberal democracy, socialism, and indeed anarchism. He sees the democratic movement as an expression of the herd-animal morality derived from the Judeo-Christian revaluation of values.[6] Anarchism is for Nietzsche the most extreme heir to democratic values—the most rabid expression of the herd instinct. It seeks to level the differences between individuals, to abolish class distinctions, to raze hierarchies to the ground, and to equalize the powerful and the powerless, the rich and the poor, the master and the slave. To Nietzsche this is bringing everything down to the level of the lowest common denominator—to erase the pathos of distance between the master and slave, the sense of difference and superiority through which great values are created. Nietzsche sees this as the worst excess of European nihilism—the death of values and creativity.

6. Slave morality is characterized by the attitude of ressentiment—the resent-

ment and hatred of the powerless for the powerful. Nietzsche sees this attitude as an entirely negative sentiment—the attitude of denying what is life-affirming, saying 'no' to what is different, what is 'outside' or 'other.' Ressentiment is characterized by an orientation to the outside, rather than the focus of noble morality, which is on the self.[7] While the master says 'I am good' and adds as an afterthought, 'therefore he is bad,' the slave says the opposite—'He (the master) is bad, therefore I am good.' Thus the invention of values comes from a comparison or opposition to that which is outside, other, different. Nietzsche says: "...in order to come about, slave morality first has to have an opposing, external world, it needs, psychologically speaking, external stimuli in order to act all,—its action is basically a reaction."[8] This reactive stance, this inability to define anything except in opposition to something else, is the attitude of ressentiment. It is the reactive stance of the weak who define themselves in opposition to the strong. The weak need the existence of this external enemy to identify themselves as 'good.' Thus the slave takes 'imaginary revenge' upon the master, as he cannot act without the existence of the master to oppose. The man of ressentiment hates the noble with an intense spite, a deep-seated, seething hatred and jealousy. It is this ressentiment, according to Nietzsche, that has poisoned the modern consciousness, and finds its expression in ideas of equality and democracy, and in radical political philosophies, like anarchism, that advocate it.

7. Is anarchism a political expression of ressentiment? Is it poisoned by a deep hatred of the powerful? While Nietzsche's attack on anarchism is in many respects unjustified and excessively malicious, and shows little understanding of the complexities of anarchist theory, I would nevertheless argue that Nietzsche does uncover a certain logic present in anarchism's oppositional, Manichean thinking. It is necessary to explore this logic that inhabits anarchism—to see where it leads and to what extent it imposes conceptual limits on radical politics.

Anarchism

8. Anarchism as a revolutionary political philosophy has many different voices, origins and interpretations. From the individualist anarchism of Stirner, to the collectivist, communal anarchism of Bakunin and Kropotkin, anarchism is diverse series of philosophies and political strategies. These are united, however, by a fundamental rejection and critique of political authority in all its forms. The critique of political authority—the conviction that power is oppressive, exploitative and dehumanizing—may be said to be the crucial politico-ethical standpoint of anarchism. For classical anarchists the State is the embodiment of all forms of oppression, exploitation and the enslavement and degradation of man. In Bakunin's words, "the State is like a vast slaughterhouse and an enormous cemetery, where under the shadow and the pretext of this abstraction (the common good) all the best aspirations, all the living forces of a country, are sanctimoniously immolated and interred."[9] The State is the main target of the anarchist critique of authority. It is for anarchists the fundamental oppression in society, and it must be abolished as the first revolutionary act.

9. This last point brought 19th-century anarchism into sharp conflict with Marxism. Marx believed that while the State was indeed oppressive and exploitative, it was a reflection of economic exploitation and an instrument of class power. Thus political power was reduced to economic power. For Marx the economy rather than the State was the fundamental site of oppression. The State rarely had an independent existence beyond class and economic interests. Because of this the State could be used as a tool of revolution if it was in the hands of the right class—the proletariat.[10] The State was only dominating, in other words, because it was presently in the hands of the bourgeoisie. Once class distinctions have disappeared, the State will lose its political character.[11]

10. Anarchists like Bakunin and Kropotkin disagreed with Marx precisely on this point. For anarchists, the State is much more than an expression of class and economic power; it has its own logic of domination and self-perpetuation, and is autonomous from class interests. Rather than working from the society to the State, as Marx did, and seeing the State as the derivative of economic relations of capitalism and the rise of the bourgeoisie, anarchists work from the State to society. The State constitutes the fundamental oppression in society, and economic exploitation is derived from this political oppression. In other words, it is political oppression that makes economic oppression possible.[12] Moreover for anarchists, bourgeois relations are actually a reflection of the State, rather than the State being a reflection of bourgeois relations. The ruling class, argues Bakunin, is the State's real material representative. Behind every ruling class of every epoch there looms the State. Because the State has its own autonomous logic it can never be trusted as an instrument of revolution. To do this would be to ignore its logic of domination. If the State is not destroyed immediately, if it is used as a revolutionary tool as Marxists suggest, then its power will be perpetuated in infinitely more tyrannical ways. It would operate, as Bakunin argues, through a new ruling class—a bureaucratic class that will oppress and exploit workers in the same manner as the bourgeois class oppressed and exploited them.[13]

11. So the State, for anarchists, is *a priori* oppression, no matter what form it takes. Indeed Bakunin argues that Marxism pays too much attention to the forms of State power while not taking enough account of the way in which State power operates: "They (Marxists) do not know that despotism resides not so much in the form of the State but in the very principle of the State and political power."[14] Oppression and despotism exist in the very structure and symbolism of the State—it is not merely a derivative of class power. The State has its own impersonal logic, its own momentum, its own priorities: these are often beyond the control of the ruling class and do not necessarily reflect economic relations at all. So anarchism locates the fundamental oppression and power in society in the very structure and operations of the State. As an abstract machine of domination, the State haunts different class actualizations—not just the bourgeoisie State, but the workers' State too. Through its economic reductionism, Marxism neglected the autonomy and pre-eminence of State—a mistake that would lead

to its reaffirmation in a socialist revolution. Therefore the anarchist critique unmasked the hidden forms of domination associated with political power, and exposed Marxism's theoretical inadequacy for dealing with this problem.

12. This conception of the State ironically strikes a familiar note with Nietzsche. Nietzsche, like the anarchists, sees modern man as 'tamed,' fettered and made impotent by the State.[15] He also sees the State as an abstract machine of domination, which precedes capitalism, and looms above class and economic concerns. The State is a mode of domination that imposes a regulated 'interiorization' upon the populace. According to Nietzsche the State emerged as a "terrible tyranny, as a repressive and ruthless machinery," which subjugated, made compliant, and shaped the population.[16] Moreover the origins of this State are violent. It is imposed forcefully from without and has nothing to with 'contracts.'[17] Nietzsche demolishes the "fantasy" of the social contract—the theory that the State was formed by people voluntarily relinquishing their power in return for the safety and security that would be provided by the State. This idea of the social contract has been central to conservative and liberal political theory, from Hobbes to Locke. Anarchists also reject this theory of the social contract. They too argue that the origins of the State are violent, and that it is absurd to hold that people voluntarily gave up their power. It is a dangerous myth that legitimizes and perpetuates State domination.

The Social Contract
13. Anarchism is based on an essentially optimistic conception of human nature: if individuals have a natural tendency to get on well together then there is no need for the existence of a State to arbitrate between them. On the contrary, the State actually has a pernicious effect on these natural social relations. Anarchists therefore reject political theories based on the idea of social contract. Social contract theory relies on a singularly negative picture of human nature. According to Hobbes, individuals are naturally selfish, aggressively competitive and egotistic, and in a state of nature they are engaged in a war of "every man, against every man" in which their individual drives necessarily bring them into conflict with one another.[18] According to this theory, then, society in a state of nature is characterized by a radical dislocation: there is no common bond between individuals; there is in fact a constant state of war between them, a constant struggle for resources.[19] In order to put a stop to this state of permanent war, individuals come together to form a social contract upon which some kind of authority can be established. They agree to sacrifice part of their freedom in return for some kind of order, so that they can pursue their own individual ends more peacefully and profitably. They agree on the creation of a State with a mandate over society, which shall arbitrate between conflicting wills and enforce law and order.

14. The extent of the State's authority may vary from the liberal State whose power is supposedly tempered by the rule of law, to the absolute State power—the Leviathan—dreamt up by Hobbes. While the models may vary, anarchists

argue that the result of this social contract theory is the same: a justification of State domination, whether it be through the rule of law or through the arbitrary imposition of force. For anarchists, any form of State power is an imposition of force. The social contract theory is a sleight of hand that legitimates political domination—Bakunin calls it an "unworthy hoax!"[20] He exposes the central paradox in the theory of the social contract: if, in a state of nature, individuals subsist in a state of primitive savagery, then how can they suddenly have the foresight to come together and create a social contract?[21] If there is no common bond in society, no essence within humans which brings them together, then upon what basis can a social contract be formed? Like Nietzsche, anarchists argue that there is no such agreement that the State was imposed from above, not from below. The social contract tries to mystify the brutal origins of the State: war, conquest and self-enslavement, rather than rational agreement. For Kropotkin the State is a violent disruption of, and an imposition upon, a harmoniously functioning, organic society.[22] Society has no need for a 'social contract.' It has its own contract with nature, governed by natural laws.[23]

15. Anarchism may be understood as a struggle between natural authority and artificial authority. Anarchists do not reject all forms of authority, as the old cliché would have it. On the contrary, they declare their absolute obedience to the authority embodied in what Bakunin calls 'natural laws.' Natural laws are essential to humanity's existence according to Bakunin—they surround us, shape us and determine the physical world in which we live.[24] However this is not a form of slavery because these laws are not external to us: "those (natural) laws are not extrinsic in relation to us, they are inherent in us, they constitute our nature, our whole being physically, intellectually and morally."[25] They are, on the contrary, what constitute humanity—they are our essence. We are inextricably part of a natural, organic society according to Kropotkin.[26] Anarchism, then, is based on a specific notion of human essence. Morality has its basis in human nature, not in any external source: "the idea of justice and good, like all other human things, must have their root in man's very animality."[27]

16. Natural authority is implacably opposed to "artificial authority." By artificial authority Bakunin means power: the political power enshrined in institutions such as the State and in man-made laws.[28] This power is external to human nature and an imposition upon it. It stultifies the development of humanity's innate moral characteristics and intellectual capacities. It is these capacities, the anarchists argue, which will liberate man from slavery and ignorance. For Bakunin, then, political institutions are "hostile and fatal to the liberty of the masses, for they impose upon them a system of external and therefore despotic laws."[29]

17. In this critique of political authority, power (artificial authority) is external to the human subject. The human subject is oppressed by this power, but remains uncontaminated by it because human subjectivity is a creation of a nat-

ural, as opposed to a political, system. Thus anarchism is based on a clear, Manichean division between artificial and natural authority, between power and subjectivity, between State and society. Furthermore political authority is fundamentally repressive and destructive of man's potential. Human society, argue the anarchists, cannot develop until the institutions and laws which keep it in ignorance and servitude, until the fetters which bind it, are thrown off. Anarchism must, therefore, have a place of resistance: a moral and rational place, a place uncontaminated by the power that oppresses it, from which will spring a rebellion against power. It finds this in an essential human subjectivity. Human essence, with its moral and rational characteristics, is an absent fullness that lies dormant in man, and will only be realized once the political power negating it is overthrown. It is from this place of absent fullness that will emanate the revolution against power. The innate morality and rationality of man will counteract political power, which is seen as inherently irrational and immoral. According to anarchist theory, natural law will replace political authority; man and society will replace the State. For Kropotkin, anarchism can think beyond the category of the State, beyond the category of absolute political power, because it has a place, a ground from which to do so. Political power has an outside from which it can be criticized and an alternative with which it can be replaced. Kropotkin is thus able to envisage a society in which the State no longer exists or is needed; a society regulated not by political power and authority, but by mutual agreements and cooperation.[30]

18. Such a society is possible, according to anarchists, because of the essentially cooperative nature of man.[31] Contrary to the Darwinist approach that insists on an innate competitiveness in animals—the 'survival of the fittest'—Kropotkin finds an instinctive cooperation and sociability in animals, particularly in humans. This instinct Kropotkin calls mutual aid and he says: "Mutual aid is the predominant fact of Nature."[32] Kropotkin applies these findings to human society. He argues that the natural and essential principle of human society is mutual aid, and that man is naturally cooperative, sociable and altruistic, rather than competitive and egotistic. This is the organic principle that governs society, and it is out of this that notions of morality, justice and ethics grow. Morality, Kropotkin argues, evolves out of the instinctive need to band together in tribes, groups—and an instinctive tendency towards cooperation and mutual assistance.[33] This natural sociability and capacity for mutual aid is the principle that binds society together, providing a common basis upon which daily life can be conducted. Therefore society has no need for the State: it has its own regulating mechanisms, its own natural laws. State domination only poisons society and destroys its natural mechanisms. It is the principle of mutual aid that will naturally replace the principle of political authority. A state of 'anarchy,' a war of "all against all" will not ensue the moment State power has been abolished. For anarchists, a state of 'anarchy' exists now: political power creates social dislocation, it does not prevent it. What is prevented by the State is the natural and harmonious functioning of society.

19. For Hobbes, State sovereignty is a necessary evil. There is no attempt to make a fetish of the State: it does not descend from heaven, preordained by divine will. It is pure sovereignty, pure power, and it is constructed out of the emptiness of society, precisely in order to prevent the warfare immanent in the state of nature. The political content of the State is unimportant as long as it quells unrest in society. Whether there be a democracy, or a sovereign assembly, or a monarchy, it does not matter: "the power in all forms, if they be perfect enough to protect them, is the same."[34] Like the anarchists, Hobbes believes that the guise taken by power is irrelevant. Behind every mask there must be a pure, absolute power. Hobbes's political thought is centered around a desire for order, purely as an antidote to disorder, and the extent to which individuals suffer under this order is incomparable to the suffering caused by war.[35] For anarchists, on the other hand, because society regulates itself according to natural laws and because there is a natural ethics of cooperation in man, the State is an unnecessary evil. Rather than preventing perpetual warfare between men, the State engenders it: the State is based on war and conquest rather than embodying its resolution. Anarchism can look beyond the State because it argues from the perspective of an essential point of departure—natural human sociality. It can, therefore, conceive of an alternative to the State. Hobbes, on the other hand, has no such point of departure: there is no standpoint that can act as an alternative to the State. Society, as we have seen with Hobbes, is characterized by rift and antagonism. In fact, there is no essential society to speak of—it is an empty place. Society must therefore be constructed artificially in the shape of the absolute State. While anarchism can rely on natural law, Hobbes can only rely on the law of the State. At the heart of the anarchist paradigm there is the essential fullness of society, while at the heart of the Hobbesian paradigm there is nothing but emptiness and dislocation.

Manicheism

20. However it may be argued that anarchism is a mirror image of Hobbesianism in the sense that they both posit a commonality that derives from their indebtedness to the Enlightenment. Both emphasize the need for a fullness or collectivity, some legitimate point around which society can be organized. Anarchists see this point of departure in the natural law which informs society and human subjectivity, and which is impeded by the State. Hobbes, on the other hand, sees this point of departure as an absence, an empty place that must be filled by the State. Hobbes's thought is caught within the paradigm of the State, which functions as the absolute conceptual limit. Outside of it are the perils of the state of nature. Political theories such as this, based on the social contract, are haunted by the threat that if one gets rid of the State, one will revert back to a state of nature. Anarchism, because it proceeds from a radically different conception of society and human nature, claims to be able to transcend this quandary. But can it?

21. Anarchism operates within a Manichean political logic: it creates an essential, moral opposition between society and the State, between humanity and

power. Natural law is diagrammatically opposed to artificial power; the morality and rationality immanent in human subjectivity comes into conflict with the irrationality and immorality of the State. There is an essential antithesis between anarchism's uncontaminated point of departure, constituted by essential human subjectivity, and State power. This logic which establishes an absolute opposition between two terms—good and evil, black and white, humanity and the State—is the central feature of Manichean thought. Jacques Donzelot argues that this logic of absolute opposition is endemic to radical political theory:

> Political culture is also the systematic pursuit of an antagonism between two essences, the tracing of a line of demarcation between two principles, two levels of reality which are easily placed in opposition. There is no political culture that is not Manichean.[36]

22. Moreover, anarchism, in subscribing to this logic and making power the focus of its analysis, instead of economy as Marxism did, has perhaps fallen into the same reductionist trap as Marxism. Has it not merely replaced the economy with the State as the essential evil in society, from which other evils are derived? As Donzelot argues:

> No sooner has one decided on good or bad grounds—no matter which—that capitalism is not the unique or even principle source of evil on earth that one rushes to substitute for the opposition between capital and labour that between State and civil society. Capital, as foil and scapegoat, is replaced by the State, that cold monster whose limitless growth 'pauperises' social life; and the proletariat gives way to civil society, that is to say to everything capable of resisting the blind rationality of the State, to everything that opposes it at the level of customs, mores, a living sociability, sought in the residual margins of society and promoted to the status of motor of history.[37]

23. Opposing living sociability to the State, in the same way that Marxism opposed the proletariat to capitalism, suggests that anarchism was unable to transcend the traditional political categories which bound Marxism. As Donzelot argues, Manicheism is the logic that skewers all these theories: it is the undercurrent that runs through them and circumscribes them. It does not matter if the target is the State, or Capital, or anything else; as long as there is an enemy to destroy and a subject who will destroy it; as long as there is the promise of the final battle and final victory. Manichean logic is, therefore, the logic of place: there must be an essential place of power and an essential place of revolt. This is the binary, dialectical logic that pervades anarchism: the place of power—the State—must be overthrown by the essential human subject, the pure subject of resistance. Anarchism 'essentializes' the very power it opposes.

24. Manichean logic thus involves a reverse mirroring operation: the place of resistance is a reflection, in reverse, of the place of power. In the case of anarchism, human subjectivity is essentially moral and rational while the State is essentially immoral and irrational.[38] The State is essential to the existence of the revolutionary subject, just as the revolutionary subject is essential to the existence of the State. One defines itself in opposition to the other. The purity of revolutionary identity is only defined in contrast to the impurity of political power. Revolt against the State is always prompted by the State. As Bakunin argues, "there is something in the nature of the State which provokes rebellion."[39] While the relationship between the State and the revolutionary subject is one of clearly defined opposition, the two antagonists could not exist outside this relationship. They could not, in other words, exist without each other.

25. Can this paradoxical relationship of reflection and opposition be seen as a form of ressentiment in the Nietzschean sense? I would argue here that, although there are differences, the Manichean relationship of opposition between the human subject and political power that is found in anarchism obeys the general logic of ressentiment described above. This is for two reasons. Firstly, as we have seen, it is based on the moral prejudice of the powerless against the powerful—the revolt of the 'slave' against the 'master.' We can see this moral opposition to power clearly in anarchist discourse, which pits the essentially 'moral' and 'rational' human subject against the essentially 'immoral' and 'irrational' quality of political power. It is evident in the opposition of natural to artificial authority that is central to anarchism. Secondly, ressentiment is characterized by the fundamental need to identify oneself by looking outwards and in opposition towards an external enemy. Here, however, the comparison to anarchism is not so clear-cut. For instance, one could conceivably argue that anarchist subjectivity and ethics—the notion of mutual aid and assistance—is something that develops independently of political power, and that therefore it does not need an oppositional relationship with the State in order to define itself. However, I would suggest that although anarchist subjectivity does develop in a 'natural' system which is radically exterior to the 'artificial' system of political power, it is precisely through this assertion of radical exteriority that ressentiment emerges. Anarchism subscribes to a dialectical logic, according to which the human species emerges from an 'animal-like' state, and begins to develop innate moral and rational faculties in a natural system.[40] However, the subject finds this development impeded by the 'irrational,' 'immoral' power of the State. Thus the subject cannot achieve his full human identity as long as he remains oppressed by the State. This is why, for Bakunin: "The State is the most flagrant negation... of humanity."[41] The realization of the subject is always stultified, deferred, put off, by the State. This dialectic of Man and State suggests that the identity of the subject is characterized as essentially 'rational' and 'moral' only insofar as the unfolding of these innate faculties and qualities is prevented by the State. Paradoxically the State, which is seen by anarchists as an obstacle to the full identity of man, is, at the same time, essential to the formation of this

incomplete identity. Without this stultifying oppression, the anarchist subject would be unable to see itself as 'moral' and 'rational.' His identity is thus complete in its incompleteness. The existence of political power is therefore a means of constructing this absent fullness. I would argue, then, that anarchism can only posit the subject as 'moral' and 'rational' in opposition to the 'immorality' and 'irrationality' of political power. In the same way the identity of the 'slave' is consolidated as 'good' by opposing itself to the identity of the 'master' which is 'evil.' Nietzsche would see in this an attitude of ressentiment *par excellence*.

26. So the Manicheism that inhabits anarchist discourse is a logic of ressentiment that for Nietzsche is a distinctly unhealthy outlook, emanating from a position of weakness and sickness. Revolutionary identity in anarchist philosophy is constituted through its essential opposition to power. Like Nietzsche's reactive man, revolutionary identity purports to be unpolluted by power: human essence is seen as moral where power is immoral, natural where power is artificial, pure where power is impure. Because this subjectivity is constituted within a system of natural law—as opposed to artificial law—it is a point which, while oppressed by power, remains outside power and unpolluted by it. But is it?

27. Bakunin himself throws some doubts on this when he talks about the power principle. This is the natural lust for power which Bakunin believes is innate in every individual: "Every man carries within himself the germs of the lust for power, and every germ, as we know, because of a basic law of life, necessarily must develop and grow."[42] The power principle means that man cannot be trusted with power, that there will always be this desire for power at the heart of human subjectivity. While Bakunin intended to warn others of the corrupting danger inherent in power, he has perhaps unconsciously exposed the hidden contradiction that lies at the heart of anarchist discourse: namely that, while anarchism bases itself upon a notion of an essential human subjectivity uncontaminated by power, this subjectivity is ultimately impossible. Pure revolutionary identity is torn apart, subverted by a 'natural' desire for power, the lack at the heart of every individual. Bakunin suggests that this desire for power is an essential part of human subjectivity. Perhaps the implication of Bakunin's power principle is that the subject will always have a desire for power, and that the subject will be incomplete until it grasps power. Kropotkin, too, talks about the desire for power and authority. He argues that the rise of the modern State can be attributed in part to the fact that "men became enamored of authority."[43] He implies, then, that State power is not completely an imposition from above. He talks about self-enslavement to law and authority: "Man allowed himself to be enslaved far more by his desire to 'punish according to law' than by direct military conquest."[44] Does the desire to "punish according to law" grow directly out of humanity's natural sense of morality? If this is the case, can human essence still be seen as unpolluted by power? While anarchism's notion of subjectivity is not entirely undermined by this contradiction, it is nevertheless destabilized by it: it is made ambiguous and incomplete. It forces one to question anar-

chism's notion of a revolution of humanity against power: if humans have an essential desire for power, then how can one be sure that a revolution aimed at destroying power will not turn into a revolution aimed at capturing power?

Will to Power

28. Has anarchism as a political and social theory of revolution been invalidated because of the contradictions in its conception of human subjectivity? Not necessarily. This paper has exposed a hidden strain of ressentiment in the essentialist categories and oppositional structures that inhabit anarchist discourse—in notions of a harmonious society governed by natural law and man's essential communality, and its opposition to the artificial law of the State. However, if anarchism can free itself from these essentialist and Manichean categories, it can overcome the ressentiment that poisons and limits it. Classical anarchism is a politics of ressentiment because it seeks to overcome power. It sees power as evil, destructive, something that stultifies the full realization of the individual. Human essence is a point of departure uncontaminated by power, from which power is resisted. There is a strict Manichean separation and opposition between the subject and power. However it has been shown that this separation between the individual and power is itself unstable and threatened by a 'natural' desire for power—the power principle. Nietzsche would argue that this desire for power—will to power—is indeed 'natural,' and it is the suppression of this desire that has had such a debilitating effect on man, turning him against himself and producing an attitude of ressentiment.

29. However perhaps one could argue that this desire for power in man is produced precisely through attempts to deny or extinguish relations of power in the 'natural order.' Perhaps power may be seen in terms of the Lacanian 'Real'—as that irrepressible lack that cannot be symbolized, and which always returns to haunt the symbolic order, disrupting any attempt by the subject to form a complete identity. For Jacques Lacan: "...the real is that which always comes back to the same place—to the place where the subject in so far as he thinks, where the *res cogitans*, does not meet it."[45] Anarchism attempts to complete the identity of the subject by separating him, in an absolute Manichean sense, from the world of power. The anarchist subject, as we have seen, is constituted in a 'natural' system that is dialectically opposed to the artificial world of power. Moreover, because the subject is constituted in a 'natural' system governed by ethical laws of mutual cooperation, anarchists are able to posit a society free from relations of power, which will replace the State once it is overthrown. However, as we have seen, this world, free of power, is jeopardized by the desire for power latent in every individual. The more anarchism tries to free society from relations of power, the more it remains paradoxically caught up in power. Power here has returned as the real that haunts all attempts to free the world of power. The more one tries to repress power, the more obstinately it rears its head. This is because the attempts to deny power, through essentialist concepts of 'natural' laws and 'natural' morality, themselves constitute

power, or at least are conditioned by relations of power. These essentialist identities and categories cannot be imposed without the radical exclusion of other
identities. This exclusion is an act of power. If one attempts to radically exclude
power, as the anarchists did, power 'returns' precisely in the structures of
exclusion themselves.

30. Nietzsche believes that this attempt to exclude and deny power is a form of
ressentiment. So how does anarchism overcome this ressentiment that has
shown to be so self-destructive and life-denying? By positively affirming power,
rather than denying it—to 'say yes' to power, as Nietzsche would put it. It is only
by affirming power, by acknowledging that we come from the same world as
power, not from a 'natural' world removed from it, and that we can never be
entirely free from relations of power, that one can engage in politically-relevant
strategies of resistance against power. This does not mean, of course, that anarchism should lay down its arms and embrace the State and political authority.
On the contrary, anarchism can more effectively counter political domination by
engaging with, rather than denying, power.

31. Perhaps it is appropriate here to distinguish between relations of power and
relations of domination. To use Michel Foucault's definition, power is a "mode
of action upon the action of others."[46] Power is merely the effect of one's actions
upon the actions of another. Nietzsche, too, sees power in terms of an effect
without a subject: "...there is no being behind the deed, its effect and what
becomes of it; 'the doer' is invented as an afterthought."[47] Power is not a commodity that can be possessed, and it cannot be centered in either the institution
or the subject. It is merely a relationship of forces, forces that flow between different actors and throughout our everyday actions. Power is everywhere, according to Foucault.[48] Power does not emanate from institutions like the State—
rather it is immanent throughout the entire social network, through various discourses and knowledges. For instance, rational and moral discourses, which
anarchists saw as innocent of power and as weapons in the struggle against
power, are themselves constituted by power relations and are embroiled in practices of power: "Power and knowledge directly imply one another."[49] Power in
this sense is productive rather than repressive. It is therefore senseless and
indeed impossible to try to construct, as anarchists do, a world outside power.
We will never be entirely free from relations of power. According to Foucault:
"It seems to me that... one is never outside (power), that there are no margins
for those who break with the system to gambol in."[50]

32. However, just because one can never be free from power does not mean that
one can never be free from domination. Domination must be distinguished from
power in the following sense. For Foucault, relations of power become relations
of domination when the free and unstable flow of power relations becomes
blocked and congealed—when it forms unequal hierarchies and no longer allows
reciprocal relationships.[51] These relations of domination form the basis of insti-

tutions such as the State. The State, according to Foucault, is merely an assemblage of different power relations that have become congealed in this way. This is a radically different way of looking at institutions such as the State. While anarchists see power as emanating from the State, Foucault sees the State as emanating from power. The State, in other words, is merely an effect of power relations that have crystallized into relations of domination.

33. What is the point of this distinction between power and domination? Does this not bring us back to original anarchist position that society and our everyday actions, although oppressed by power, are ontologically separated from it? In other words, why not merely call domination 'power' once again, and revert back to the original, Manichean distinction between social life and power? However the point of this distinction is to show that this essential separation is now impossible. Domination—oppressive political institutions like the State—now comes from the same world as power. In other words it disrupts the strict Manichean separation of society and power. Anarchism and indeed radical politics generally, cannot remain in this comfortable illusion that we as political subjects, are somehow not complicit in the very regime that oppresses us. According to the Foucauldian definition of power that I have employed, we are all potentially complicit, through our everyday actions, in relations of domination. Our everyday actions, which inevitably involve power, are unstable and can easily form into relations that dominate us.

34. As political subjects we can never relax and hide behind essentialist identities and Manichean structures—behind a strict separation from the world of power. Rather we must be constantly on our guard against the possibility of domination. Foucault says: "My point is not that everything is bad, but that everything is dangerous... If everything is dangerous, then we always have something to do. So my position leads not to apathy but to a hyper- and pessimistic activism."[52] In order to resist domination we must be aware of its risks—of the possibility that our own actions, even political action ostensibly against domination, can easily give rise to further domination. There is always the possibility, then, of contesting domination, and of minimizing its possibilities and effects. According to Foucault, domination itself is unstable and can give rise to reversals and resistance. Assemblages such as the State are based on unstable power relations that can just as easily turn against the institution they form the basis of. So there is always the possibility of resistance against domination. However resistance can never be in the form of revolution—a grand dialectical overcoming of power, as the anarchists advocated. To abolish central institutions like the State with one stroke would be to neglect the multiform and diffuse relations of power they are based on, thus allowing new institutions and relations of domination to rise up. It would be to fall into the same reductionist trap as Marxism, and to court domination. Rather, resistance must take the form of what Foucault calls agonism—an ongoing, strategic contestation with power—based on mutual incitement and provocation—without any final hope of being

free from it.[53] One can, as I have argued, never hope to overcome power completely—because every overcoming is itself the imposition of another regime of power. The best that can be hoped for is a reorganization of power relations—through struggle and resistance—in ways that are less oppressive and dominating. Domination can therefore be minimized by acknowledging our inevitable involvement with power, not by attempting to place ourselves impossibly outside the world of power. The classical idea of revolution as a dialectical overthrowing of power—the image that has haunted the radical political imaginary—must be abandoned. We must recognize the fact that power can never be overcome entirely, and we must affirm this by working within this world, renegotiating our position to enhance our possibilities of freedom.

35. This definition of power that I have constructed—as an unstable and free-flowing relation dispersed throughout the social network—may be seen as a non-ressentiment notion of power. It undermines the oppositional, Manichean politics of ressentiment because power cannot be externalized in the form of the State or a political institution. There can be no external enemy for us to define ourselves in opposition to and vent our anger on. It disrupts the Apollonian distinction between the subject and power central to classical anarchism and Manichean radical political philosophy. Apollonian Man, the essential human subject, is always haunted by Dionysian power. Apollo is the god of light, but also the god of illusion: he "grants repose to individual beings... by drawing boundaries around them." Dionysus, on the other hand is the force that occasionally destroys these "little circles," disrupting the Apollonian tendency to "congeal the form to Egyptian rigidity and coldness."[54] Behind the Apollonian illusion of a life-world without power, is the Dionysian 'reality' of power that tears away the "veil of the maya."[55]

36. Rather than having an external enemy—like the State—in opposition to which one's political identity is formed, we must work on ourselves. As political subjects we must overcome ressentiment by transforming our relationship with power. One can only do this, according to Nietzsche, through eternal return. To affirm eternal return is to acknowledge and indeed positively affirm the continual 'return' of same life with its harsh realities. Because it is an active willing of nihilism, it is at the same time a transcendence of nihilism. Perhaps in the same way, eternal return refers to power. We must acknowledge and affirm the 'return' of power, the fact that it will always be with us. To overcome ressentiment we must, in other words, will power. We must affirm a will to power—in the form of creative, life-affirming values, according to Nietzsche.[56] This is to accept the notion of 'self-overcoming.'[57] To 'overcome' oneself in this sense, would mean an overcoming of the essentialist identities and categories that limit us. As Foucault has shown, we are constructed as essential political subjects in ways that dominate us—this is what he calls subjectification.[58] We hide behind essentialist identities that deny power, and produce through this denial, a Manichean politics of absolute opposition that only reflects and reaf-

firms the very domination it claims to oppose. This we have seen in the case of anarchism. In order to avoid this Manichean logic, anarchism must no longer rely on essentialist identities and concepts, and instead positively affirm the eternal return of power. This is not a grim realization but rather a 'happy positivism.' It is characterized by political strategies aimed at minimizing the possibilities of domination, and increasing the possibilities for freedom.

37. If one rejects essentialist identities, what is one left with? Can one have a notion of radical politics and resistance without an essential subject? One might, however, ask the opposite question: how can radical politics continue without 'overcoming' essentialist identities, without, in Nietzsche's terms, 'overcoming' man? Nietzsche says: "The most cautious people ask today: 'How may man still be preserved?' Zarathustra, however, asks as the sole and first one to do so: 'How shall man be overcome?'"[59] I would argue that anarchism would be greatly enhanced as a political and ethical philosophy if it eschewed essentialist categories, leaving itself open to different and contingent identities—a post-anarchism. To affirm difference and contingency would be to become a philosophy of the strong, rather than the weak. Nietzsche exhorts us to 'live dangerously,' to do away with certainties, to break with essences and structures, and to embrace uncertainty. "Build your cities on the slopes of Vesuvius! Send your ships into unchartered seas!" he says.[60] The politics of resistance against domination must take place in a world without guarantees. To remain open to difference and contingency, to affirm the eternal return of power, would be to become what Nietzsche calls the Superman or Overman. The Overman is man 'overcome'—the overcoming of man: "God has died: now we desire—that the Superman shall live."[61] For Nietzsche the Superman replaces God and Man—it comes to redeem a humanity crippled by nihilism, joyously affirming power and eternal return. However I would like to propose a somewhat gentler, more ironic version of the Superman for radical politics. Ernesto Laclau speaks of "a hero of a new type who still has not been created by our culture, but one whose creation is absolutely necessary if our time is going to live up to its most radical and exhilarating possibilities."[62]

38. Perhaps anarchism could become a new 'heroic' philosophy, which is no longer reactive but, rather, creates values. For instance, the ethic of mutual care and assistance propounded by Kropotkin could perhaps be utilized in the construction of new forms of collective action and identities. Kropotkin looked at the development of collective groups based on cooperation—trade unions, associations of all kinds, friendly societies and clubs, etc.[63] As we have seen, he believed this to be the unfolding of an essential natural principle. However, perhaps one could develop this collectivist impulse without circumscribing it in essentialist ideas about human nature. Collective action does not need a principle of human essence to justify it. Rather it is the contingency of identity—its openness to difference, to singularity, to individuality and collectivity—that is itself ethical. So the anarchist ethics of mutual aid may be taken from its essen-

tialist foundations and applied to a non-essentialist, constitutively open idea of collective political identity.

39. An alternative conception of collective action may for instance, be developed from a re-articulation of the relationship between equality and freedom. To anarchism's great credit it rejected the liberal conviction that equality and freedom act as limits upon each other and are ultimately irreconcilable concepts. For anarchists, equality and freedom are inextricably related impulses, and one cannot conceive of one without the other. For Bakunin:

> I am free only when all human beings surrounding me—men and women alike—are equally free. The freedom of others, far from limiting or negating my liberty, is on the contrary its necessary condition and confirmation. I become free in the true sense only by virtue of the liberty of others, so much so that the greater the number of free people surrounding me the deeper and greater and more extensive their liberty, the deeper and larger becomes my liberty.[64]

40. The interrelatedness of equality and liberty may form the basis of a new collective ethos, which refuses to see individual freedom and collective equality as limits on each other—which refuses to sacrifice difference in the name of universality, and universality in the name of difference. Foucault's anti-strategic ethics may be seen as an example of this idea. In his defense of collective movements like the Iranian revolution, Foucault said that the anti-strategic ethics he adopts is "to be respectful when something singular arises, to be intransigent when power offends against the universal."[65] This anti-strategic approach condemns universalism when it is disdainful of the particular, and condemns particularism when it is at the expense of the universal. Similarly, a new ethics of collective action would condemn collectivity when it is at the expense of difference and singularity, and condemn difference when it is at the expense of collectivity. It is an approach that allows one to combine individual difference and collective equality in a way which is not dialectical but which retains a certain positive and life-affirming antagonism between them. It would imply a notion of respect for difference, without encroaching on the freedom of others to be different—an equality of freedom of difference. Post-anarchist collective action would, in other words, be based on a commitment to respect and recognize autonomy, difference and openness within collectivity.

41. Furthermore, perhaps one could envisage a form of political community or collective identity that did not restrict difference. The question of community is central to radical politics, including anarchism. One cannot talk about collective action without at least posing the question of community. For Nietzsche, most modern radical aspirations towards community were a manifestation of the 'herd' mentality. However it may be possible to construct a ressentiment-free notion of community from Nietzsche's own concept of power. For Nietzsche,

active power is the individual's instinctive discharge of his forces and capacities which produces in him an enhanced sensation of power, while reactive power, as we have seen, needs an external object to act on and define itself in opposition to.[66] Perhaps one could imagine a form of community based on active power. For Nietzsche this enhanced feeling of power may be derived from assistance and benevolence towards others, from enhancing the feeling of power of others.[67] Like the ethics of mutual aid, a community based on will to power may be composed of a series of inter-subjective relations that involve helping and caring for people without dominating them and denying difference. This openness to difference and self-transformation, and the ethic of care, may be the defining characteristics of the post-anarchist democratic community. This would be a community of active power—a community of 'masters' rather than 'slaves.'[68] It would be a community that sought to overcome itself—continually transforming itself and reveling in the knowledge of its power to do so.

42. Post-anarchism may be seen, then, as a series of politico-ethical strategies against domination, without essentialist guarantees and Manichean structures that condition and restrict classical anarchism. It would affirm the contingency of values and identities, including its own, and affirm, rather than deny, will to power. It would be, in other words, an anarchism without ressentiment.

Notes

1 Friedrich Nietzsche, *On the Genealogy of Morality*, ed. Keith Ansell-Pearson (Cambridge, UK: Cambridge University Press, 1994), p. 52.
2 Ibid., p. 161.
3 Ibid., p. 12.
4 Ibid.
5 Ibid., p. 19.
6 Ibid., p. 161.
7 Ibid., p. 21.
8 Ibid., pp. 21-22.
9 Mikhail Bakunin, *Political Philosophy: Scientific Anarchism*, ed. G.P. Maximoff (London: Free Press of Glencoe, 1984), p. 207.
10 Karl Marx, "Critique of the Gotha Program," in *The Marx-Engels Reader, 2nd ed.*, ed. Robert C. Tucker (New York: W.W. Norton & Co., 1978), p. 538.
11 Marx, "After the Revolution: Marx Debates Bakunin," in *The Marx-Engels Reader*, p. 545.
12 Bakunin, *Marxism, Freedom and the State* (London: Freedom Press, 1950), p. 49.
13 Bakunin, *Political Philosophy*, p. 228.
14 Ibid., p. 221.
15 Nietzsche, *On the Genealogy of Morality*, p. 61.
16 Ibid., pp. 62-63.
17 Ibid., p. 63.
18 Thomas Hobbes, *Leviathan* (Oxford: Basil Blackwell, 1947), p. 83.
19 Ibid., p. 82.
20 Bakunin, *Political Philosophy*, p. 165.
21 Ibid.
22 Peter Kropotkin, *The State: Its Historic Role* (London: Freedom Press, 1946), p. 37.
23 Bakunin, *Political Philosophy*, p. 166.
24 Ibid., p. 239.

25 Ibid.
26 Kropotkin, *The State: Its Historic Role*, p. 12.
27 Bakunin, *Political Philosophy*, p. 121.
28 Ibid., p. 212.
29 Ibid., p. 240.
30 Kropotkin, *Revolutionary Pamphlets,* ed. Roger N. Baldwin (New York: Benjamin Blom, 1968), p. 157.
31 Kropotkin, *Ethics: Origin & Development* (New York: Tudor, 1947), p. 14.
32 Ibid.
33 Ibid., p. 45.
34 Hobbes, *Leviathan*, p. 120.
35 Ibid.
36 Jacques Donzelot, "The Poverty of Political Culture," *Ideology & Consciousness* 5, 1979, 73-86, p. 74.
37 Ibid.
38 Bakunin, *Political Philosophy*, p. 224.
39 Ibid., p. 145.
40 Ibid., p. 172.
41 Ibid., p. 138.
42 Ibid., p. 248.
43 Kropotkin, *The State: Its Historic Role*, p. 28.
44 Ibid., p. 17.
45 Jacques Lacan, *The Four Fundamental Concepts of Psychoanalysis,* ed. Jacques-Alain Miller, (London: Hogarth Press, 1977), p. 49.
46 Michel Foucault, "The Subject and Power," in Hubert L. Dreyfus and Paul Rabinow, *Michel Foucault: Beyond Structuralism and Hermeneutics* (Brighton: Harvester Press, 1982), p. 221.
47 Nietzsche, *On the Genealogy of Morality*, p. 28.
48 Foucault, *The History of Sexuality Vol. I: Introduction* (New York: Vintage Books, 1978), p. 93.
49 Foucault, *Discipline and Punish: the Birth of the Prison* (London: Penguin Books, 1991), p. 27.
50 Foucault, "Power and Strategies," in *Power/Knowledge: Selected Interviews and Other Writings 1972-77,* ed. Colin Gordon (New York: Harvester Press, 1980), p. 141.
51 Foucault, "The Ethic of Care for the Self as a Practice of Freedom," in *The Final Foucault,* eds. J. Bernauer and D. Rasmussen (Cambridge: MIT Press, 1988), p. 3.
52 Foucault, "On the Genealogy of Ethics," in *The Foucault Reader,* ed. Paul Rabinow, (New York: Pantheon Books, 1984), p. 343.
53 Foucault, *History of Sexuality*, p. 96.
54 Friedrich Nietzsche, *Birth of Tragedy*, in *Basic Writings*, trans. Walter Kaufmann (New York: Modern Library, 1968), p. 72.
55 See Allan Megill, *Prophets of Extremity: Nietzsche, Heidegger, Foucault, Derrida* (Berkeley: University of California Press, 1985), p. 39.
56 Nietzsche, *On the Genealogy of Morality*, pp. 55-56.
57 See Nietzsche, *Thus Spoke Zarathustra*, trans. R.J. Hollingdale (London: Penguin, 1969), pp. 28-29.
58 Foucault, "The Subject and Power," p. 212.
59 Nietzsche, *Thus Spoke Zarathustra*, p. 297.
60 Nietzsche, *The Gay Science*, trans. Walter Kaufmann (New York: Vintage), p. 228.
61 Nietzsche, *Thus Spoke Zarathustra*, p. 297.
62 Ernesto Laclau, "Community and Its Paradoxes: Richard Rorty's 'Liberal Utopia'" in *Emancipations,* ed. Ernesto Laclau (London: Verso, 1996), p. 123.
63 Kropotkin, *Mutual Aid: A Factor of Evolution* (London: Penguin Books Ltd., 1939), p. 210.
64 Bakunin, *Political Philosophy*, p. 267.
65 Foucault, "Is It Useless To Revolt?" *Philosophy and Social Criticism* 8 (1), 1981, p. 9.

66 See Paul Patton "Power in Hobbes and Nietzsche," in *Nietzsche, Feminism & Political Theo-ry*, ed. Paul Patton (Sydney: Allen & Unwin, 1993), p. 152.
67 Ibid., p. 156.
68 Ibid., p. 154.

Attentat Art

Anarchism and Nietzsche's Aesthetics

John Moore

Anarchism is an anti-systemic philosophy. Nietzsche's philosophy is anti-systemic. This common antipathy to systems provides a point of contact between the two. And although the conclusions drawn from this shared emphasis are sometimes divergent, nevertheless there are distinct points of congruence between anarchist and Nietzschean philosophy. Aesthetics remains one of those junctures.

Due to its anti-systemic nature, Nietzsche's philosophy, including his aesthetic philosophy, remains multiple and varied.[1] Although it possesses intellectual cogency, there is no attempt to make a fetish of coherence. The sentiment voiced by Nietzsche's contemporary, Walt Whitman, "Do I contradict myself?/ Very well, I contradict myself/I contain multitudes," fits Nietzsche perfectly. A number of strands can be discerned in Nietzsche's thought on a range of issues, and depending on how far one is prepared to follow these Ariadne threads and how one interprets their meanings, one can arrive at a multiplicity of destinations. Such is the richness and complexity of the textual strategies employed within his work that the reader finds few hermeneutic limits. This is crucial to Nietzsche's perspectivism. It is also the strength and the weakness of his work, in that it allows a range of ideological appropriations, some of them compatible with liberatory projects, others compatible with the repressive project.

As the primary liberatory project, anarchism—the project which aims at the abolition of all forms of power, control and coercion—remains entitled to appropriate the work of one of the greatest iconoclasts of all time. And although Nietzsche was rather harsh on his anarchist contemporaries—or more precisely on a type of contemporary anarchist—he nevertheless in some respects shared with them a vision of total transformation. The notion of a transvaluation of all values clearly remains not merely compatible with, but an integral component of the anarchist project, and the idea of philosophy with a hammer underlies the anarchist commitment to radical social transformation.

Further, twice in his final work, *Ecce Homo* (1888), Nietzsche makes positive use of the key contemporaneous anarchist term, *attentat* (roughly 'outrage' or 'attack'). The *attentat* was designed as a blow against bourgeois society, but also as a wake-up call for the proletariat. After the 1881 congress in London, many anarchists were promoting the use of propaganda by the deed, and when

Nietzsche wrote *Ecce Homo* he must have been aware of the infamous *attentat* which had taken place only two years previously in the United States. In May 1886, during a violent nationwide strike campaign for an eight-hour workday, an explosive device was thrown into a rank of advancing police in Chicago's Haymarket. The subsequent judicial murder of five prominent anarchists led to widespread outrage, both in the United States and Europe. "Haymarket," as John Zerzan remarks, "was the opening blow in 25 years of anarchist violence from Chicago to St. Petersburg."[2]

Nietzsche's use of the term *attentat* occurs with reference to *The Birth of Tragedy* and to *Untimely Meditations*. The latter is merely a passing characterisation of the quartet of meditations as 'four *attentats*.'[3] But the former, more significant reference occurs explicitly in relationship to aesthetic issues. Re-evaluating his earliest book twenty-six years after its publication, Nietzsche says of *The Birth of Tragedy*:

> A tremendous hope speaks out of this writing. I have in the end no reason whatever to renounce the hope for a Dionysian future of music. Let us look a century ahead, let us suppose that my *attentat* on two millennia of anti-nature and the violation of man succeeds. That party of life which takes in hand the greatest of all tasks, the higher breeding of humanity, together with the remorseless destruction of all degenerate and parasitic elements, will again make possible on earth that *superfluity of life* out of which the Dionysian condition must again proceed. I promise a *tragic age*: the supreme art in the affirmation of life, tragedy will be reborn when mankind has behind it the consciousness of the harshest but most necessary wars *without suffering from it*.[4]

From his mature perspective, Nietzsche reinterprets *The Birth of Tragedy* as an "*attentat* on two millennia of anti-nature and the violation of man"—in other words, as an *attentat* in words that in some respects complements the anarchist propaganda of the deed. Both types of *attentat* aim at the eradication of human alienation and violation. Although there are differences (certainly in terms of terminology), there are also broad compatibilities between the Nietzschean and anarchist perspectives because both—although Nietzsche would have denied this point—are of the "party of life." Both see that radical psychosocial transformation can only be effectuated through "necessary wars," whatever the nature of those conflicts might be.[5] Both recognise that a higher "breeding" (or human development, in anarchist terms) can only come about through the destruction of limits (power) and the eradication of parasitic elements (or the entire ensemble of State and Capital, in anarchist terms).[6] And both acknowledge that only through such a process can there come about the conditions for creating a superfluity of life which in turn is capable of generating the Dionysian condition (or anarchy, in anarchist terms).

In the present context, however, the most significant point remains the role envisaged for art in this scenario. Nietzsche confidently foresees "a Dionysian future of music." Clearly Dionysian art (in contradistinction to any other type of art) remains an integral part of a transformed future, when it will become "the supreme art in the affirmation of life." But this passage also begs the question regarding the role to be played by art in effecting the social transformation that emerges from the transvaluation of all values. This question can only be answered once the nature of Dionysian art, as it is conceptualised in Nietzsche's work, becomes clear. But before addressing this question, it is necessary to understand the status and social function of non-Dionysian art as Nietzsche understands it.

In *The Birth of Tragedy*, Nietzsche seeks in a renewal of tragic—or Dionysian—art a solution to the problem of suffering and existential absurdity. Art is "the supreme task," and "the supreme and properly serious task of art" is "that of rescuing the eye from gazing into the horrors of night and releasing the subject, with the healing balm of illusion, from the convulsive stirrings of the will."[7] Art is conceived in terms of liberation ('release'), but not through an exertion of will which might transform the human subject and social conditions, but rather in a Schopenhauerian renunciation of the will in an acceptance of therapeutic aesthetic illusion. The beautiful dream of art becomes the medium "through which life is made both possible and worth living."[8] As helper, healer and consoler, art makes life bearable, and indeed in the famous formulation "it is only as *an aesthetic phenomenon* that existence and the world are eternally *justified*."[9] Without the metaphysical consolation provided by art, life remains meaningless and death seems attractive: only art "can turn these thoughts of repulsion at the horror and absurdity of existence into ideas compatible with life."[10]

Art provides the necessary illusions that make living endurable, but only at the cost of inaction. Affirming Kant's notion of disinterested aesthetic contemplation, Nietzsche renounces action, above all for the tragic or Dionysian hero: "Both have truly seen to the essence of things, they have *understood*, and action repels them; for their action can change nothing in the eternal essence of things, they consider it ludicrous or shameful that they should be expected to restore order to the chaotic world."[11] The politics of this quietist stance are clear: in *The Birth of Tragedy* "Nietzsche holds [that] social life depends upon the confinement of Dionysian ecstasy to symbolic, artistic expression."[12] The Dionysian energies invoked through tragic art, due to their amoral nature, need the boundaries of Apollonian form if they are not to overflow the bounds of art and threaten the integrity of the social order itself.

The reawakening of the Dionysian spirit in the modern world through art points to a "new mode of existence,"[13] but the unstable Dionysian energies are not to be channeled toward human regeneration directly, but in the mediated form of art. The Wagnerian *Gesamtkunstwerke*, with its reunification of discrete art forms, acts as a medium through which the holistic experience of the Dionysian spirit is to be reconstituted:

Now the slave is a free man, now all the rigid and hostile boundaries that distress, despotism or "impudent fashion" have erected between man and man break down. Now, with the gospel of world harmony, each man feels himself not only united, reconciled, and at one with his neighbour, but *one* with him, as if the veil of Maya had been rent and now hung in rags before the mysterious primal Oneness.

Singing and dancing, man expresses himself as a member of a higher community: he has forgotten how to walk and talk, and is about to fly dancing into the heavens. His gestures express enchantment. Just as the animals now speak, and the earth yields up milk and honey, he now gives voice to supernatural sounds: he feels like a god, he himself now walks about enraptured and elated as he saw gods walk in dreams. Man is no longer an artist, he has become a work of art: the artistic power of the whole of nature reveals itself to the supreme gratification of the primal Oneness amidst the paroxysms of intoxication. The noblest clay, the most precious marble, man, is kneaded and hewn here, and to the chisel-blows of the Dionysiac world-artist there echoes the cry of the Eleusinian mysteries, "Do you bow low, multitudes? Do you sense the Creator, world?"[14]

In subsequent texts Nietzsche refines and revises his attitudes to art, and abjures mystical worldviews and terminologies. Nevertheless, despite the comprehensive changes that follow, the emphasis on liberation from despotism, world harmony and holism—the core of the Dionysian condition—remain, albeit in drastically reformulated shape. Similarly, although radically transformed, the emphasis on the momentous role of art in radical social transformation remains constant. In *The Birth of Tragedy*, the Dionysian artist is no longer confined to the art work, but becomes a world-creator, a world-artist, and a work of art himself. The project of Dionysian art, then, emerges not merely as a renewal of art, but as the regeneration of humanity itself. At this stage of Nietzsche's thought, however, such regeneration can occur only through the medium of art, not through social activity.

In the four years following the publication of *The Birth of Tragedy*, Nietzsche published separately his four *Untimely Meditations*. The last of these, *Richard Wagner in Bayreuth*, was published in July 1876, the same month in which he left the first Bayreuth festival in disgust and broke with Wagner. These surface events are indicative of the profound subterranean changes taking place in Nietzsche's philosophy and his aesthetics in particular at this time. Nietzsche learned much from Wagner about the relationship between art, politics and power, but came to feel stultified by his mentor's Schopenhauerian insistence on social inaction. Julian Young summarises Nietzsche's thought at this transitional stage:

...power, *all* power, is, as Wotan shows us in the Ring cycle, evil; Wotan's renunciation of power is a model for us all to follow. At the beginning of *Wagner at Bayreuth* Nietzsche says that the most vital question for philosophy is the extent to which the world is alterable; vital, he says, making an active-*sounding* remark, so that once it is answered we may "set about *improving that part of it recognised as alterable*. But at the end of the work it turns out not to be the world but only our attitudes to it that are capable of alteration. One can believe in the future, he says, only because the Socratic attitudes of our modern culture towards art and the metaphysical are, at least possibly, capable of being changed, not because any changes in the fundamental character of human existence are possible.[15]

Power—that is to say, coercion and control—needs to be renounced and abolished. (This notion of power should not be confused with Nietzsche's later emphasis on the Will to Power, i.e., self-affirmation and enablement—an unfortunate terminological failure on Nietzsche's part which results in all kinds of misunderstandings.) The abolition of power would seem to require social activism. However, still under the spell of Wagnerian ideology, Nietzsche rejects the possibility of effecting socio-material changes and confines himself to a form of idealist alteration through art.

This edging toward social activism, and the posing of a relation between art and activism, remained in check until Nietzsche's infamous break with Wagner. Upon quitting Bayreuth, Nietzsche began work on the psychological observations that would form *Human, All Too Human* (1878), a work which Wagner interpreted as evidence of its author's mental breakdown. Young refers to 'the radical change of stance [toward art] represented by *Human, All Too Human*,'[16] compared to earlier works, and this is nowhere more apparent than in a passage which marks a turning point in Nietzsche's aesthetics:

> *The twofold struggle against misfortune.* When a misfortune strikes us, we can overcome it either by removing its cause or else by changing the effect it has on our feelings, that is, by reinterpreting the misfortune as a good, whose benefit may only later become clear. Religion and art (as well as metaphysical philosophy) strive to effect a change in our feeling, in part by changing the way we judge experiences (for example, with the aid of the tenet, "Whom the Lord loves, he chastens") and in part by awakening a pleasure in pain, in emotion generally (which is where tragic art has its starting point). The more a person tends to reinterpret and justify, the less will he confront the causes of the misfortune and eliminate them; a momentary palliation and narcotization (as used, for example, for a toothache) is also enough for him in more serious suffering. The more the rule of religions and all narcotic arts decreases, the more squarely do men confront the real elimination of misfortune—of course, this is bad for the tragic poets (there being less and less material for tragedy, because the realm of inexorable, invincible fate grows ever smaller)

but it is even worse for the priests (for until now they fed on the nar-
cotization of human misfortunes).[17]

As in *The Birth of Tragedy*, Nietzsche's starting point remains the problem of
suffering—here cast in the guise of misfortune. Two starkly opposed responses
are regarded as possible to this problem: either the consolations afforded by
metaphysics—whether religious, artistic or philosophical—or confronting the
causes of misfortune and eliminating them. In other words, a passive acceptance
of suffering as unavoidable, necessary and even beneficial, or an active removal
of its causes. In *The Birth of Tragedy*, Nietzsche affirmed the former response; in
Human All Too Human he makes a complete *volte face* and affirms the latter. In
terms of aesthetics, this shift in emphasis is important because it seems to
involve a renunciation of art. Even tragic art, the crucial redemptive element in
The Birth of Tragedy, appears doomed as the need for metaphysical consolation
recedes in the face of an advancing extirpation of the causes of suffering.

This apparent rejection of art is, however, an illusion. In swinging like a pen-
dulum from one extreme to another, Nietzsche seems to switch from asserting
the quintessential importance of art to denouncing art as redundant. But in actuality Nietzsche's characterisation of art as narcotic is merely a judgment on
presently existing art, not on art *per se*. Art *as it is currently practised*, he suggests,
has a specific social control function: it prevents social transformation by nar-
cotising people, by numbing their pain or (like an opium pipe) providing them
with beautiful but illusory dreams. Explicitly linking art and religion, Nietzsche
converges on Marx's point that religion—or art—is the opium of the people. But
in aesthetic terms, Nietzsche proceeds further: contemporary or narcotic art is
not aesthetic at all, but rather (as the toothache image makes plain) anaesthetic.
In *Human All Too Human*, Nietzsche does not reject aesthetics, but anaesthetics—that is to say, the social anaesthetics provided by contemporary art.

Recoiling in horror from his new-found insights into Wagner's art—always
regarded by Nietzsche as the key art works of the era—Nietzsche's other comments on art in *Human All Too Human* remain subsidiary to this crucial recognition of art as social anaesthetic. In the two supplements to the volume, *Assort-
ed Opinions and Maxims* (1879) and *The Wanderer and his Shadow* (1880), and in
Dawn (1881), however, a subtle shift begins to take place as Nietzsche begins to
discern the emergence of a form of art that is not anaesthetic and contemporary,
but aesthetic and untimely. As Young comments: "Though the observations on
art made in *Dawn* are uniformly hostile, it nevertheless shares... that valuing of
a certain kind of art which distinguished both *Opinions* and *Wanderer* from
Human."[18] In *Dawn*, however, Nietzsche more importantly broadens and deep-
ens his critique of narcotic or metaphysical art, as Young makes plain when he
comments: "in *Dawn*... metaphysical art is represented as a form of 'intoxication' that is both effect and cause of alienation from human reality."[19]

The hostility to narcotic art which Young discerns in *Dawn* is tempered by
Nietzsche's identification of himself as an artist—albeit of a non-narcotic stripe.
In the Preface, added in 1886, Nietzsche notes his hostility towards "the pleas-

ure-seeking and lack of conscience of the artists which would like to persuade us to worship where we no longer believe—for we are artists."[20] Contemporary metaphysical artists inauthentically seek to embroil their audiences in hedonistic illusions and the self-renunciations and social disempowerments of a discredited religious sensibility. In contrast, the kind of art which Nietzsche proposes—for which, as yet, he has no name (except perhaps the unstable category of the Dionysian), nor clear definition—is evidently to differ markedly from this conception.

The blame for narcotic art lies, however, not with the artist, but with the contemporary audience.

> *Better people!*—They tell me that contemporary art is directed at the greedy, insatiable, undisciplined, disgusted, harassed men of the present day and exhibits to them a picture of blissful exultation and unworldliness to set beside their own dissoluteness: so that they can forget themselves and breathe again, perhaps indeed to bring back with them out of this forgetting an incitement to flight and reformation. Poor artists who have such a public! Whose hidden intentions have to be half priestly, half psychiatric! How much more fortunate was Corneille—"our great Corneille," as Madame de Sévigné exclaims in the accents of a woman in the presence of a complete *man*—how much more exalted was *his* audience, whom he could improve with pictures of knightly virtue, stern duty, magnanimous self-sacrifice, the heroic restraining of himself! How differently did he and they love existence: not out of a blind, dissolute "will" which is cursed because it cannot be killed, but as a place where greatness and humanity are *possible* together and where even the strictest constraint of form, subjection to princely and clerical arbitrariness, can suppress neither the pride, nor the chivalry, nor the charm, nor the spirit of every individual, but is felt rather as an antithetical spur and stimulus to an inborn self-reliance and nobility, to an inherited power of will and passion![21]

The contemporary audience demands narcotic art and the artist, in order to prosper, must meet that requirement. Such an audience needs to forget itself and the social conditions it creates and inhabits, and thus the art it requires remains thoroughly escapist. The debased—or as Nietzsche will subsequently call them, *décadent*—audience debases the artist by forcing her to produce debased art. In contrast, artists such as Corneille were blessed with an audience more commensurate with his artistry, with the result that—in stark contrast with present tendencies to fragmentation—both audience and artist found mutual completion. Through the dialectical interaction of artist and audience, humanity and greatness, along with self-reliant individuality, are made possible, and this despite the constraints of social power ("subjection to princely and clerical arbitrariness"). Audiences, instead of being amused, entertained or anaesthetised, can be "improved" by such an art, and thus the point is made that not all art is necessarily narcotic art. Nonetheless, narcotic art is the dominant art of the era, and the narcotics are necessary because the audience-patients are sick, both spiritually and physiologically. Using the metaphor of ill-health (which is not entirely figurative, as Nietzsche claims a materialist basis to his cultural diagnosis—"Aesthetics is certainly nothing but applied Physiology."[22]), *Dawn* proclaims:

> *Art and the sick.*—To counter any kind of affliction or distress of soul one ought in the first instance to try change of diet and hard physical labour. But in those cases men are accustomed to resort to means of intoxication: to art, for example—to the detriment of themselves and of art as well! Do you realise that if you demand art when you are sick you make sick the artists?[23]

Metaphysical art narcotises and intoxicates. It allows individuals to accommodate themselves to social alienation, to continue preying on others, and it allows power to work on and programme them. But it does not prevent the contagion from spreading, from audience to artist to art work. This is the process Nietzsche discerned in Wagner, the archetypal artist of the age. As Young comments, for Nietzsche "the business of art, as we saw in *Opinions*, is to improve the future. It is, as *Dawn* continues the theme, to 'improve' its audience... With Wagner, however, we find the reverse of what we should find. Artist as legislator of high values for the future has been replaced by artist as panderer to low tastes of the present."[24] And not only as panderer, but as plague-carrier—and given the intensity of Nietzsche's involvement with Wagner, no one was more susceptible to infection than Nietzsche himself.

The Gay Science (1882), Nietzsche's next work, is clearly signaled as a work of convalescence. In the Preface to the Second Edition, penned in 1886, Nietzsche talks of the text explicitly in terms of a convalescence: "'Gay Science': that signifies the saturnalia of a spirit who has patiently resisted a terrible, long pressure—patiently, severely, coldly, without submitting, but also without hope—and who is now all at once attacked by hope, the hope for health, and the *intoxication* of health."[25] In contrast to the intoxicant of metaphysical art, Nietzsche talks of an intoxication of health—and to accompany and inform it a new life-affirming art:

> How maliciously we listen now to the big county-fair boom-boom with which the "educated" person and city dweller today permits art, books, and music to rape him and provide "spiritual pleasures"—with the aid of spiritous liquors! How the theatrical scream of passion now hurts our ears, how strange to our taste the whole romantic uproar and tumult of the senses have become, which the educated mob loves, and all its aspirations after the elevated, inflated, and exaggerated! No, if we convalescents still need art, it is another kind of art—a mocking, light, fleeting, divinely untroubled, divinely artificial art that, like a pure flame, licks into unclouded

skies. Above all, an art for artists, for artists only! We know better afterwards what above all is needed for this: cheerfulness, any cheerfulness, my friends—also as artists: let me prove it. There are a few things we now know too well, we knowing ones: oh, how we now learn to forget well, and to be good at *not* knowing, as artists![26]

Metaphysical or narcotic art is now cast as violating as well as creating an unhealthy nervous excitement.[27] With an explicit reference to the *Gesamtkunstwerke* ("the whole romantic uproar and tumult of the senses"), Nietzsche condemns the Wagnerian and every lesser kind of contemporary art. In contrast to the heavy Germanic beer of the North, Nietzsche recommends the light sparkling wine of the South. The projected art is still an intoxicant—it is an art for the convalescent, not the recovered, and is thus something of a way-station— but it is a step away from inebriation and toxicity. It is an art associated, not with memory and what elsewhere Nietzsche terms *ressentiment*,[28] but with forgetting and looking away. But, as Nietzsche says, above all, it is an art for artists only. This statement begs the question of who is capable of becoming an artist in this sense and what this revised category of the artist then means.

In passing, Nietzsche poses the question in the Preface of whether convalescents still need art, and the possible reasons why they continue to need art. The answer to this question appears in the text at the climactic ending of Book Two. Under the heading *"Our ultimate gratitude to art,"* Nietzsche celebrates art as a "cult of the untrue" which sustains humanity in the face of science's exposure of "general untruth and mendaciousness." Art combats the tendencies to nausea and suicide which emerge as a response to scientific honesty:

> But now there is a counterforce against our honesty that helps us to avoid such consequences: art as the *good* will to appearance... As an aesthetic phenomenon existence is still *bearable* to us, and art furnishes us with eyes and hands and above all the good conscience to be *able* to turn ourselves into such a phenomenon. At times we need a rest from ourselves by looking upon, by looking *down* upon, ourselves and, from an artistic distance, laughing *over* ourselves.... [W]e need all exuberant, floating, dancing, mocking, childish, and blissful art lest we lose the *freedom above things* that our ideal demands of us. It would mean a *relapse* for us, with our irritable honesty, to get involved entirely in morality... We should be *able* to stand *above* morality—and not only to stand with the anxious stiffness of a man who is afraid of slipping and falling at any moment, but also to *float* above it and *play*. How then could we possibly dispense with art— and with the fool?[29]

Nietzsche amends the key statement of *The Birth of Tragedy*—"it is only as *an aesthetic phenomenon* that existence and the world are eternally *justified"*—to read "as an aesthetic phenomenon existence is still *bearable* to us." Existence is no longer justified, but at least endurable as an aesthetic phenomenon. Art's function is no longer so grandiose, but more practical. Art provides the means through which humans are enabled to transform their lives into aesthetic phenomenon, and thus fulfil the liberatory project. As Young comments: "Such a transformation of outlook... demands, is equivalent to, nothing less than the transformation of the self. We must turn not just the world but also the self into an 'aesthetic phenomenon.' We must, says Nietzsche... become artists who produce not (or not primarily) 'the art of works of art' but rather their own lives."[30] Such a project remains incompatible with the banal roles and routines characteristic of life in the control complex, and thus represents a radical challenge and alternative to current social arrangements.

For Nietzsche, the fearless confrontation with morality facilitated by science tends to draw the convalescent into conditions of being characterised by solemnity, heaviness and seriousness. Although this confrontation remains necessary to effect an ultimate recovery, it involves the risk of triggering a relapse. The role of art for the convalescent is to combat this possibility. Blissful, ludic art provides the convalescent with aesthetic distance from morality and from herself. Through art, she can gain the requisite perspective which allows her to achieve an aesthetic distance, a certain lightness of being, a capacity to look down upon herself and the profundities of existence—and laugh at both. Although in some respects a will to appearance, the will to life as an aesthetic phenomenon remains an impulse toward freedom, an affirmation of a necessary *"freedom above things."* And as such, at least for the convalescent, art remains indispensable.

Clearly, the blissful, ludic, life-affirming art prescribed for the convalescent is envisaged as the opposite of narcotic metaphysical art. The former aims at aiding recovery, while the latter merely serves to allay the symptoms—in order that the patient can continue to function while the disease spreads further. "This kind [of art] is designed for those everyday souls who in the evening are not like victors on their triumphal chariots but rather like tired mules who have been whipped too much by life."[31] Such art is for "Men whose lives are not an 'action' but a business, [who] sit before the stage and observe strange creatures for whom life is no business[.] 'That is decent,' you say; 'that is entertaining; that is culture.'"[32] Narcotic art is designed for the defeated, those who conform to the immiserating routines of work and business. Culture, in this sense of the term, entertains, consoles, narcotises and intoxicates in order that the work-machine may continue. But what of those who refuse the social order?

> What are the Fausts and Manfreds of the theater to someone who is somewhat like Faust or Manfred? But it may give him something to think about that characters of that type should ever be brought upon the stage. The strongest ideas and passions brought before those who are not capable of ideas but only of intoxication! Theater and music as the hashish-smoking and betel-chewing of the European! Who will ever relate the whole history of narcotica?—It is almost the history of "culture," of our so-called higher culture.[33]

The *Übermensch*—those who live life as an aesthetic phenomenon, as perhaps a Faust or a Manfred, those who *become* tragic or Dionysian figures, ego-
ists engaged in a titanic struggle with the forces of limitation and control—have
no need for such an art, indeed it is inimical to them. Such individuals want to
practise the art of life and living ("we want to be the poets of our life—first of
all in the smallest, most everyday matters"[34]), rather than be consumers of alien-
ated images of life. Narcotic art reinforces social domination by providing alien-
ated images which emphasise the gulf between art and daily life. The disparity
alienates the spectator from herself, her creativity and thus the possibilities of a
liberated life. In the West, at least, such an experience remains central to the
experience of culture. Culture, in the dominant understanding of the term,
remains for Nietzsche a synonym of alienation, domestication and control. As
he later remarks in *On the Genealogy of Morals* (1887): "Supposing that what is
at any rate believed to be the 'truth' really is true, and the *meaning of all culture*
is the reduction of the beast of prey 'man' to a tame and civilized animal, a
domestic animal, then one would undoubtedly have to regard all those instincts
of reaction and ressentiment through whose aid noble races and their ideals
were finally confounded and overthrown as the *actual instrument of culture*...
These 'instruments of culture' are a disgrace to man and rather an accusation
and counterargument against 'culture' in general!"[35]

In contrast, Nietzsche suggests that a different kind of art—a tragic,
Dionysian art which goes beyond the blissful art necessary for convalescents—
restores the human being to herself and to health: "*What should win our gratitude.*—Only artists, and especially those of the theater, have given men eyes and
ears to see and hear with some pleasure what each man *is* himself, experiences
himself, desires himself; only they have taught us to esteem the hero that is con-
cealed in everyday characters; only they have taught us the art of viewing ourselves as heroes—from a distance and, as it were, simplified and transfigured—
the art of staging and watching ourselves."[36] Narcotic art serves as a distraction,
not only from the misery of daily life in conditions of power, but from the care,
articulation and enhancement of the self. Dionysian art, on the other hand, fos-
ters the aesthetic distance necessary for living life as an aesthetic phenomenon,
i.e., for a staging of the self as hero—and more particularly as tragic hero, in
Nietzsche's understanding of the term. As he later comments in *Twilight of the
Idols* (1889), the tragic artist displays "precisely the condition of fearlessness in
the face of the fearsome and questionable."

> Bravery and composure in the face of a powerful enemy, great hard-
> ship, a problem that arouses aversion—it is this *victorious* condition
> which the tragic artist singles out, which he glorifies. In the face of
> tragedy the warlike in our soul celebrates its Saturnalias; whoever is
> accustomed to suffering, whoever seeks out suffering, the *heroic*
> man extols his existence by means of tragedy—for him alone does
> the tragic poet pour this draught of sweetest cruelty.[37]

While narcotic art anaesthetises existential pain and thus permits the continued operation of power, and blissful ludic art creates sustaining illusions for the convalescent as she disentangles herself from control structures, Dionysian or tragic art—an art for those restored to health—confronts the social sources of pain and stimulates the individual to affirm herself in and through her tragic conflict with control. The warlike soul is the individual who heroically affirms her individuality through a transvaluation of all values—i.e., a willing into existence of values constructed solely on the basis of one's unique individuality. In undergoing this process, the individual transforms her life and the world around her into an aesthetic phenomenon. She becomes the artist and life becomes her art work. As Nietzsche later comments in *The Will to Power* (1901): "One should not play with artistic formulas: one should remodel life so that afterward it *has* to reformulate itself."[38]

Nietzsche, however, seeks the origins of the division between narcotic and non-narcotic art at a more profound, psychological level. He talks of tracing "the backward inference from the work to the maker, from the deed to the doer, from the ideal to those who need it, from every way of thinking and valuing to the commanding need behind it."[39] This genealogical methodology leads him to conclude that:

> Every art, every philosophy may be viewed as a remedy and an aid in the service of growing and struggling life; they always presuppose suffering and sufferers. But there are two kinds of sufferers: first, those who suffer from the over-fullness of life—they want a Dionysian art and likewise a tragic view of life, a tragic insight—and then those who suffer from the impoverishment of life and seek rest, stillness, calm seas, redemption of themselves through art and knowledge or intoxication, convulsions, anaesthesia, and madness.[40]

This passage occurs in a section in which Nietzsche explicitly sets out to rectify the errors committed in *The Birth of Tragedy*, and as in that text he frames his discussion in terms of suffering. The concept of the Dionysian has clearly undergone a transformation, however, as it is no longer the counterpart of the Apollonian, but the opponent of the Romantic and the Christian. Dionysian art, characterised by its tragic worldview, becomes a product of an abundance of vitality; narcotic art, marked by its desire for stasis, emerges from a scarcity of life-energy. "Regarding all aesthetic values I now avail myself of this main distinction: I ask in every instance, 'is it hunger or superabundance that has here become creative?'"[41] Nietzsche denies that this distinction can be reduced to a conflict between change and stasis, or creative and destructive impulses:

> The desire for *destruction*, change, and becoming can be an expression of an overflowing energy that is pregnant with future (my term for this is, as is known, "Dionysian"); but it can also be the hatred of the ill-constituted, disinherited, and underprivileged, who

destroy, who *must* destroy, because what exists, indeed all existence, all being, outrages and provokes them. To understand this feeling, consider our anarchists closely.[42]

Nietzsche should have followed his own advice here: what he says is certainly true of *some* anarchists, but not of all. The contrast between Dionysian and narcotic art derives from the nature of the impulse that becomes manifest in each aesthetic type. The informing impulse can be derived from either an abundance or lack of vitality. The presence or absence of this vitality is accorded a determining role: it determines the nature of aesthetic expression, but also character structure, cultural patterns, and ultimately history itself. Further, the future prospects of humanity hinge upon it: whether it is creative, destructive, or both, the presence of vitality can spark radical human transformation ("an overflowing energy that is pregnant with future"), whereas an absence of vitality may result in a nihilistic destruction of the world.

In this passage Nietzsche sees Dionysian art as emerging from what he will refer to in *Ecce Homo* as "that *superfluity of life* out of which the Dionysian condition must again proceed." Moreover, from the above discussion it remains clear that Dionysian art has a key role to play if the Dionysian condition is indeed to "again proceed." But in a sense Nietzsche had reached an impasse. Although recommending Dionysian art as "the great stimulus to life,"[43] Nietzsche could not authentically claim to be a Dionysian artist himself. His claims to being an artist ring hollow, and a tacit recognition of this failure appears in a passage of *The Gay Science* which contains obvious autobiographical resonances. Nietzsche refers to a nameless poet whose works "never wholly express what he would like to express and what he would *like to have seen*: it seems as if he had had the foretaste of a vision and never the vision itself": "...he lifts his listeners above his work and all mere 'works' and lends them wings to soar as high as listeners had never soared. Then, having themselves been transformed into poets and seers, they lavish admiration upon the creator of their happiness... as if he had attained his goal and had really *seen* and communicated his vision. His fame benefits from the fact that he never reached his goal."[44] Nietzsche sees his work as attaining the Dionysian goal of transforming his audience into artists, but there is a sense of dissatisfaction in this passage. Nietzsche was not content to play the role of John the Baptist. He wanted to be the (Anti-)Christ. He wanted to reach "his goal."

In *Human, All Too Human*, he had spoken of *"Books that teach us to dance. There are writers who, by portraying the impossible as possible, and by speaking of morality and genius as if both were merely a mood or a whim, elicit a feeling of high-spirited freedom, as if man were rising up on tiptoe and simply had to dance out of inner pleasure."*[45] In order to write such a (profoundly anarchist) book, to represent the impossible as possible, to reach his goal, Nietzsche needed to make a leap into the unknown. He had to abandon philosophical discourse, at least in its dominant form, and make the transition to becoming an artist.

In writing *Thus Spoke Zarathustra*, Nietzsche transformed himself from a philosopher into a *Dichterphilosoph* (a poet-philosopher). In making the translation, Nietzsche's aesthetics reached their apotheosis. In *Nietzsche's Philosophy of Art*, Young sees a further trajectory for Nietzsche's aesthetics beyond *Zarathustra*. For me, however, Nietzsche's post-*Zarathustra* meditations on aesthetics merely reiterate and amplify points already made. *Zarathustra* embodies Nietzsche's aesthetics: it has nothing to say about the issue of aesthetics. There is nothing more to say, and subsequent texts have nothing further to add.

Adequate engagement with the aesthetic of *Zarathustra* remains beyond the scope of this essay. Nietzsche himself recognises the singularity of this work in *Ecce Homo* when he writes: "This work stands altogether alone. Let us leave the poets aside: perhaps nothing at all has ever been done out of a like superfluity of strength. My concept 'Dionysian' has here become the *supreme deed*; compared with it all the rest of human activity seems poor and conditional."[46] For Nietzsche, in *Zarathustra* words and deeds become one, such is the transformative capacity of the text. Written out of an unparalleled superfluity of energy ("*great health*,"[47] rather than convalescence), it is a perfect exemplification of Dionysian art and of "that *superfluity of life* out of which the Dionysian condition must again proceed."

In *On The Genealogy of Morals*, Nietzsche attacks artists, those purveyors of narcotics and domesticating "culture": "they do not stand nearly independently enough in the world and *against* the world for their changing valuations to deserve attention *in themselves!* They have at all times been valets of some morality, philosophy, or religion.... They always need at the very least protection, a prop, an established authority: artists never stand apart; standing alone is contrary to their deepest instincts."[48] In *Zarathustra*, Nietzsche shows that the Dionysian artist can stand alone, in and against the world, refusing to serve any abstract system, and rejecting all authority. Indeed, the textual strategies of *Zarathustra* are markedly and deliberately anti-authoritarian, indeed anarchistic. The text demonstrates Nietzsche's "honest willingness to employ an openly fictional mode (in the traditional sense of the word) to render philosophical propositions comprehensible and illustrate their applicability."[49] The synthesis of the philosophical and the fictional in order to construct "a narrative whose aesthetic criteria [are] not objective nor merely subjective, but rather thoroughly perspectivistic"[50] remains Nietzsche's greatest achievement in aesthetic terms. In *Zarathustra* Nietzsche finally locates an aesthetic form commensurate with the practice of Dionysian art—with "the art of works of art"—and with the art of life for which such Dionysian art provides the stimulant.

Notes

1   As Julian Young comments: "...there is, in Nietzsche, no single view of art (or of very much else). Rather his career divides up into different periods distinguished from each other by sharply contrasting attitudes to and about art." Even if one disagrees with Young's theses on and periodisation of Nietzsche's aesthetics, this point remains indisputable. Julian Young, *Nietzsche's Philosophy of Art* (Cambridge, UK: Cambridge University Press, 1992), p. 1.

2 John Zerzan, "Afterword" to Frank Harris, *The Bomb* (Portland, OR: Feral House, 1996), p. 210.

3 Friedrich Nietzsche, *Ecce Homo*, trans. R. J. Hollingdale (Harmondsworth: Penguin, 1986), p. 85.

4 Ibid., 81-82.

5 The comparability of the "necessary wars" envisaged by Nietzsche and the social revolution envisaged by anarchism becomes apparent in *Ecce Homo*: "For when truth steps into battle with the lie of millennia we shall have convulsions, an earthquake spasm, a transposition of valley and mountain such as has never been dreamed of. The concept politics has then become completely absorbed into a war of spirits, all the power-structures of the old society have been blown into the air—they one and all reposed on the lie: there will be wars such as there have never yet been on earth. Only after me will there be *grand politics* on earth.—" (*Ecce Homo*, 127). Nietzsche and the anarchists clearly share a common vision of a revolutionary upheaval resulting in the destruction of power and the initiation of a *"grand politics."*

6 The compatibility of anarchist and Nietzschean perspectives emerges clearly in a later passage, where Nietzsche proclaims: "For when truth steps into battle with the lie of millennia we shall have convulsions, an earthquake spasm, a transposition of valley and mountain such as has never been dreamed of. The concept politics has then become completely absorbed into a war of spirits, all the power-structures of the old society have been blown into the air—they one and all reposed on the lie: there will be wars such as there have never yet been on earth." *Ecce Homo*, p. 127. Both anarchists and Nietzsche share a vision of a revolutionary anti-politics which engages in social upheaval to effect a destruction of *all* power structures.

7 Nietzsche, *The Birth of Tragedy*, trans. Shaun Whiteside (Harmondsworth: Penguin, 1993), pp. 13, 93-94.

8 Ibid., p. 16.

9 Ibid., p. 32.

10 Ibid., p. 40.

11 Ibid., p. 39.

12 Young, p. 34.

13 Nietzsche, *The Birth of Tragedy*, p. 95.

14 Ibid., pp. 17-18.

15 Young, p. 56. By "Socratic attitudes," Nietzsche refers to nineteenth-century positivism.

16 Ibid., p. 55.

17 Nietzsche, *Human, All Too Human*, trans. Marion Faber and Stephen Lehmann (Harmondsworth: Penguin, 1994), p. 77.

18 Young, p. 88.

19 Ibid., p. 89.

20 Nietzsche, *Daybreak: Thoughts on the Prejudices of Morality*, trans. R.J. Hollingdale (Cambridge: Cambridge University Press, 1995), p. 4. *Dawn* is sometimes, as here, given the alternative translation title *Daybreak*.

21 Ibid., pp. 112-13.

22 Nietzsche, *Nietzsche Contra Wagner* in *The Case of Wagner, Nietzsche Contra Wagner, The Twilight of the Idols, The Anti-Christ*, trans. Thomas Common (London: T. Fisher Unwin, 1899), p. 67.

23 Nietzsche, *Daybreak*, p. 147.

24 Young, p. 91.

25 Nietzsche, *The Gay Science*, trans. Walter Kaufmann (New York: Vintage, 1974), p. 32.

26 Ibid., p. 37. This passage initiates Nietzsche's rejection of the Kantian notion of disinterested aesthetic contemplation. His most sustained critique of this notion occurs in *On the Genealogy of Morals* in *On the Genealogy of Morals* and *Ecce Homo*, trans. Walter Kaufmann and R.J. Hollingdale (New York: Vintage, 1989), pp. 103-5.

27 As Nietzsche subsequently points out: "Beautiful feelings, sublime agitations, are, physio-

logically speaking, among the narcotics: their misuse has precisely the same consequences as the misuse of any other opiate—neurasthenia." Friedrich Nietzsche, *The Will to Power*, trans. Walter Kaufmann and R.J. Hollingdale (New York: Vintage, 1968), p. 249.

28 The connection between art, suffering, (social) anaesthesia, physiology and ressentiment is made apparent when Nietzsche later maintains: "For every sufferer instinctively seeks a cause for his suffering; more exactly, an agent; still more specifically, a *guilty* agent who is susceptible to suffering—in short, some living thing upon which he can, on some pretext or other, vent his affects, actually or in effigy: for the venting of his affects represents the greatest attempt on the part of the suffering to win relief, *anaesthesia*—the narcotic he cannot help desiring to deaden pain of any kind. This alone, I surmise, constitutes the actual physiological cause of ressentiment, vengefulness, and the like: a desire to *deaden pain by means of affects*." (Nietzsche, *On the Genealogy of Morals* and *Ecce Homo*, p. 127).

29 Nietzsche, *The Gay Science*, pp. 163-64.

30 Young, p. 99.

31 Nietzsche, *The Gay Science*, p. 141.

32 Ibid., p. 142.

33 Ibid.

34 Ibid., p. 240.

35 Nietzsche, *On the Genealogy of Morals* and *Ecce Homo*, pp. 42-43.

36 Nietzsche, *The Gay Science*, pp. 132-33.

37 Nietzsche, *Twilight of the Idols* and *The Anti-Christ*, trans. R.J. Hollingdale (Harmondsworth: Penguin, 1979), p. 82.

38 Nietzsche, *The Will to Power*, p. 447. A tripartite conception of art thus emerges in Nietzsche's work which can be schematically summarised as follows: 1) Narcotic art maintains a strict distinction between the artist (the artist-as-genius) and the spectator, and (thus) reinforces the dominant social system; Blissful ludic art, an intermediary stage, encourages the spectator to become an artist of her own life by providing a forum for visions of psychosocial transformation. (Artists in this phase are "an intermediary species: they at least fix an image of that which ought to be; they are productive, to the extent that they actually alter and transform; unlike men of knowledge, who leave everything as it is." [Nietzsche, *The Will to Power*, p. 318.]) But for convalescents art still remains something external to themselves; lacking self-energy, they require the inspiration provided by the creative energies of artists; 3) Dionysian art engages in conflict with the dominant social system through collapsing the distinction between artist and spectator, and thus generates a generalisation of creativity—thus fulfilling Lautrémont's demand that "poetry [should be] made by all, not just by one."

39 Nietzsche, *The Gay Science*, p. 329.

40 Ibid., p. 328.

41 Ibid., p. 329

42 Ibid.

43 Nietzsche, *Twilight of the Idols*, p. 81.

44 Nietzsche, *The Gay Science*, p. 133.

45 Nietzsche, *Human, All Too Human*, pp. 124-25.

46 Nietzsche, *Ecce Homo*, p. 106.

47 Ibid., p. 101.

48 Nietzsche, *On the Genealogy of Morals*, p. 102.

49 John Carson Pettey, *Nietzsche's Philosophical and Narrative Styles* (New York: Peter Lang, 1992), p. 42.

50 Ibid., p. 74.

Crazy Nietzsche

Peter Lamborn Wilson

[To Peter Gast:] Turin, January 4, 1889

To my maëstro Pietro,

Sing me a new song: the world is transformed and all the heavens are full of joy.

—The Crucified

This is one of Nietzsche's last insane letters, written after his collapse in Turin, early in January 1889, but before his final lapse into silence. His letter to Overbeck (in which he says he has ordered "all anti-Semites shot") is signed "Dionysus"; and another to Cosima Wagner (whom he'd never ceased to love) was signed "Dionysus and the Crucified One." It appears that Nietzsche's descent into madness took the form of a religious mania in which he attempted to reconcile Dionysus and Christ by becoming them. In the letter to Burckhardt he says, "I am the god who has made this caricature."

Whether Nietzsche's collapse was caused by syphilis, or by the unbearable burden of his thought, the final letters were not meaningless babble. The synthesis of Dionysus and Jesus represents a way out of the conflict between Dionysus and Apollo first explored in 1872 in *The Birth of Tragedy*, and brought to an ultimate pitch in *The Anti-Christ* (1888), which in a sense pits Dionysus against the Crucified, and also against reason as an apollinine function. It was not necessarily 'mad' of Nietzsche to believe that he could 'overcome' such a dichotomy in the form of a higher unity. He had already given a religious sense to his philosophy in *Thus Spoke Zarathustra* (1883-85); one obvious solution to the problem of the death of God is to become god. The Myth of Eternal Return constitutes something of a theological disappointment in the Zarathustran context, however, due to its static configuration. It solves the stoic/existentialist crisis, but not the problem of will and becoming.

Scattered through Nietzsche's uncollected notes in *The Will to Power* one detects the proposal for a materialist religion with dynamic potential.

Nietzsche's brilliant scientific analysis of the difference between *survival* and *expression* points away from deterministic reductionism to a spiritual principle inherent in or identical to Nature (so to speak)—the will to expression, to power, which Nietzsche exemplifies as creativity and desire. Here too is found Nietzsche's attempt to overcome the alienation of the individual in the social, in the discovery of a principle of *communitas*. Even the strange notes on race-mixing as a solution to the problem of the social can be seen in this 'religious' light, as a proposal for the deliberate creation of self-overcoming humanity (*übermensch*) through desire and synthesis—almost a messianic concept.

A Dionysan/Christian *coincidentia* makes good historical and philological sense, too, as Nietzsche would certainly have known. If early Christianity owes anything to Hellenism, it came through Orphic/Dionysan sources—and even in the basic symbol of *wine*, an identity can be traced between the two rival saviors. The Neo-Platonic aspects of such a synthesis would have had little appeal for Nietzsche, I imagine, but the images of transcendence, ecstasy, supra-rationality, and violence common to both traditions would have intrigued him. The themes of immortality and morality would have been less useful to his project than the more immediate themes of 'the kingdom of this world' and *entheogenesis*, 'birth of the god within.'

If we have not read too much into the last insane letters, it would appear that the prophet of the death of God was about to become infused with the divine, perhaps even the would-be founder of a new religion. What then had become of the thinker who once promised to build his project on 'nothing'? It would be easy to say that the impossibility of such a project finally drove him to lunacy—but in this case we would have to condemn both his starting point ('nothing') and his end point ('religion'). Such judgment amounts to saying that Nietzsche was *always* crazy. We should examine other hypotheses.

Nietzsche spoke well of Islam, interpreting it (and to some extent misinterpreting it) according to the Freethinker tradition as a kind of heroic anti-Christianity. Although he criticized Judaism as the source of Christianity, he also lavished praise on its obvious 'pagan' elements—in part to sting the anti-Semites, but also with obvious sincerity. In this Nietzsche can be compared with an early Deist like John Toland, with roots in heretical occultism (Giordano Bruno), pantheism, masonic freethought, and anticlericalism—rather than with later rationalist/atheist/materialist philosophers. Toland, too, admired Islam and Judaism (and the pagan Druids!). Nietzsche's 'Zarathustra' in fact belongs to this old Renaissance tradition, rather than to any knowledge of actual Zoroastrianism. In any case it's clear that he was not 'against religion' in some vulgar sense; his dialectic was much more complex.

Nietzsche's 'nothing' constitutes the definitive breakthrough into a universe devoid of entelechy. Up to that point we have metaphysics; after it, we don't. In one sense we now have physics, in which expression takes precedence over consciousness. But in another sense it is by no means clear that the disappearance of entelechy presupposes the disappearance of meaning, or that consciousness is to be considered 'impossible' (or a mere epiphenomenon of matter). Is it possible that life's expression of itself created meaning, or that it may even be considered *as* meaning? And are we permitted to imagine a consciousness in harmony with this emergent meaning, devoid of God but (for all practical purposes) now itself becoming the divine?

Nietzsche is always and everywhere ready to bear the horrendous weight of nihilism—never once does he invoke a *deus ex machina*. However, to build a project on nothing does not necessitate ending it with nothing. He speaks first of 'necessary illusions,' through which life expresses its will to power. But Nietzsche's personal tragedy arose from his own inability to embrace these illusions (friendship, love, power itself). His philosophy required an anti-pessimistic stance, a 'Yes to Life'—but he could not locate this in psychology any more than in metaphysics. His thought required *real* transcendence, not merely an existential leap of commitment. He sought this principle in overcoming, and in the Eternal Return—a kind of absolute without entelechy. Finally, I believe, he was faced with the problem of skepticism. The Dionysus he had approached (and the Christ he had reproached) so often finally 'took two steps towards him' (as the Sufis say); he received the *experience* of transcendence already implicit in *The Anti-Christ* in the explicit form of a spiritual materialism, a mysticism of life in self-expression as mystery. And somehow it killed him.

Ultimately it would seem that one can only overcome religion *through* religion—perhaps a kind of simultaneous suppression/uplifting process in the neo-Hegelian sense of the term *aufhebung*. This image bears some relation to the alchemical term *sublimatio*, in which a substance disappears (or is overcome) at one level to appear at a higher level in a different form. Inasmuch as a program can be detected in the last insane letters, this is it.

A rejection of religion based on experience (of the 'nothing') will itself be infused with what it opposes if the Nothing suddenly appears as a dynamic void or *Tao* in the Chinese sense of this term. (What a pity that Nietzsche, unlike Oscar Wilde, never read Chuang Tzu.) Beyond the dichotomy of spirit and matter proposed by western religions and philosophies there persists something about which nothing can be said, a nothing that is neither spirit nor matter. Consciousness in a sense forms a barrier against the positive experience of this dynamic void (or 'chaos'), but in another (paradoxical) sense it can be attuned to the tao and even speak from its position. In the agonistic harmony of Dionysus and the Crucified lies a dramatized experience of such a taoist dialectics.

In a sense Nietzsche was the first Nietzschean, the first convert to his own religion—the texts of the letters memorialize this moment and emphasize its destructiveness. Nietzsche failed to survive his own most authentic (or in any case final) expression. 'Becoming god' is not quite the same thing as 'attaining the *tao*' (or perhaps it is, since taoists are also said to be 'mad'). In any case, Nietzsche's solution seems to have backfired. Or perhaps not; after all, we shouldn't fetishize his madness, which may have been purely physiological and not moral. Perhaps if Nietzsche had lived (as something other than a vegetable) he could have worked it out. But where he failed, are we cursed to have to succeed?

It is possible to believe that religion is simply an infantile illusion and that humanity will outgrow it—as predicted by all the great 19th-century materialists, Nietzsche included. This evolutionist concept of human consciousness, however, can be questioned (also on a Nietzschean basis). And we could say that 'religion' represents a recurrent and emergent actuality in consciousness that cannot be erased but rather only transformed. Transformations are inevitable—but not entirely deterministic in nature. 'Will' plays a role—not causative, perhaps, but 'co-creative.' Religion *returns*—but not always perhaps as the same thing again (even recurrent cycles have spirals of becoming within their compass). From the point of view of history, religion refuses to go away. Hostility to this process might be pointless; more effective would be an attempt at transformation. This attempt would necessitate a certain radius of identity with the process itself—hence the appearance of Dionysus/Christ in 1889.

In view of everything we've learned about the history of religions since the late 19th century we might be able to suggest many such coincidences, some perhaps even more precise and effective than Nietzsche's. In any case we should hesitate to propose a cult (always a danger with Nietzsche, who was after all a prophet). Nevertheless I believe one could at least take Nietzsche's project seriously, despite its appearance at the very moment of his 'crucifixion.' As a theologian Nietzsche has the distinction of proposing a religion honestly based on 'nothing'—on the very 'nothing' which has become our own theological world in the 19th and 20th centuries. Material bottom, so to speak. The rockless bottom.

Nietzsche signed himself to Burckhardt as 'Nietzsche,' but speaks as divinely-infused: "What is disagreeable and offends my modesty is that at bottom I am every name in history.... I consider with some mistrust whether it is not the case that all who come *into* the kingdom of God also come *out* of God.... Dear Professor, this edifice you should see: since I am utterly inexperienced in the things which I create, you are entitled to any criticism; I am grateful without being able to promise that I shall profit. We artists are incorrigible." Certainly a god frolics in these words (along with a wounded madman)—suitable material for a liturgy.

We've already imagined the worst results of a Dionysus/Crucified cult: the possibility that it drove Nietzsche insane. Beyond that particular abyss (so akin to Rimbaud's Abyssinia) we may consider the cases of some utopian possibilities (always bearing in mind that we take the Dionysus/Crucified model as inspirational rather than dogmatic). The advantages of a theological Nietzsche were explored by the briefly popular, now forgotten 'God is Dead' School of Christian Theology, who had a few interesting ideas, particularly in the realm of ethics. Speaking generally, the Dionysus/Crucified model as entheogenic is a religion 'without authority,' radically antinomian, somewhat as Toland envisioned his Revived Druidry, a faith for the free. And as in Toland's pantheism (he introduced the word into English), it envisions the microcosm as both full emblem and full substance of the macrocosm—immanence *as* transcendence. This explains Toland's and Nietzsche's paganity, their tendency to accept an infinite diffraction of the divine light, every center as 'the' center (and this is a sign of the Late Hellenism both thinkers share). Toland in imagining the Druid, and

Nietzsche in speaking of the 'primitive rhapsodist,' already intuited a theory of shamanism as religion without separation, based on experience rather than authority, a kind of theological self-empowerment. Shamanism is frequently based in entheogenic practices involving sacred plants, which (in combination with valuative ritual) provide an efficacious sacrament or democracy of enlightenment.

The 'God is Dead' School pointed out the logical consequences of a situational crisis (the death of God) in a situational ethics. In traditional Sufi terms one might speak of an ethics based on Imagination, Will, and Risk—rather than on categorical morality. And where there is an ethics there will be a *politique*, here rooted in the principle of upholding human becoming over all principles of stasis. Moreover, the Dionysus/Crucified model's agonistic consciousness predestines it for the antagonistic role in millennial history—religion as revolution. Only in struggle can the Dionysus/Crucified model come to saturate its own individual identity—a saturation that points directly at the social (or Harmony, as Fourier called it)—for the realization of utopian desires. In short, as Capital triumphs over the Social as against all spiritualities, spirituality itself finds itself re-aligned with revolution. Money as the final form of stasis (the ultimate platonic solid) has moved into a stage of gnostic numispherics, in which 90% of all money refers only to other money—the solid is in fact a global bubble. Money is totally spiritualized and yet retains all power in the world—something not even God could accomplish. Religion now is of no use to Capital except as a storehouse of images for commodification and consumption. In such a situation 'religion' as we're envisioning it can only capitulate or resist; there is no third way.

The revolt of religion could take the form of conservative revolution, and this danger must be considered in any *imaginaire* based on Nietzschean theology. *Communitas* can veer into ecstatic *communion* and the promethean cult of the (Cartesian) ego. But there have always been Left Nietzscheans, and I need not repeat their arguments—Nietzsche himself mockingly excoriated those who believe that 'beyond good and evil' means *to do evil*. Freedom lies in the ambiguities.

In Turin in 1889 Nietzsche saw a coachman flogging a horse, rushed forward, and threw his arms around the beast to protect it—then fainted. When he awoke he wrote the Last Insane Letters. These absurd images have the crude surrealistic power of a messianic moment—suitable for post-millennial stained glass, or a 'shrine of the book.' Nietzsche's recurrent modernity reveals him as prophet, saint. And as a modern scripture Nietzsche's Last Letters must of course be crazy.

—NYC, November 1996

Guy Aldred (UK) was an important but relatively neglected British theorist who was active in the movement for over fifty years. A member of the Glasgow Anarchist Group (later the Anti-Parliamentary Communist Federation), he was the editor of the newspapers *The Herald of Revolt*, *The Spur*, *The Commune*, *The Council* and *The Word*. His works include many pamphlets, articles, and his autobiography *No Traitor's Gate*. He died in 1963.

Allan Antliff (Canada) is a Canada Research Chair in Modern Art at the University of Victoria. He edited *Only a Beginning: An Anarchist Anthology* (Arsenal Pulp Press, 2004), and is the author of *Anarchist Modernism: Art, Politics and the First American Avant-Garde* (University of Chicago Press, 2001), a member of the *Alternative Press Review* editorial collective, and art editor at *Anarchist Studies*.

Max Cafard (US), a surre(gion)alist writer and pre-ancientist philosopher, lives on the Île de la Nouvelle-Orléans, a Floating Island in what some call "The Dream State." His book *The Surre(gion)alist Manifesto and Other Writings* was recently published by Exquisite Corpse.

Daniel Colson (France) teaches Philosophy at the University of St.-Etienne and is a researcher with the CRESAL, which is associated with the CNRS (National Center for Scientific Research). He is the author of *La Compagnie des Fonderies, Forges et Aciéries de Saint-Etienne (1865-1914)* (Publications de l'Université de Saint-Etienne, 1997), *Petit Lexique Philosophique de l'Anarchisme: De Proudhon à Deleuze* (Le Livre de Poche, 2001) and *Trois Essais de Philosophie Anarchiste* (Editions Léo Scheer, 2004).

Andrew M. Koch (US) is currently an Associate Professor of Political Philosophy at Appalachian State University in Boone, North Carolina. He is the author of a number works on anarchism, poststructuralism, and the links between epistemology and political ideas.

John Moore (UK) was a lecturer in Creative Writing at the University of Luton, the author of works such as *Anarchy & Ecstasy* (1987), *Lovebite* (1990) and *The Book of Levelling* (1995) (all on Aporia Press), and an associate editor at *Anarchist Studies*. He passed away suddenly in October 2002 at age 45.

Saul Newman (Australia) is a Research Associate in Politics at the University of Western Australia. His research is in the area of radical political and social theory, particularly that which is informed by perspectives such as poststructuralism, discourse analysis and psychoanalytic theory. His works include *From Bakunin to Lacan: Anti-authoritarianism and the Dislocation of Power* (2001) and *Power and Politics in Poststructuralist Thought* (Routledge, forthcoming).

Jonathan Purkis (UK) is a lecturer in Media and Cultural Studies at John Moores University in Liverpool. He has edited (with James Bowen) the anthologies *Twenty-First Century Anarchism* (Cassell, 1997) and *Changing Anarchism* (Manchester University Press, 2004).

Franco Riccio (Italy) teaches Philosophy at the University of Palermo. His works include *Introduzione ad una Lettura della modernità* (1994), *Verso un pensare nomade* (1997) and *Eclissi della teoria unica* (2002), all on Franco Angeli.

Leigh Starcross (UK) is an anarchist theorist whose work has appeared in *Green Anarchy* and *Anarchist Studies*.

Salvo Vaccaro (Italy) teaches Political Philosophy at the University of Palermo. His main interest is the conjunction of critical theory and so-called poststructuralist thought. His recent works include *Globalizzazione e diritti umani* (Mimesis, 2004) and *Anarchismo e modernità*, (BFS, 2004). Currently he is working issues regarding Foucault, GIP, prisons and surveillance.

Peter Lamborn Wilson (US) has written histories of piracy, sufism, the "Assassins," and spiritual anarchism in colonial America, including *Pirate Utopias* (Autonomedia, 1997), *Sacred Drift: Essays on the Margins of Islam* (City Lights, 1993), and *Scandal: Essays in Islamic Heresy* (Autonomedia, 1993).

Index of names

More Books from Autonomedia

Visit our web site at www.autonomedia.org for online ordering,
topical discussion, events listings, book specials, and more.

More Books from Autonomedia

*Visit our web site at www.autonomedia.org for online ordering,
topical discussion, events listings, book specials, and more.*

More Books from Autonomedia

Autonomedia • PO Box 568, Williamsburgh Station • Brooklyn, NY
11211-0568 • T/F 718-963-2603 • info@autonomedia.org

*Visit our web site at www.autonomedia.org for online ordering,
topical discussion, events listings, book specials, and more.*